JEWEL
TEA

Sales and Houseware Collectibles

C. L. Miller

With Value Guide

77 Lower Valley Road, Atglen, PA 19310

DEDICATION

To my father, Walter L. Miller (1911-1965), the true scavenger, historian, archaeologist, collector and spinner of yarns. This is for you, for allowing mother to shop the Jewel way!

Jewel customers looked for the Mark of Quality when purchasing the "Green Key" pattern china. This china appeared in the August 1926 issue of the Jewel News, Vol. 4 No. 8, and may be even older. The border was designed with a dainty Grecian key in green coloring, with a narrow gold outline. On the back of this china appears a Bavarian backstamp as well as the letter "J" in a laurel wreath with the word "Bavarian" below the wreath. The china set included: cup and saucer, bread and butter plate, breakfast plate, dinner plate, round soup, vegetable saucer, gravy boat, salad bowl, uncovered vegetable dish, small and large platter, sugar and creamer. Pieces were sold separately, as every piece could be secured or replaced the Jewel way. *Hamilton Collection.*

Printed in China.
ISBN: 0-88740-898-2

Library of Congress Cataloging-in-Publication Data

Miller, C. L. (Charles L.) 1941-
    Jewel Tea: sales and houseware collectibles / C.L. Miller.
      p. cm. -- (A Schiffer book for collectors)
    "With value guide."
    Includes bibliographical references.
    ISBN 0-88740-898-2 (hard)
    1. Jewel Tea Company--Collectibles--Catalogs. 2. Grocery trade-Collectibles--United States--Catalogs. 3. Hall China Company--Catalogs. 4. Pottery--20th century--Collectors and collecting--United states--Catalogs. I. Title. II. Series.
NK808.M57   1995
683'.8'0973075--dc20   95-35253
                    CIP

Published by Schiffer Publishing, Ltd.
77 Lower Valley Road
Atglen, PA 19310
Please write for a free catalog.
This book may be purchased from the publisher.
Please include $2.95 postage.
Try your bookstore first.

We are interested in hearing from authors with book ideas on related subjects.

ACKNOWLEDGMENTS

After the completion of my first volume, *The Jewel Tea Company, Its History and Products,* collectors across the United States continued to send correspondence. Both N.A.L.C.C. members and private collectors sent beautiful photographs of items from their own collections and copies of Jewel documents for this second major project.

I am grateful to each of you who took time to acknowledge my letter of introduction. Without your collections, scholarship, facts, and theories this second volume on the company would never have been possible. Only time will tell what remains hidden behind cabinet doors, in dust-covered boxes stored in some forgotten attic, or on shelves in some antique shop off the beaten path.

I wish to acknowledge the endorsement of many people, both N.A.L.C.C. members, private collectors, members of my own family, and friends. Without your support this second volume would not have been possible. Through the development of the first volume I made many friends across the United States, and I appreciate each of you. Your friendship is bound between the pages of this book.

I wish to acknowledge the friendship of Lon and Lynda Lemons and their support of this major project. I was asked by these fine people to prepare a video to promote the first volume for their Western Regional Meeting in California. I warned Lon and Lynda in advance that the video tape would be far from a Hollywood production. But it was made, and I do appreciate their asking. After all, what are friends for? These fine collectors never once hesitated to contribute to the framework of this project.

To Robert and Sharon Poggemiller for sharing one of the most beautiful pieces, and my favorite, the Zephyr butter dish. Of all Autumn Leaf butter dishes, I believe this is the most sought-after piece with the famous motif; there are so few!

To Don and Joyce DeJong for sharing their exceptionally beautiful rare items. I appreciate their support and thoughtfulness in sharing their collections.

Upon undertaking this project, Bernard and Norma Busch were the second to contact me after my letter of introduction arrived at their Illinois home. Their endorsement and help in both volumes was appreciated and I value their friendship.

To Shirley Easley for her patronage, sharing, and defense. This gracious lady never hesitated when I requested items from her vast Jewel collection. I appreciated her friendship and support in this emotionally tiring experience.

To Mr. Michael Williams and Mr. Matt McManaman of the J.T. Merchandise Services, Inc., for allowing me access to the Jewel Archives. Without their support I could never have offered readers the numerous historical black and white photographs that appear throughout this publication.

To Hall China president John Thompson, Mr. Everson Hall, and Commercial Decal of Ohio president David Dunn, and to the Jewel Food Stores, for their endorsement of both volumes.

To a couple of the finest friends a writer could ever have, Bill and NanSue Hamilton. Their collection is one of the most extensive I have encountered. They never hesitated to share photographs, information, or to search through their extensive collection of Jewel News. I appreciated their letters, phone calls, advice, and indulgence of my many requests. This gracious couple continued to share more of their growing collection of unusual Jewel items after I had met my contract. I appreciate their kindness and endorsement; a writer could never turn them down.

To Suzan Fausset, who continues to meticulously support, encourage, and assist me in my effort to preserve history for future generations. Suzan was always reassuring, and I appreciate her help and her belief in me and my project. To her husband, Larry — now you know the price of the Batter Bowl!

To Neal and Patti Byerly for opening their home and allowing me to photograph their incredible collection. Neal and Patti shared their collection of Jewel Home Shopping Service catalogues and various documents for my research and contributed to both the first and second volume. Her direction to reliable sources paid off in both publications.

To Mrs. Eva Zeisel, for her correspondence and endorsement.

To collector Opal Hancock for her assistance and encouraging phones calls during the past years and for sharing numerous documents from her private collection.

To Ohio residents Bill and Dee Hedges for their full support and encouragement during those hectic years. I appreciate their support, friendship, and knowledge.

To Mike and Cindy Schneider, who believed in me: look what happened! My first book was so large, Schiffer Publishing Ltd. and my editor Jeffrey B. Snyder were able to develop not one volume but two. What a challenge! -- well worth all those long hours. Thanks for your support, I love you both.

To Schiffer Publishing Ltd., and to the finest editor a writer could have, Jeffrey B. Snyder. I appreciate your professional advice, phone calls, letters, and your work in developing two superior books. Thanks for allowing a novice into the publishing world.

To Doug B. Dupler, who handled over 1600 photographs and continued to record the vast amount that arrived after the deadline. He ran errands, monitored incoming phone calls and sorted an enormous amount of mail. I appreciate your time, encouragement and your faith in me.

To close friends Gary and Carol Eisnaugle, my thanks for your support, care, and encouragement after the release of my first book; and most of all, for your friendship and assistance with this second book.

To Michael Harkins, Executive Director Barrington Area Historical Society, for his support. Today those priceless

Jewel archives are now maintained by this organization, of which I am pleased to be a part.

Through their work in the Jewel Homemakers' Institute Kitchen, Mary Reed Hartson and Leone Rutledge Carroll provided a vast amount of historical foundation for the development of this book. Without them, most of this would not have been possible. I would appreciate hearing from anyone who might have further information concerning these two Jewel women.

Finally, to Cecelia Androsky, Jack and Emy Barringer, B.J.'s Antiques, Fred Beghul, Doug and Margaret Belmonte, Rod and Sally Blackstone, Charles and Thelma Blow, Charles and Elizabeth J. Boyce, Joan Brinkman, Dan and Char Casey, Cascade Iowa Public Library, Betty Carson, Columbus Ohio Public Library, Russ and Donna Colwell, Sharon Costanza, Craig and Sue Cross, Sandra Hooper Edwards, Jim and Nita Kinder, Julie Kuhse, Ben Lail, Mike and Laurel Long, Rick and Karen Marshall, E. Jane Matson, Annie Mercer, Curt Miller, Ralph and Linda Miller, Jack and Sarah Miller, Dave and Susie Mills, Bonnie Nemluvil, Oak Park Illinois Public Library, Jewel Payton, The Pottery Perengrinators, Paul H. and Olly Preo, Harry and Judy Pomroy, Art and Barbara Randall, Pansy C. Ramsey, Lorraine Zeno Rippey, Rolls Antiques, Larry and Bernetta Scott, Richard C. Schwartz, Emery E. Seider, Larry and Sylvia Sivils, Richard H. Smith, Bob Stokes — Illustrations, Matt Sullivan, Randall and June Weales, Joel Wilson, Virginia Wilson, Randy and Marsha Vogel, Grace Zeno, Herb and Janey Zolliner, to every Mrs. Brown, and to those who wish to remain anonymous.

For everyone's support, encouragement, and dedication, I will be forever grateful. If I have overlooked anyone I am truly sorry. From the bottom of my heart, my thanks go out to each of you.

In a 1932 edition of The Jewel News, Vol. 10 No. 6, the "Bavarian Climbing Rose" pattern appeared. Shown here are a cup and saucer with a 10" plate. The backstamp of the china is a crown below the words "H&Co., Selb Bavaria Heinrich & Co." in green lettering. *Hamilton Collection.*

CONTENTS

A 10" dinner plate in the "Floral Dresden" pattern, made in Germany. Distributed in the U.S.A. during the mid- to late 1930s. Jewel offered a complete dinner service in this pattern. Marked "EPIAG" with a bent arm holding a sword, "CZECHOSLOVAKIA 9954," and "41." This pattern was used in various Jewel promotional photographs and may be even older. *Hamilton Collection.*

INTRODUCTION

It has always been my intention to preserve history regarding the reputable Jewel Tea company for future generations. Of course, no history can ever be *completely* finished. I did not have access to all Jewel booklets, brochures, Jewel News editions, or catalogues, and many dates cannot be pinpointed, so research remains to be done by future Jewel scholars. I used what was available, and as always would appreciate hearing from collectors who can supply material missing throughout this publication. Even with your help, however, I fear it is impossible to list or photograph every Jewel item ever offered to Mrs. Brown!

As you build your collection, it is wise to pay close attention to marks. Remember that "Distributed by Jewel" means that someone else manufactured the product, while "Manufactured by Jewel" indicates that the product was made by Jewel itself. I personally believe that if an item says "JEWEL," it qualifies as a Jewel product, whether they were the manufacturer or just the distributor.

The mark "Jewel Park" indicates a date after 1930, when Jewel moved into their Barrington headquarters. Many Jewel logos overlap, since an old product had to be used up before the new product was marketed. The seal "TESTED AND APPROVED BY MARY DUNBAR JEWEL HOMEMAKERS INSTITUTE" appears only on those items that passed an extensive testing process.

Jewel, liks many other companies, placed their name before the public as much as possible. Customers paid attention when items were imprinted with the famous "JEWEL" name, so the company was aware that they would be secure as a business as long as "Jewel" remained a household word. Most of their items are marked with the company name, but as in most cases there are exceptions to the rule. It may be helpful to have both volumes on this historical company, to cross-reference marks and items.

A Journey Through History

In this book, you will meet the founders of Jewel, a young solicitor and his partner, and hear the famous story.

You will become acquainted with R.E. Durham, Hancock and Karker, Frank Talbot and Billy Whalen, and relive those horse and wagon days and winter weather. Be electrified with the company's purchase of "The Big Building," and feel the tension of the era's most difficult financial times. Be saddened at the death of Frank P. Ross. Indulge yourself in this fascinating history; it is part of our heritage.

In this book you will finally meet the matriarch of the Jewel Tea Company, and discover that she was a real person.

You will meet Hall China designer Eva Ziezel, who was responsible for so many beautiful Jewel items.

Roam the Barrington building into hidden places, and walk the corridors where a chronicle of portraits hang. Explore every nook and cranny. You may even feel the presence of Mary Dunbar, hear voices from the past and savor the fragrance of roasting coffee and the aroma of vanilla. The term "coffee break twice a day" was originated by the Jewel Tea Company, in connection with the operation of the ration packing line. During World War II, the Jewel Tea Company used its facilities for packaging food and coffee for the troops overseas. Take a break in the Barrington cafeteria, or hear the faint sound of a bowling ball in the former employee bowling alley. Wander on the grounds where history was written. Sing Jewel songs; listen to Jewel music.

Meet the Jewel salesmen, and examine their awards and carrier cases. Engage in conversation with "the Coffee Man" to learn about Jewel's three ways of saving. Examine the photographs of salesmen from the archives. Let yourself become an unseen passenger in a Jewel wagon or truck. Feel the movement of the wheels beneath the wagon, and the breath of the horse or mule against your cheek.

Look through the lens of a "Speed Graphic" or "View Camera" and become part of the Jewel test kitchen. You will see everyday kitchen items offered through the Jewel Tea Company to make living more simple. You will be introduced to staff members and behold spectacular items that appeared in many of the test kitchen photographs. You may stare in amazement at the many Jewel products and premiums which are actually being used in these photographs. Take time to examine each picture carefully (at times a magnify glass may help), for each photograph holds a vast amount of historical data. In addition, you will examine the contents of a trunk that was associated with Mary Dunbar.

Some of the most exceptional "Unusual" pieces ever offered by Jewel (or rejected by them) are now in private collections. I hope you will be fascinated and appreciate them as much as I do when you discover them on these pages.

One of the most valuable chapters for Jewel researchers is the one focusing on paper and plastic, offerng a wealth of Jewel information. As I did for my first volume, I cut apart the crumbling pages of my Jewel News collection from the late 1920s and early 1930s to allow them to appear in this publication.

As you read this book, you will realize that all Jewel products, premiums, and services made the perfect gift for a wedding, anniversary, or any other occasion.

I hope you will comprehend the concern that Jewel and Mary Dunbar had for children. You may be fortunate to discover hidden memories from your own childhood. It was impossible to list, photograph or describe the many Jewel toys and merchandise offered for children. This book show only begins to touch upon the items available.

You will learn how much faith many customers had in Mary Dunbar, when they turned to her for advice concerning household tasks, especially sewing, laundry, and cleaning. This book shows how the task of housework could be made easy with Jewel shears, irons, sewing baskets, dustpans, and cleaning supplies.

Mary Dunbar also taught her readers how to set the perfect table, using the finest glassware, the appropriate china and linens, and the proper placement of silverware.

Discover the designer David Douglas, the "Madrid" pattern from The Federal Glass Co., and experience a chronicle adventure in "ChicagoLand." Search for "Go-Along" pieces of china and glassware manufactured by the Salem Co. of Salem, Ohio.

Enjoy the story of Ephraim the mule, who will intrigue you as he heads for the finish line in the hope of winning his symbol of distinction.

You will meet Mrs. Brown's husband, the real Granny Hartney, and Admiral Richard E. Byrd. You will soon realize every Jewel customer was a real Mrs. Brown!

As you explore this volume, I hope you capture a glimpse of yesterday, and realize how important it is to preserve history for future generations. As you read this second volume of Jewel history, I hope you develop "wings"!

The yellow three-cup rainbow bowl; this bowl is backstamped "Hall Radiant Ware." This set of all-purpose bowls gave a bright touch to any kitchen. *Eisnaugle Collection.*

In 1942 the American housewife found numerous uses for Hall Rainbow Bowls. Listed as No. 320, the 1-1/2 cup bowl came in green, the 3-cup size came in yellow, the 5-cup in royal blue, and a 2-quart in deep orange. These Rainbow Bowls can be seen on the countertop in a black and white Jewel photograph from 1939, appearing on page 121 in the first volume. *Hamilton Collection.*

8

CHAPTER 1
THE HISTORY OF JEWEL

Frank Vernon Skiff.

The Jewel Tea Company sold groceries directly to a million American homes, with the inducement of sharing profits through premiums distributed in advance. Jewel reached the housewife in her own home through well-trained salesmen who traveled established routes by motorcar. Salesmen called on each customer every two weeks, delivering the groceries ordered two weeks previously and taking an order to be dropped off on the next regular visit.

This operation had its beginnings at the turn of the century. Frank Vernon Skiff (1870-1933) was a young solicitor for the India Tea Company in Chicago when he set up his own tea wagon operation in 1899. Mr. Skiff's only assets were a horse and wagon, $700, and an idea. He planned to operate a door-to-door route to regular customers selling them fresh coffee from the roaster. His idea was to call on them every week on the same day and approximately the same hour.

At the turn of the century coffee was purchased from bins or large tin canisters from the local grocery store. The coffee may have been out of the roaster for weeks or even months, affecting the quality and freshness.

When the customers found the coffee to be good, they got into the habit of dealing with Mr. Skiff. Soon he was delivering spices, tea, and other staple grocery items to their doors. He would take orders for both coffee and grocery items on one trip, and deliver them two weeks later.

Frank P. Ross.

Frank Skiff was joined in 1901 by his brother-in-law, Frank P. Ross (1869-1947), as a partner in the business. Frank P. Ross's job was to secure new customers for the growing business. Mr. Skiff was a quiet man with a wry sense of humor, while Mr. Ross was an energetic extrovert; both men worked well together in forming the company in those early days.

Together they named their new company the "Jewel Tea Company." The name "Jewel" was chosen because in those days, anything special (be it a thing or even an idea) was called a "jewel."

In 1903, just four years after Skiff and Ross founded the Jewel Tea Company, the firm hired a young man by the name of Frank Talbot. On March 3, 1938, Mr. Talbot completed his 35th year with the Jewel Tea Company. He was given a service button set with two diamonds and three rubies. At that time Mr. Talbot was senior purchasing agent.

Frank Talbot.

The horse and wagon of the Jewel Tea Company, photographed in Chicago, Illinois on March 1, 1903. Billy Whalen was a combination barn boss and wagon driver.

When coffee sales surged upward, Jewel customers paid the 8¢ a pound more than stores were charging.

As the service prospered under the guidance of the two men, routes inside the city were expanded and new routes opened outside the city. In 1903 Jewel Tea was incorporated in Illinois. Within two years the Company had outgrown its old building, at which time they acquired a three-story building for the roasting of their own coffee. During this time manufacturing equipment was bought and by 1906 they were producing the first products under their own label, including baking powder and extract.

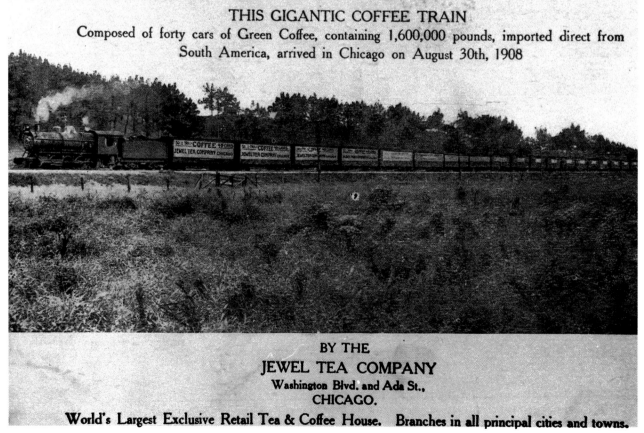

THIS GIGANTIC COFFEE TRAIN

Composed of forty cars of Green Coffee, containing 1,600,000 pounds, imported direct from South America, arrived in Chicago on August 30th, 1908

BY THE
JEWEL TEA COMPANY
Washington Blvd. and Ada St.,
CHICAGO.

World's Largest Exclusive Retail Tea & Coffee House.   Branches in all principal cities and towns.

This picture postcard shows a train that arrived in Chicago on August 30, 1908, containing 1,600,000 pounds of coffee. *Byerly Collection.*

As 1909 approached they were in need of more space. Skiff and Ross erected their first manufacturing company, which was to expand the range of products manufactured under the Jewel label. Jewel reached the million-dollar mark in annual sales in 1910 and had established 400 routes.

By 1915, what had first started as a one-wagon operation had developed into 850 routes and produced over $8 million in annual sales.

The Wausau, Minnesota Jewel Tea Co. horse and wagon shown here is dated pre-1910. Note the sign above the woman's head in the doorway. It reads: "Jewel Tea Co., Wausau."

The Company ceased giving coupons by 1914, and instead allocated profit-sharing credits for groceries purchased as cash credits to the customers' premium account balances.

With a capitalization of $16 million, the owners incorporated Jewel Tea under the laws of the State of New York in 1916. At this time, they listed Jewel common and preferred stock on the New York Stock Exchange.

Then they expanded into new areas, including New England, the Rocky Mountain states, and the West Coast. At the end of 1916 sales had reached nearly $13 million, with 1645 routes in operation.

When World War I began, it became difficult for Jewel to recruit manpower. Costs of raw materials increased and strikes by union drivers on bread and milk routes crippled operations in major cities, forcing Jewel to shut down operations in many of those cities.

By the end of 1917, Jewel had curtailed 1,714 of their own routes. The government commandeered the Jewel plant in Hoboken, New Jersey for war material production, which pushed costs higher. Jewel profits fell by the year's end but sales held.

Disrupted by World War I, Jewel continued retiring the last of its horses and mules, preparing for the "numerous automobiles" they had boasted about in their advertising. Jewel employees felt that the truck could never replace the horse and wagon on certain routes. They believed that the truck might be practical where there were long distances to cover, but a horse and wagon would be more useful in jobs having many stops in one locality.

Management decided to gamble on the automobile and in 1926 sold their last horse and wagon. Many Jewel employees still believed that the new "horseless carriage" could never replace the reliable old horse and wagon.

Taken in 1911, this photograph shows Emery Seider, Sr. when he opened up the territory for Jewel Tea in Toledo, Ohio. *Rhodes Collection.*

This historical black and white photograph was found in the Barrington archives. The photograph was not dated and the two men can not be identified. *Barrington Archives.*

Jewel's connection with the Hall China Company of East Liverpool, Ohio dates to the mid-1920s. Hall teapots began to be used as premiums during this decade. The famous Autumn Leaf appeared in the 1930s. In the 1940s, the Morning Glory pattern appeared, and in the 1950s came Cameo Rose. Of all the Jewel premiums, however, Autumn Leaf remains the highest in demand.

The Homemakers' Institute was launched in 1924 with a new concept that linked customers with the Jewel headquarters. At the Institute they tested recipes, developed new ones, and collected household ideas to be published in the Jewel News. For the first time Jewel cookbooks were published and the household name—"Mary Dunbar"—that would become famous was adopted.

By 1930 the company owned a block of government bonds valued at $1,500,000. Maurice Karker still felt that the company was losing its earning power.

Because of inadequate accounting controls and expansion, Skiff and Ross were forced out of their operation by 1919. Managerial talents were brought in when a banker named Raymond E. Durham was elected interim president in 1919, and a 19-year Navy veteran named John M. Hancock joined as administrative vice president.

By the end of 1920, the company's New Orleans and the San Francisco plants, routes and branches were reduced by a third.

J. M. Hancock became Jewel's president in 1922 after pulling the ailing company out of the red. He resigned this position in 1924, but remained as Chairman of the Board.

Maurice Karker succeeded Hancock as president; under Mr. Karker's leadership, Jewel was a more closely controlled operation.

This photograph shows one Hartford, CT street in 1928, with the three sales units which had just begun the distribution of Jewel Cup Coffee to the grocery stores in Hartford, a subsidiary of the Brooklyn, N. Y. division. *Barrington Archives.*

The company purchased 211 acres of farmland in 1928 at the edge of Barrington, Illinois. When they acquired an additional 100 acres, they named the area "Jewel Park."

On June 27, 1929, Jewel officially broke ground for a new building on the site, and nine months later the Barrington building was completed. In April 1930, Jewel made a complete surprise announcement to most Jewel customers and friends: they were moving into their new General Headquarters Office and Midwest Plant at Barrington, Illinois.

The Barrington building was a architectural masterpiece of limestone, marble, and brass. Employees could bowl, play handball or squash, have a game of tennis on the outdoor courts, or fish in a stocked lake behind the building. Jewel was taking care of their people's needs. The building has undergone numerous additions over the years.

Maurice Karker.

The headquarters in Barrington, Illinois. *Barrington Archives.*

Jewel Stores

Although The Jewel Tea Company began in 1899 primarily as a home delivery service featuring coffee, tea, spiices, and premiums, they did have a few stores set up to show and sell their product lines. These were not really grocery stores, though; they were more like advertising showcases for various wares, existing only in certain areas.

In 1932 a law was enacted in Green River, Wyoming that was to change the history of Jewel. This ordinance prohibited salesmen from making uninvited calls at the homes or prospective customers. The ordinance spread like an epidemic through the country, threatening to stop Jewel's business, since they relied so heavily on salesmen going door-to-door to sign up new customers.

Jewel wanted to purchase a small chain of food stores as a defensive measure against the Green River Ordinance. At this time, they learned that the Loblaw Groceterias of Canada were over-expanded in Chicago because of the Depression. The Loblaw chain was a little larger than Jewel wanted, but in 1932 Jewel became the owner of 77 Loblaw stores in Chicago, and four other midwestern stores, for approximately one million dollars.

Unfortunately, this was the worst possible time for a move of this sort. The economy of the country was struggling. By the end of its first year of operations, Jewel had lost as much money as they had paid for the stores.

The new business was forced to move cautiously in the relatively unfamiliar surroundings of the retail grocery store trade. For two years Jewel struggled but seemed to slip two strides back for every one taken forward. Because the company had little previous experience in this particular type of retail merchandising, management studied the methods used by other chains and decided to improve departments in their stores which appeared to be relatively unproductive for competitors.

The situation had reached a critical point. Jewel hired Robert Updegraff, who advised Karker to "liquidate or fight it out." Mr. Karker decided to fight it out. This decision marked the turning point in Jewel's method of doing business, and opened the way for future expansion.

Here is an announcement Jewel made to its customers in The Jewel News about the new facility:

> The Barrington Midwest Plant means vast improvements in groceries, premiums, service, and the ultimate satisfaction of Jewel customers. It stands for more satisfied employees, and near the Barrington Plant, Jewel employees are building a number of attractive homes in Jewel Park and in other adjacent subdivisions.
>
> The Plant is located in pure, clean, sunshine, light and air of this small city of Barrington, Illinois with a population of 3,000. The Jewel Tea Company takes its manufacturing activities into ideal surroundings and conditions. Barrington is located thirty-eight miles northwest of Chicago.

John Bell was the landscape architect for the Jewel development, which included 55,000 trees, shrubs and brushes.

The 160 members shown gathered in Barrington, Illinois to attended the thirteenth annual branch managers' convention from June 25-28, 1934. (Front row left to right) G. H. Sibley, Robert Updegraph, Jim O'Connor, Joe Friedlander, Allen Hunt, C. W. Kaylor, W. D. Smith, John Hancock, M. H. Karker, Robert Hilton and R. W. Muir. Also appearing are Mrs. L. R. Carroll and Mrs. J. J. Goddard; can you find them? *Barrington Archives*

Jewel also turned to its potential customers—the housewives—to find out how they could be better served. Jewel conducted a survey of 18,000 housewives in the Chicago area, and formulated the "Ten Commandments of Jewel" based on the responses. In May of 1934 Jewel closed all the Loblaw Groceterians' stores for renovations. When they reopened three days later, they all bore the Jewel name.

For the first four years, these stores were a drain on the routes' earnings. Not until 1938 did they made significant contributions to the company's earnings.

Total sales reached a new all-time high by 1937 and new route branches opened on the West Coast and in Harrisburg, Pennsylvania. In Chicago, at 2617 S. Ashland Avenue, Jewel Food Stores were in their own Jewel-owned headquarters.

Jewel, Employees, & The Community

Jewel Retirement Estates was formulated and adopted in 1938, starting with a contribution of $80,555.90 from the company. Over 1,700 Jewel employees elected to join.

Jewel had one of the first group life insurance policies and medical plans for their employees, dating back to 1918. The company was to adopt the Jewel Package Plan (medical insurance) in 1950, and added it to the list of benefits.

In 1938 over 300 citizens from the Barrington community learned about Jewel when they were invited to visit the headquarters plant on Thursday, September 29.

This was the first "open house" invitation since the Barrington building had open eight years earlier. The invitation was extended through the Barrington newspapers.

C. N. Watkins, chief of the publications division, Charles Kunz, the pressroom foreman, and J. Walker Black, a general printing executive, review proofs of the grocery order card.

In October of 1938 a newly published edition of a selling tool was received by Jewel salesman. The publication was the 1939 grocery order card.

The inside spread displayed Jewel's standard grocery items. The front cover advertises "the most complete coffee service in America," as did the last edition of the grocery order card. The back cover was startlingly different and new, with full color photographs telling "what the product will do." In addition to these sales-boosting pictures, the back cover employs another feature in helping to sell the product. A 3" x 5" black space is provided for customers to attach pictures that were clipped from The Jewel News. It was pointed out that in every issue of The Jewel News there were illustrations designed to fit into this space and tie in with the current sales program, including the World's Fair campaign.

On November 30, 1938, Robert W. Muir, Secretary and General Counsel of Jewel Tea Co., Inc. died as the result of a cerebral hemorrhage. Mr. Muir's interment was in Barrington.

Mr. Muir had joined the Jewel Tea Co., Inc. on May 14, 1924 as a special counsel. On April 21, 1925 he was elected assistant secretary and made general counsel, then was elected secretary of the company on July 14, 1931. Mr. Muir was first vice-president of both the National Retail Tea and Coffee Merchants Association and the National Association of Direct Selling Companies. He was also a director of the First National Bank in Barrington.

World War II shaped Jewel's future, as women replaced men in staffing both routes and stores. Women were successfully handling more than one-third of all the Jewel jobs by the end of 1942. One-fourth of all Jewel Food Stores had women managers and over 700 women were running the routes during 1944.

When Mr. Karker resigned as president to go to Washington in order to aid the war efforts, Jewel replaced him with 36-year-old Franklin J. Lunding. Mr. Lunding had been with Jewel since 1931 as general counsel. Due to the efforts of Mr. Lunding during those troubled years, sales volume and earnings were kept stable.

Franklin J. Lunding.

When sugar and coffee were rationed, Jewel was hit hard because the major plant operation had been to process coffee.

Routes were reduced to 1591, and only 154 stores were in operation by the end of 1942.

By the late '40s, the company had a reputation for quality products and a concern for customers. The early '50s saw route expansion efforts taken away from rural areas and concentrated in metropolitan areas, where salesmen could locate customers with a minimum of travel.

FRANK V. SKIFF, FOUNDER OF TEA COMPANY, DIES

June 3, 1933

Frank Vernon Skiff, 63 years old (1869-1933), one of the organizers of the Jewel Tea Company and for nineteen years a resident of Oak Park, died yesterday morning at the Harbor sanitarium, New York, following a long illness. Mr. Skiff was born in 1869 at Newton, Ia., the son of a grocer. He is survived by his widow, the former Ida Catherine Rowe of St. Joseph, Mich.

From 1900, the year before the tea company was organized, until 1917 Mr. Skiff made his home in Oak Park, Il. Since then he had alternately lived in his winter home at Palm Beach, Fla., and at his summer home in Millburn, N.J. He retired from active work in the Jewel Tea Company in 1919.

Interment Sunday at Millburn, N.J.

The above death notice appeared in the Chicago Tribune 1933 paper.

FRANK P. ROSS, JEWEL TEA CO-FOUNDER, DIES

Services for Frank P. Ross, 531 North East Avenue, widely known co-founder of the Jewel Tea company, will be conducted at 2:30 on Friday afternoon at his home. Interment will be at Bronswood, in Hinsdale (Illinois).

Mr. Ross, well known and beloved in the community where he was an early resident, died suddenly Sunday morning at the Corey Hill hospital in Brookline, Mass. He had undergone a serious operation a fortnight ago and was thought to be recovering satisfactorily, although still gravely ill.

Mrs. Ross and their son-in-law, Dr. John Orndorff, were with him in Brookline during his operation, and Dr. Orndorff remained with him until a day or two before his sudden death, leaving only when his recovery was anticipated and a safe convalescence was assured.

"Mr. Ross' death is a loss to the community, where he had lived for so many years, and his benevolence endeared him to many whom he aided quietly, in many ways," a friend said Monday.

Before his retirement in 1919, Mr. Ross and his brother-in-law, the late Frank V. Skiff, had built a business empire and developed a horse and wagon venture into an $88,000,000 enterprise with branches throughout the country.

Mr. Ross was born in Wind Ridge, Greene County, Pa., on July 22, 1869. He was the son of Asa and Mary Fonner Ross. He was the youngest of 11 children.

Mr. Ross never lost his love for his home community and returned to his hometown often. He was a great benefactor to the community, and in respect to all he has done, schools will be closed there on the day of his funeral, and flags at half-staff. Memorial services will be conducted there at the same time as the service takes place in Oak Park.

It was at the age of 17 when Mr. Ross decided to "go west." He located in Oskaloosa, Iowa, where he learned telegraphy. In the early part of 1887, he took his first position with the Iowa Central Railroad, now the M. & St. L. Railway in Latimer, Iowa, and he subsequently held similar positions for the road at Alexander, Centerville, and Newton, Iowa.

He was later promoted to traveling freight agent. It was in Newton, Iowa where he met Blanche Skiff, with whom he was united in marriage on February 7, 1899.

In 1901, Mr. Ross resigned from the M. & St. L. Railway and came to Chicago. With his brother-in-law, the late Frank V. Skiff, a small store on the south side of Chicago was rented and the Jewel Tea company was started.

They had one horse and wagon at that time, from which they sold tea and coffee, and originated the premium in-advance plan. The company grew steadily and by 1916 was sufficiently successful to engage eastern investment bankers in a plan of reorganization, pursuant to which they purchased preferred and part of the common stock of the company. The Skiff and Ross interests, however, retained control and continued in the management of the business until 1919 when they relinquished control to the bankers and turned over to them the active management of the company. Mr. Ross, however, continued until his death to hold a substantial interest in the common stock of the company. He also continued as a director of the company until about 1922.

After his retirement in 1919, Mr. and Mrs. Ross spent considerable time traveling, taking many world tours. For the past 15 years they have spent their winters in Tucson, Ariz., with occasional trips to California. It was on the scheduled day of departure that Mr. Ross learned it would be necessary for him to undergo a serious operation.

During his years of retirement Mr. Ross took great pleasure in quietly giving aid to many people, and he was particularly interested in the educational advancement of the younger generation. He made many gifts to the Richill Township High School at Wind Ridge, Pa. He equipped the school with a complete band, furnished a library, and annually gave awards for the students receiving the highest grades. He also granted annual scholarships to the Waynesburg College of Waynesburg, Pa. from which college Mr. Ross later received an honoary degree of Doctor-of-Law.

He is survived by his widow, Blanche Skiff Ross, two daughers (Mrs. John R. Orndorff and Mrs. Arthur C. Fennekohl) and six grandchildren. Dr. and Mrs. Orndorff and their three children reside in River Forest, and the Fennekohl, with their three children, reside in Houston, Texas. He is also survived by two sisters and one brother, Mrs. Sarah R. Burke, who resides in the old homestead in Wind Ridge, Pa., Mrs. Anna R. Irwin of Ridgway, Pa., and James M. Ross of Kimball, Kan.

The above death notice appeared in the Oak Leaf Newspaper in Oak Park, Illinois on Thursday, February 27, 1947. On Thursday, March 6, 1947 a small notice appeared with his photograph and the caption "Conduct Services for Frank P. Ross."

This 1933 photograph shows Jewel Tea's co-founder Frank P. Ross (fourth from the left, in a light-colored suit) with boyhood friends at the "Century of Progress" meeting.

In 1949, catalogs showing a variety of merchandise and products were distributed by the route salesmen to regular customers. Orders were taken bi-weekly and filled through the mail. Jewel was the first home shopping service to introduce a catalog.

In 1966, the Jewel Home Shopping Service of the Jewel Tea Co., Inc. became a division of Jewel Companies, Inc., making it the 12th largest retailer in the nation.

The Jewel Home Shopping Service was the original shopping service of the Jewel business; even later, when the company's name was changed to the Jewel Companies, Inc., they retained the Home Shopping Service as one of several diversifications.

On January 29, 1981, Jewel Companies, Inc. announced their intention to discontinue ownership of the Jewel Home Shopping Service. They planned to transfer the assets of the business to a cooperative organization which would be formed and managed by certain Jewel employees. At the same time, the Company stated it expected the balance of its operations to achieve record earnings in the fiscal year ending January 1981.

Under the formulated plan of 1981, Jewel agreed to sell each route to the employee who would operate it, and

transfer the inventory and other assets to a cooperative which would serve the newly independent route operators.

On March 24, 1981 Jewel Home Shopping Service became a dealer-owned cooperative, named IHSS, Inc. (In Home Shopping Service). After becoming a Co-op, a committee was formed to work on a new name and identification program. One of the conditions of the purchase was that the Jewel name be phased out over a three year period as a development of a new identity took place.

The committee was in charge of narrowing down name possibilities and deciding which single name best served the organization. A graphics design company was retained along with an advertising agency to submit ideas and designs. Dealers and employees were asked to send in suggestions, of which two hundred thirty-nine suggestions were received. The committee then selected six of those, which were tested in three focus groups: working women, homemakers who had traded with the organization, and a group of selected Jewel customers. Those members of each focus group discussed both positive and negative feelings about the six names and designs submitted, and selected "Heritage Home Shopping" and "J. T.'s General

Store." Selected people were interviewed and asked to rate each name in shopping malls in Los Angeles, Pittsburgh, and Nashville. The consensus of these interviews pointed to "J. T.'s General Store." The committee then asked all employees and dealers to approve J. T.'s General Store as the new name. Ninety-seven percent approved.

The Jewel name appeared with the new wagon logo and the subtitle until May 1983, then vanished. On October 3, 1994, J. T.'s General Store became known as "JT Dealer Sales and Services Corp" after being sold to some of the employees.

The office of the company president. *Barrington Archives.*

This photograph, taken on a winter day from the fifth floor of the Barrington building during the 1940s, shows the aerosol building. Later, J.T. used it as a sample room; then Park Coffee Service was located in it for a brief period. It is now believed to be occupied by a computer repair company.

The employees' cafeteria at the Barrington headquarters. *Barrington Archives.*

"Good Morning! Jewel Tea Co., Barrington, may I help you?" This photograph is marked "switchboard operator Sally Banks." Sally also appeared in a Jewel Baking Powder photograph in 1938, with a group of home office employees. *Barrington Archives.*

The Barrington auditorium, taken from the side of the room. *Barrington Archives.*

17

Will it be a strike or gutter ball? Barrington employees enjoy a game of bowling in the lower level bowling alley provided by Jewel. Currently, J.T.'s Print Shop occupies these quarters. *Barrington Archives.*

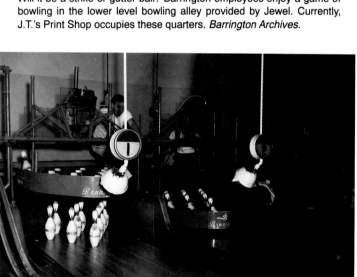

In lanes 1 and 2 of the Barrington Bowling Alley, the pins were manually reset. *Barrington Archives.*

The Jewel plant in Chicago, 1919, where Jewel-Jell, baking powder, extracts, toilet articles, and other products were manufactured and packaged. This same photograph appeared as an illustration on a 1926-1927 calendar housecard. Note the Jewel sign and the logo on the building. *Barrington Archives.*

A group of fine-looking gentlemen pose for this photograph. This unmarked photograph may be Barrington staff or branch managers attending a seminar. *Barrington Archives.*

The back of this photograph reads "Jewel Tea Co., Inc. Washington and Ada Street Chicago, Illinois 1909." Can you find the five different signs indicating Jewel Tea Co.? This building underwent different stages of renovations. The original building is on the corner with the entrance. Next to this entrance, to the right of the automobile, is a later addition. *Barrington Archives.*

Thirteen of the men from the previous group photograph.

The group of men and women shown below posed for this historical photograph in front of Jewel Tea Co., Inc. building. Location and date unknown. *Barrington Archives.*

This photograph shows a large group of Jewel Tea Co. personnel. Though it is dated 1916-1918 on the back, no place or names are indicated. *Barrington Archives.*

Plant personnel from Hoboken, New Jersey, photographed on October 7, 1926. *Barrington Archives.*

This historical Barrington photograph shows the Main Power Control for the building. No date or other information appears on this photograph. *Barrington Archives.*

The Jewel Tea Company boiler room basement in Barrington, no date given. *Barrington Archives.*

CHRONOLOGICAL BUSINESS & RESIDENCE TABLE

[Additional notes made in italics]*

In Chicago in 1899, Frank V. Skiff boards in a house at 4003 S. Drexel. *[No mention is made of the business. Ross is still in Iowa where he married Blanche Skiff on February 7, 1899.]*

In 1901 Skiff has a house at 2221 S. Wabash Avenue. *[No mention is made of the business. No reference is made of Frank P. Ross. Ross resigned from the Iowa railroad in 1901.]*

In 1902, Skiff and Frank P. Ross are listed selling "Teas, Coffees and Spices" under the name "Skiff and Ross" at 643 E. 43rd Street. Skiff has a house at 742 E. 46th and Ross has a house at 4105 S. Indiana. *[An historical photograph of this company at the 643 E. 43rd Street address shows on the overhead awning — 643 JEWEL TEA COMPANY 643, below COMPANY appears, NOT INC. This also appears on the front window with the names SKIFF AND ROSS, PROPS. below along with the legend TEAS, COFFEES, BAKING POWDERS AND EXTRACTS. Date of this photograph unknown.]*

In 1903, they are listed selling "Teas, Coffees and Spices — Skiff and Ross (Frank V. Skiff and Frank P. Ross)" at the 643 E. 43d Street address. Skiff has changed residence and has a house at 4602 S. Prairie and Ross is at 462 E. 41 Street. *[Skiff and Ross became prosperous enough to expand outside of the Chicago area.]*

In 1904, Teas, Coffees and Spices are sold under the name Jewel Tea Co. at 641 E. 43d Street. *[Note change in number.]* Skiff is listed as Sec. Jewel Tea Co. and Ross listed as Pres. Jewel Tea Co., 641 E. 43d Street. Both Skiff and Ross are living together at 430 E. 41 Street.

In 1905, both men are working out of 641 E. 43rd Street, "Teas, Coffees and Spices — Jewel Tea Co." Frank V. Skiff is now listed as President and Frank P. Ross is Secretary. Skiff has a house back on S. Prarie but this time at number 4413 S. Prairie. Ross is still living in the house at 430 E. 41 Street. *[Began roasting their own coffee and packaging baking powder.]*

In 1906, Skiff and Ross are listed as selling "Teas, Coffees and Spices — Jewel Tea Co." at 18 N. May Street. Frank V. Skiff is President and Frank P. Ross is Secretary. Skiff has a house at 137 S. Pine Avenue and Ross remains in the house at 430 E. 41 Street.

In 1907, the listing and address remain the same for the company, as do the offices of President and Secretary. This time both Skiff and Ross are living together at the 137 S. Pine Avenue address.

In 1908, Teas, Coffees and Spices — Jewel Tea Co. 426 W. Washington Blvd. Earlier in 1908 they were listed still at the 18 N. May Street address. Frank V. Skiff is President and Frank P. Ross is Secretary. Both still resided together at the house at 137 Pine Avenue. *[August 30, 1908 a train containing 1,600,000 pounds of coffee imported directly from South America arrived in Chicago for the Jewel Tea Co.]*

In 1909, Teas, Coffees and Spices — Jewel Tea Co. at 426 W. Washington Blvd — Skiff is listed as Pres. Jewel Tea Co., and Ross is listed as Sec. Both Skiff and Ross are living together still at 137 S. Pine Avenue. *[It is believed the new headquarters are built in Chicago, Illinois on Washington Blvd. and Ada Street, note Washington Blvd. address above.]*

In 1910, "Teas, Coffees and Spices — Jewel Tea Co., at 1327 W. Washington." Skiff is listed as President and Ross as Secretary. Skiff is listed at 1327 W. Washington, while Ross is listed working out of 426 W. Washington. Note different business address for Skiff and Ross. Both still are living together at the 137 S. Pine Avenue address.

In 1911, "Teas, Coffees and Spices — Jewel Tea Co.," is still listed at 1327 W. Washington. Skiff is listed as President and Ross as Secretary. Both listed at the Washington Street address and both still resided at the house at 137 S. Pine Street.

From 1912-1913 the information remains the same as it was in 1911. *[Scotty Gellately began a career with the Jewel Tea Co., in 1912.]*

In 1914, "Teas, Coffees and Spices — F.V. Skiff Pres.; F.P. Ross Sec.," at 1327 W. Washington Blvd. Frank P. Ross now has a house in Oak Park. Frank V. Skiff (no home address given) only appears in the business listings.

From 1915 to 1916 no listing can be found. *[Stock was purchased in 1916 by Goldman, Sachs & Co., and Lehmann Brothers when Jewel became a New York Corporation.]*

In 1917, "Teas, Coffees and Spices — F.V. Skiff Pres. and F.R. Ross Sec.," location 1327 W. Washington Blvd. Frank P. Ross is still listed in a house in Oak Park. Frank V. Skiff (no home address given) only appears in the business listings. *[Frank V. Skiff was living in Oak Park for 19 years, address unknown.][By this time, Jewel had a variety of 20 different flavors of extracts.]*

In 1919, Frank P. Ross retires from the Jewel Tea Co. but is director of the company until about 1922.

The next listing is 1921 for Jewel Tea Co., Pershing and Robey (Damen Ave.) Rd.

In 1923, Frank P. Ross is at an office at 1555 Madison with a house at 531 North East Ave., Oak Park. *Frank P. Ross died at this address in 1947. Mrs. Frank Blanche Skiff would die at the same address in 1969. No listing for Frank V. Skiff.*

[In 1924, Mary Reed Hartson was designated "The Jewel Lady."]

[In 1926, Mary Reed Hartson gave exclusive rights to her maiden name, Mary Dunbar.]

In 1927, C.M.D.* lists Jewel Tea Co., at 3930 S. Winchester Avenue with a telephone number of LAF0928.

In 1930, Jewel moved into its Barrington, Illinois headquarters. Jewel Tea Co., C.M.D.* reports sales for the four weeks ending November 30, 1929 were $1,386,486 compared with $1,370,971 for the parallel weeks in 1928, an increase of 1.13 percent.

In 1933, Frank V. Skiff died in New York.

*C.M.D. = Central Manufacturing District
Chicago City Directories - Individual and Business Listings

21

CHAPTER 2
THE HISTORY OF HALL CHINA

This trademark is known worldwide. It is the mark of the Hall China Company of East Liverpool, Ohio. They are the manufacturers of a secretly processed fireproof cooking china.

It was in the year 1903 that the former partners in the inoperative East Liverpool Potteries Company came together at the stately residence of Robert Hall on Thompson Lane. On the afternoon of July 7 they met to settle the affairs and distribute the physical assets of the company. This stately residence and area was razed for the construction of the present freeway.

Ownership of the plant on the southeast corner of East Fourth and Walnut Streets was accepted by Robert Hall. The plant had previously been known as the West, Hardwick, and George Pottery.

On August 14, 1903 Mr. Hall founded The Hall China Company, just thirty-eight days after that afternoon meeting. Three oven kilns were fired, and with thirty-three potters they began to make bedpans and combinets, and the first chinaware to bear the famous Hall China trademark.

At first the company struggled. Suffering from a lack of capital, they scrambled in stiff competition with other small potteries. Less than a year after the founding of the company, in 1904, Mr. Hall died. His plans for the future of the company would never be known.

Assuming the responsibilities of management right from the beginning, his son, Robert Taggart Hall, began investigating the possibilities of developing a glaze that would stand the required heat for bisque firing, making possible single-fire ware that would be craze-proof. Mr. Hall had no precedent to follow and little to guide him. During the period from 1905 to 1911, Robert T. Hall experimented to develop the single-fire process. The struggling company continued to produce, at a profit, sufficient ware to keep the company in operation. From 1908 until 1914, dinnerware was added to the line and was made in small quantities.

After the death of the founder, Robert Hall, Francis I. Simmers became associated with Robert Taggart Hall. Mr. Simmers is credited with keeping orders coming in and laid the groundwork for the development that was to come.

On Memorial Day of 1910, vandals entered the sliphouse and inflicted damages to the extent of $3000. Neither the vandals nor the motive were ever discovered. This was an almost catastrophic loss for the company.

In 1911, after intensified research, Mr. Hall and Superintendent Jackson Moore, who had succeeded one Mr. Meakin, began to succeed. They witnessed the first successful leadless glaze. Mixed in a mortar with a pestle, the quantity was sufficient to dip half a mug. Placing the mug in the hottest part of the kiln (approximately 2200 F), they received a fair result, but further efforts were encouraging. They prepared more glaze and the pans were fired with promising results. They proceeded to load an entire kiln with the glaze-dipped unfired bisque. Pieces fired in the hottest part were almost perfect, with those in the coolest part being unsatisfactory. A hotter fire was needed. They again loaded and fired the kiln at a temperature of 2400 F. When the door of the kiln opened, a new era was to begin.

Those pieces that came out of the kiln in 1911 were strong, hard, nonporous, and craze-proof. Production grew in the following months from two dozen to sixteen dozen pieces per day.

In 1914, because of the war, European potteries were unable to continue to make or ship their products to the United States. The Hall company took advantage of the situation, turning all available production facilities to the manufacture of casseroles, teapots, coffeepots, and various items for the institutional trade. At the end of the war, cheap imports began entering the country. By then, customers realized that Hall products were less expensive in cost per year and cheaper in terms of food preservation. Hall by then had begun to establish their famous name.

In 1919 Hall increased their facilities through the purchase of the Goodwin Pottery Company at East Sixth and Broadway and introduced a new line — gold-decorated teapots. They became the world's largest manufacturer of decorated teapots.

In the quiet surrounding hills of East Liverpool, Ohio, approximately one mile from the tract of twenty-three acres that was first occupied in 1930, is located the Riverview Cemetery. Upon entering the peaceful grounds of this cemetery, it is easy to locate massive granite monuments chiseled with the prestigious name "HALL." Around many of these monuments rest members of this famous East Liverpool family.

Mr. Hall succumbed to a heart attack at his Park Boulevard residence on November 18, 1920, at the age of 43 years. After that, Mr. Francis T. Simmers served continuously as the company's president.

In 1920 Malcolm W. Thompson joined the company and became treasurer and general manager. Also in 1920, William J. Hocking, became purchasing agent.

A new line was introduced after the opening of Hall's third facility in 1927. They were to produce soda-fountain jars, and later decorate cooking china which was distributed through retail trade channels.

In 1929 it was decided to erect an entirely new factory facility and abandon the three old plants upon the completion of this new building.

The building was 250 feet wide by 680 feet long, with approximately 170,000 square feet of floor space located on one floor. This open space provided for continuous movement of work. The new facility consisted of three tunnel kilns, one open-fired multi-burner, one muffle-fire, and one semi-muffle-fire glost kiln fired with natural gas.

When the building was opened, the open-fire unit was turned on, followed by the glost kiln the next year, and in 1933 the muffle-fired unit was placed into operation.

In 1933 Hall engaged in the manufacture of decorated china, teapots, and coffee makers.

By 1936, Hall brought further expansion into their product line and, for the first time since 1914, their dinnerware

In 1930, Hall China occupied the new facility located on twenty-three acres in the East End that had been chosen for the new site. The facility's front entrance is shown here.

23

took shape. As the company's activities grew it was necessary to add eight additions to the building and install four other firing units. The first was made in 1934 and the last addition, completed in 1941, provided 385,000 square feet of floor space.

World War II brought new problems, but Hall continued and solved their war and postwar problems.

Since its early years the Hall China Company has been recognized as an industry leader in the production of quality hotel and restaurant china. Skillful designers translate customer demands into aesthetic yet well-engineered shapes. Craftsmen and craftswomen manufacture these shapes to tightly-controlled specifications. Laboratory personnel kept careful watch over quality, ensuring that high standards were maintained in all steps of manufacturing Hall China.

During 1991 a complete restoration in the west end section of the Hall China Company building took place. During the refurbishing of this section their old Hall Closet Retail Outlet prepared to close its doors and made provisions to relocate. While packaging and moving various pieces of china, Hall Closet conducted a half-price sale on the few remaining items that had not been moved.

The Hall Closet site is now a parking lot.

In the refurbished section of the main building, The Hall Closet Retail Outlet opened under the same name on August 29, 1991. The main entrance to the new outlet is shown here. *Boyce Photograph*

Commercial Decal of Ohio

The famous Autumn Leaf decal that appeared on old Autumn Leaf and on today's pieces offered by the N.A.L.C.C. and by China Specialties, Inc., is produced by the Commerical Decal of Ohio, Inc. in East Liverpool, Ohio. Approximately 75 years ago the company was located in downtown East Liverpool. However, there was much criticism over the smell of chemicals used in the production of decals, and in the 1960s the company built new facilities away from the center of the city. They still operate there today.

The company was orignially an importer of decals from Germany. Today Commercial Decal is an international manufacturer of decals. Operations of the organization are overseen by company president David Dunn.

Charles Boyce, husband of well-known historian Elizabeth Boyce, prepares for his last visit inside the old Hall Closet in August 1991, before it was razed. *Boyce Photograph*

CHAPTER *3*
THE JEWEL SALESMAN

The Coffee Man

Grandmother started a wonderful tradition when she gave her patronage to the "coffee man" around the turn of this century. Fifty years later, the company had become much more than coffee, though.

HALF A HUNDRED

"Over fifty food, laundry, and toilet products of the purest and finest quality are carried in the Jewel basket of service to its customers -and how many of these varied products do you purchase from your Jewel service salesman as he regularly calls for your order and makes deliveries to your door?"

"Save your order for your Jewel home service merchant. Think what a complete line of food products you can purchase from him; and with your products, thanks to the Jewel economy way of merchandising, you can enjoy the receipt of dozens and dozens of useful premiums, items you need for the kitchen, dining room, living room and bedroom."

"These premiums, which are delivered in your home and the homes of over 2,500,000 others, are put in your hands as an economy made possible by Jewel's money saving direct-to-home plan of operation. They represent the profits of middle-men — which have become your Jewel premiums."

"Over fifty products and nearly one hundred premiums, and you have uses for all of them."

— Jewel News, 1927

The Jewel Tea Salesman Needs Your Help

In 1926, the Jewel Tea salesman needed the help of the American customers. Jewel Tea issued the following statement:

"There is more in life than dollars and cents, and a friendly cooperation often helps things along wonderfully. Even so humdrum a task as buying groceries can be made pleasant and warmly human.

"Take, for instance, selecting the things you need. You can't carry them all in your head. More important matters crowd them out. So, if you trust to memory you're going to forget something — sure as fate! And chances are it's something you'll miss keenly when you do need it. So why not avoid the risk of such disappointment?"

"Sometimes it happens that folks find they can't be at home when The Jewel Man comes. That's liable to occur any time, to anyone. Something unexpected turns up — you simply can't be there. In that case, just leave your order slip and the cash or check with your neighbor. The Jewel Man will take care of the rest. He'll certainly thank you for the thought you show in helping him. An you'll be better satisfied yourself!"

No Accidents — January 1949

It was a new year again, and everyone at Jewel had started off fresh with a clean slate — NO ACCIDENTS! They were urged to keep it that way each and every day during the new year of 1949. Drivers resolved to look every time they backed up or pulled away from the curb, and to make sure the way was clear before crossing intersections.

The majority of Jewel salesmen had been driving vehicles for quite awhile and knew how to drive defensively in order to prevent accidents. They did not depend on the other fellow to stop at intersections or always do the right thing. By keeping alert at all times, these salesmen were able to protect excellent safe driving records.

In 1938, this Jewel car was junked in an accident because of reckless driving. The Jewel salesman suffered fractured ribs and multiple lacerations of the head.

The JEWEL T SAFETY AWARD for No Accidents. This metal award is heavy duty—3/16" thick with a 7/16" threaded bolt at the bottom for mounting. It could be placed on top of the hood of the truck, bolted to a steel plate for a desk or mantel decoration. There is no suggestion of a specific date on this award. For further discussion, see the "For Men Only" chapter. *Hedges Collection.*

During February 1938, the group of men shown here were honored at a banquet in the Hotel Texas in Ft. Worth. This group of men were the safest automobile drivers in Jewel's national organization for the year ending 1937. Fort Worth drivers covered approximately 225,000 miles of streets and highways.

Top Row — T.H. Cole, O.L. Woods, H.H. Kennedy, E.M. Whitehead, E.P. Hays, A.L. Pesha, J.B. Russell, F.A. Walling, Otho Nichols, J.M. Hudson, and R.B. McGibbon.

Middle Row — F.E. Gullion, B.W. Bridges, W.B. Davis, H.H. Johnson, O.J. McAlister, G.B. Humphreys, J.R. Webb, J.E. Holtz, B.O. Beach, T.L. Pack, and R.N. Sitton.

Bottom Row — O.C. Cook, J.C. Bartlett, C.F. Jones, R.F. Rogers, J.H. Williams, S.F. Ward, C.E. Rogers, H.A. Bartz, E.H. Carrington, and V.L. Stevens.

Note the illustration of the award held by the men in the center of this photograph, which is similar to the actual award shown here. *Eisnaugle Collection.*

"DAD. . . . HERE COMES OUR JEWEL MAN."

"He's a friend of all the family. . . . Mom and Dad, Sister and Brother, — and baby too. He's America's Groceryman, a friendly visitor through-out the year."

"Thanks to Jewel's Home Shopping Service. . . . the only service of it's kind in all America. . . . he is able to bring to the home many of the family's everyday needs. . . . clothing, housewares, home furnishings, toys, gifts, sports and playtime needs. Indeed, most of the good things in life that mean Better Living for More People."

— Jewel 1950

Jewel's Gallery of Salesmen

Tulsa, Oklahoma route salesman F. H. Pitt, number 2437. Note the Jewel logo on side of wagon. *Barrington Archives.*

In this historical photograph (dated 1919) C. O. Hancy stands with the basket; the other gentleman is anonymous, and the location is unknown. *Barrington Archives.*

This historical photograph is dated 1912. The wagon is marked number 1320, St. Paul, and the driver is Raymond Rumble. *Barrington Archives.*

This historical photograph of a Jewel sled is dated 1918. This photograph has been professionally retouched and appeared in a Jewel Calendar. *Barrington Archives.*

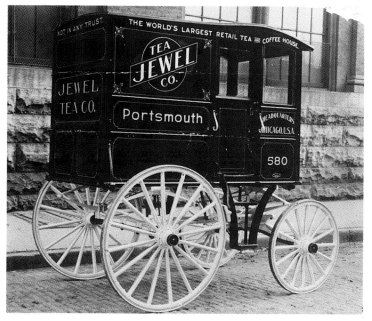

Portsmouth and number 580 appears on the side of this magnificent Jewel Tea Wagon; no information appears on the back. Note the exceptional Jewel logo. *Barrington Archives.*

This historical wagon is number 1694 Wichita. The back of the photo reads "E. J. Clark (City Route)" and "Roy Wadlow." Note scale logo. *Barrington Archives.*

The scale logo appears on the number 2071 Jewel wagon in this historical photograph. No other information appears on the back. *Barrington Archives.*

27

This historical photograph is believed to have been taken in Carbondale, Illinois, wagon number 186. No information appears on the back. *Barrington Archives.*

The above historical photograph of wagon number 249 was taken in Wichita, Kansas. No date appears on the back. *Barrington Archives.*

On close examination, this historical photograph shows the full harness team from the photograph shown earlier, but with wagon. *Barrington Archives.*

W. A. Little of Toledo, Ohio. In 1937 Mr. Little increased his sales and received a $50 prize check. Note the salesman's carrying basket.

Salesman W. A. King of Charlotte was a selling champion twice over. He won the Winged Victory Trophy in 1937 by leading his branch with two line orders and immediately repeated the victory in the tea contest.

This Jewel Truck is dated from the late 1940s. The truck is on display in an Illinois state park. *Woodruff Collection.*

Photographed in 1948, here is W. C. Bond with his daughter Barbara of the Long Beach, California branch. Mr. Bond maintained a better than $700 average and he hit $1017.58 and $919 respectively in the first and second weeks of an Anniversary Sale. Behind the gleaming Metro can be seen part of his residence. Mr. Bond knew as much about Jewel products as any man in the business and prided himself on a complete knowledge of the products he carried and sold. When not working on his route his hobby was photography.

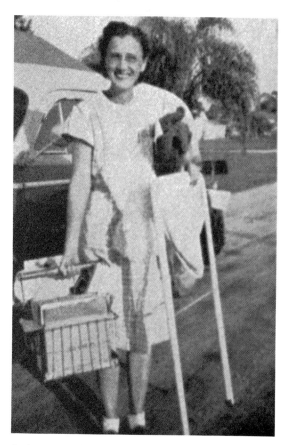

During the late 1920s, Fred Houser operated Route 05 in Reading, Pa. Fred is shown with his Jewel truck, ready to make calls upon the Pennsylvania customers.

Here she is, a real lady Jewel salesperson, Mrs. Velma Wilson from the Jackson 18 route at St. Petersburg, Florida. In the late 1940s Mrs. Wilson set an all-time high in the branch with a $907 average in the 12th period. She had $1296.75 in the final week of the 12th, another all time high for the branch.

In 1948, Wally Seidl had less than nine months' experience as a Jewel man, but in that time he had fashioned his 12 route into one of the top routes in the Duluth branch. Mr. Seidl and his family lived in Park Falls, Wisconsin. Wally enjoyed hunting, but when he couldn't find much time for it, he enjoyed watching a sporting event.

Jewel Tea Salesman Howard Hooper begins his Jewel route. *Courtesy Sandra Hooper Edwards.*

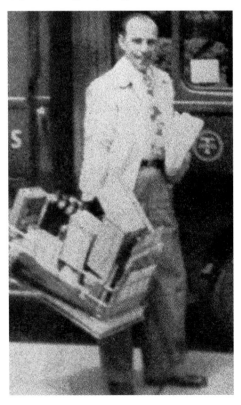

In the late 1940s Keith Johnson believed in taking a basketful of Jewel Products into each home on his Route 04 in Peoria.

A WORD ABOUT YOUR JEWEL MAN

"His title is 'Jewel Cooperative Franchise Operator.' However, your Jewel man is truly a businessman who assumes the responsibilities and enjoys the satisfaction that comes from successfully operating his own business. His qualifications are high. (We choose him as though our customers were doing the interviewing, and we might add that we welcome the fine recommendations many of our customers make). He is a man who has been carefully selected to serve you, not just sell you."

— Jewel 1952

FOUR JEWEL SERVICES — THE JEWEL WAY 1927,

FROM THE JEWEL TEA CO., INC.,

NEW YORK/CHICAGO

Jewel is more than a big business; it is a Service, giving its patrons four worth-while things for the price of one.

Quality Products

Coffees, other found products, laundry products and toilet articles-all of quality—are Jewel's first service to its customers.

Jewel products satisfy because they are always uniform and good; they are prepared with care, and quality is put into them.

The Jewel customer pays no more for Jewel products than she must pay for the same quality elsewhere, but for that price she also gets three other things, making four in all.

Quality Premiums

Jewel supplies useful household articles for the customer's home; things she needs, all of high grade, made to please and satisfy her.

With every package of Jewel products the customer receives a credit which she may apply toward payment for the household article she selects, paying for it without additional cash outlay.

This credit allowance does not increase the price she pays for her products.

She does not have to save enough credits to pay for the household article before getting it; Jewel advances it to her with her first order of coffee or other products and she uses it while she is paying for it.

Other articles, selected by the customer, are advanced, from time to time; the volume of her purchase each delivery determines the amount of premium advanced.

Quality Personal Service

Jewel brings the markets of the world direct to the customer's door; the Jewel service salesman brings them, giving her the advantages of buying in her home and of delivery at her door.

The Jewel salesman serves her intelligently, respectfully and regularly, calling once every two weeks, on the same day of the week at the same hour; if he has the customer's standing order he keeps her supplied without further care on her part.

The Jewel salesman makes his customer's interest his own, because his watchword is Service, and he must satisfy her to be successful himself; the Jewel business is built on the regular patronage of satisfied customers.

Unlimited Guarantee

Jewel stands back of its products, household articles and personal service with an absolute satisfaction or money-refunded guarantee.

Jewel guarantees all its products to be pure and of high quality, meeting the requirements of all Pure Food Laws, and going far beyond the law.

Jewel guarantees all its household articles to be high-grade, standard merchandise.

Jewel guarantees the courtesy, honesty and regularity of all Jewel salesmen.

If at any time the customer is not fully satisfied, her money will be refunded promptly, and Jewel guarantees to make satisfactory to her any part of its service with which she is not pleased.

THREE JEWEL WAYS OF SAVING

Jewel can do all this for its customers because it prefers to use what it saves, by its perfected business methods, in giving service, rather than in temporarily increasing its profits; it knows that to serve is good business and insures its continued prosperity.

Immense Purchasing Power

Jewel saves in first cost, because its nation-wide business, serving over two million people, enables it to buy in immense quantities from original sources and to manufacture on a large scale.

Direct Distribution

Jewel saves the wasteful expense and profits of all middlemen; it brings its products direct from its factories to the customer's door, a short cut in distribution.

Cash Business

Jewel does a cash business, and is able to use all its resources in providing service benefits for its customers.

Conclusion

Thus Jewel saves so much that it can give its customers the four services, products, household articles, delivery to the home, and an unlimited guarantee, for the price of the products alone.

Jewel does not claim to give something for nothing; the customer pays for what she gets, but in buying from Jewel she gets more than when she trades with others.

This Laurel logotype began appearing in the 1950s. This trademark can be seen in early Jewel Home Shopping catalogs.

Sorry We Missed You! Jewel salesmen (c. 1972) often placed tags like this on customers' doors when no one was found home. The card indicated the time the salesman had called, and an approximate time when he would return. The customer could leave a note on the reverse side of the card with instructions about when she could be reached. *Author's Collection.*

Barrington's own Mary Dunbar greets her Jewel Tea salesman at her residence in this 1938 photograph. Note the salesman carrier/basket.

A closer view of the "Economy" carrier/basket dates to 1930s. *Hamilton Collection.*

This "The Friendly Jewel Man" hotpad is believed to have been given away during the 1940s or 1950s, when "The Friendly Jewel Man" was a slogan. *Nemluvil Collection*

Salesman Carrier Cases

"This is your JEWEL HOUSE CARD" was a means for customers to record purchases and payments made. A date of 1967 is listed inside, along with lists for Premiums, Cash Sales, Budget Plans and dates. An address forwarding card was included in case the customer moved; they could fill it out and mail it to Jewel Tea Co., Inc. Jewel Park Barrington, Illinois. Postage was paid by Jewel. *Author's Collection.*

The salesman "Economy" wire carrier/basket measures 12" wide x 21" long x 7" high, and 13" at the handle.

The "Economy" carrier/basket dates to the 1930s. Note the wooden handle and side section for salesman personal material. An example of this basket can be seen in the photograph of Mary Dunbar and her Jewel Tea Salesman. *Hamilton Collection.*

"A Better Place to Work, A Better Place to Trade" appears on the side of the metal frame/pressed fiberboard 1950s Jewel Tea salesman carrier. *Marshall Collection.*

The opposite side of the 1950s salesman carrier. The carrier itself measures 12" wide x 24" long x 7" high, and with the handle it measures 11-1/2". At one end the salesman's ledgers, catalogs, and supplies were kept. *Marshall Collection.*

CHAPTER 4

THE JEWEL LADY

Home Cookery Service Free

Quality and customer satisfaction have always been by-words at Jewel. Ever since Jewel began roasting its own coffee and packaging baking powder in 1905, the emphasis was on quality.

A decision was made in 1924 to expand and improve Jewel service by establishing the Jewel Homemakers' Institute. Mrs. Mary Hartson was designated "The Jewel Lady" and through the Jewel News, a bi-weekly publication distributed to customers, she shared recipes and household suggestions and invited correspondence.

By 1925, you could ask the Jewel Lady to answer any questions and make suggestions on Home Cookery AB-SOLUTELY FREE. This was another form of service the customer received when she bought "The Jewel Way." A customer simply wrote to "The Jewel Lady, c/o Jewel Tea Co., Inc., Madison St. and Wasbash Ave., Chicago, Illinois."

It wasn't too long before management realized that The Jewel Lady needed a name; the personal touch was lacking. An old issue of the Jewel News, describes how it came about: Mrs. Hartson said, "Why not use a real name—not a coined one. Use Mary Dunbar, which is my maiden name. I will present it to the Jewel Tea Co., Inc. and renounce all future claims to its public uses."

Thus began an era.

This 3" x 5" postal card is believed to part of the original customer request. The card reads: "JEWEL TEA CO. INC. CHICAGO, ILLINOIS — Thank you for your request. I hope you will like the material I am sending, and that the Jewel Lady page in the Jewel News will continue to interest you. Cordially Yours, signed The Jewel Lady — Director, Home Service Division." *Hamilton Collection.*

"Sixteen generous servings in one package," advertised Jewel-Macaroni. It is believed this 6" x 8-1/2" pamphlet accompanied the aforementioned 3" x 5" Jewel Lady postal card. On the reverse side of the pamphlet, various recipes were given. This pamphlet also bears The Jewel Lady signature on the reverse side, and what are believed to be the first tested recipes. *Hamilton Collection.*

The reverse side of the 6" x 8-1/2" pamphlet advertisement of Jewel Quick Oats provided recipes, and like the macaroni advertisement bears The Jewel Lady signature. These two pamphlets were folded in half. *Hamilton Collection.*

The Home Service Division was the forerunner to the Jewel Homemaker's Institute. Mary Reed Hartson, shown here, used her maiden name "Mary Dunbar" to take the place of the impersonal-sounding "The Jewel Lady."

A Speech Given By Vice President O. B. Westphal — 1925

"About two weeks ago Mrs. Hartson talked with two of our head salesmen who were in the office. They talked for nearly an hour and a half Saturday afternoon. During this talk, they said:

Mrs. Hartson, tell the boys something more about yourself.

Those of us who met you last summer, and heard you talk at the hotel and at the plant, are 100% sold on the Home Service Division. But there are still some of the men who haven't seen you. They sort of visualize you a being too "high-brow" for Jewel Customers. They picture you as a cross between a school ma'am and a trained nurse.

"Now, I know most of you men realize the good that the Home Service Division has done, and the majority of the men are taking advantage of this unique and valuable sales aid. I know that most of you are showing your customers "The Jewel Lady" page in the JEWEL NEWS and building up their interest in Jewel products through it. I know that most of you are getting your questions and your customers' questions about Jewel products answered through the use of the Form 300. But I know that there are

some men who aren't doing these things. They are missing a real opportunity.

What these two Head Salesmen told Mrs. Hartson, led me to ask her to tell you some of the facts about her experience and its direct help to you. Here they are in her own words:

"I appreciate this opportunity, which Mr. Westphal has afforded, because I believe that you will be surprised to learn that I've been selling goods for twelve years.

"I've sold advertising, baking powder, milk, and mince meat, direct to the house-wife, by means of house-to-house canvassing and at fair booths.

"For nearly two years, I supervised the work of one hundred and fifty house to house canvassers, from Minnesota to Texas and Indiana to California, making fifty cent sales of baking powder.

"I've rapped on thousands of back doors and said, "Good morning, are you the lady of the house?" and these back doors represented the homes of the "Rich man, poor man, beggar man, thief, doctor, lawyer, merchant, chief.

"This gives me personal knowledge of the sale problems of our field sales force. I know, from the experience of these past twelve years, that "Women's stuff" does have a distinct sales appeal to women.

"Of course, figures are the most interesting thing to all of us, for they are concrete facts. Let's suppose then that after reading this article, each route salesman said, "I'm going to tell all of my customers about the Jewel Tea Company's wonderful free service to the housewife. I'm going to show my customers the Jewel Lady's page in the JEWEL NEWS, and see that they use the recipes and suggestions there. I'm going to see that the coupon in the JEWEL NEWS is used by each one of my customers.

"Then, let's suppose that each salesman uses the Jewel Lady recipes and suggestions in the JEWEL NEWS, as a talking point for making only one fifty-cent sale during the year to each customer. Do you know what that would total? Yes, sir -- 600 times fifty-cent is an added yearly volume of $300.00. That's worth getting! It means that if each man uses the Jewel Lady's help only once a year, and will make only one fifty-cent sale per customer, he will increase his income approximately $37.50. That wouldn't be a bit hard to take, would it? Well, it is just as easy to do that twenty-six time a year, as it is once. It is not at all an impossible thing to do; as a matter of fact, it should be very easy. Don't you think so?"

"I think Mrs. Hartson is right, men. Think it over."

The Jewel Lady's Letter—1926

In March 1926, The Jewel Lady revealed herself in the following letter.

During the two years that I have been serving you, I have received, literally, hundreds of letters saying: "Dear Jewel Lady, I do wish I had some other name for you. Just calling you "Jewel Lady" or "Dear Madam", seems so impersonal." This year my desk was loaded with Christmas cards from hundreds of you out there in the United States. I can't tell you how much I appreciated them, but I do want to tell you that among them were so many which said, "I wish I knew your real name."

From the mass of correspondence during this period of time, we have been led to believe that you really want to know me more personally or intimately and so here I am, making my bow to you with my own, really, true name at the head of this column. Just plain, everyday, housewifely, Mary, coupled up with my thrifty Scotch name of Dunbar. I hope you're going to like it. I'm sure you will find it very easy to remember, and I do hope, also, that you will visualize me as just a housewife, meeting our housewives' daily problems in your Jewel Kitchen in Chicago.

I've tried, sincerely, to serve you for two years and I want to assure you that I shall continue to do so, feeling that I have a much broader and better opportunity with this new edition of Jewel News.

signed, MARY DUNBAR

Mrs. Leone Rutledge Carroll, pre-1926.

Mary Dunbar—A Real Person

"A real, honest-to-goodness person is Mary Dunbar. She has been with us since 1923 at which time she came into our organization to establish for use our Home Service Division.

"Her influence is felt in practically every department of our business, for she and her staff are constantly at work to insure the quality of Jewel Products and Premiums.

"She is a woman old enough to have practical knowledge and experience in home making, and young enough to be thoroughly modern and up-to-date in all her views.

"She has had college training in home economics and is therefore sound in her theories of foods and nutrition.

"Her years in the world of business have given her a practical insight into the field of Home Service as it exists today between manufacturer and consumer.

"Mary Dunbar supervises a large department. She does it with dignity, tact and understanding. She is a real friend to our hundreds of thousands of customers because she is indeed such a real person herself.

"President, Jewel Tea Co., Inc."

In 1926, Mrs. Leone Rutledge Carroll came to Jewel to assume the directorship of the Jewel Homemakers' Institute, becoming the best-known Mary Dunbar. Her national reputation in the field of nutrition, her degrees in chemistry and home economics, and her teaching experience were just the background Jewel was looking for. She became Jewel's first woman executive, serving as the famous Mary Dunbar for seventeen years.

During her 1974 visit, Mrs. Carroll spoke of being women's editor of the Jewel News. Homemakers often shared household short-cuts with Mary Dunbar. Before she would print them in the paper, however, she tried them herself.

The results weren't always a resounding success. She remembered one woman who suggested a new way of starting rose bushes. She told Mary Dunbar to take a rose clipping and stuff it into a potato, which would provide the plant with nourishment and then bury the potato in the soil. "Well," said Mrs. Carroll, "I started lots of pussy willow by rooting them in water and then pouring sand around them, and I thought the potato idea would work. So, I got a great big potato and pushed the cuttings down into it and planted it. Well, I got potatoes," she laughed. "She didn't say you have to cut the eyes out."

One of Mary Dunbar's most famous efforts was *Mary Dunbar's Cookbook*, first published in 1927. Delivered personally to Jewel customers by route salesmen, the free cookbook proved so popular that several editions were printed. The last edition, published in 1943, went to 800,000 homes. Even today, there's an occasional request from a customer wanting to replace her beloved copy. See the chapters covering "Cookbooks" and "Jewel Homemakers' Institute Kitchen" for additional information.

The tradition of Mary Dunbar and the Homemaker's Institute — that of testing grocery and household articles for purity, durability, and serviceability before offering them for sale — was carried on throughout the life of the company.

It is believed that Leone Rutledge Carroll was replaced by Julia Godard, then by Olga Grebe and the others who followed in their footsteps.

In 1974, Mrs. Carroll returned to "her" Homemakers' Institute in Barrington, Illinois to reminisce about her 17-year association with Jewel. The photograph shown here is believed to be the last picture taken of the woman who served as Jewel's famous Mary Dunbar from 1926 to 1943.

September 8, 1975

Leone Rutledge Carroll, beloved wife of the late John; loving mother of Sarah (Mark) Moeller of Barrington, Ill, fond sister of Helen (Harry) Strong, of Humbolt, Iowa, grandmother of John and Robert. Memorial services Wednesday, 7:30 p.m., at the United Methodist Church of Barrington, Ill. Memorials may be made to the Church.

Mrs. Carroll, c. 1974. *Barrington Archives*

CHAPTER 5

COOKBOOKS

In March 1924, three months after the introduction of the Home Service Division, the Jewel Tea Company began providing tested recipes to Jewel customers.

The division was organized to provide salespeople with selling pointers and ideas in promoting more products. The Service also provided customers with recipes and suggestions for the uses of any Jewel product.

Mrs. Mary Reed Hartson .

Mary Reed Hartson was hired to head this new undertaking and was to be acknowledged as "The Jewel Lady." Mrs. Hartson organized a test kitchen to work with Jewel products and wrote a column in the "Jewel News." See the chapter entitled "The Jewel Lady" for more information.

The most sought after paper products of The Jewel Tea Co. are the Mary Dunbar cookbooks. Various editions were published from 1927 through about 1948 in a variety of sizes. They contained recipes, household hints, an assortment of photographs, advertisements; some cookbooks pictured pieces of Autumn Leaf. Only those cookbooks in mint condition demand a reasonably high price.

First Tested Recipes

The first tested recipes were printed on half-sheets of letter-size paper and mailed out upon customer request. These may be almost impossible to find. See "The Jewel Lady" chapter.

A "Package Insert Program" was introduced in 1924. These 4" x 2-1/2" recipe cards were inserted in packages of coffee, tea, rice and coconut. Printed in an assortment of colors, the inserts provided a recipe on one side and publicity about the "Free Home Cookery Service" from The Jewel Lady on the reverse. *Author's Collection.*

Issued in August 1926, a 20-page pamphlet entitled "Healthful Cookery by Mary Dunbar" offered a collection of recipes to be used for cooking in the Mary Dunbar Waterless Cooker. It was packed with the cooker. This booklet was issued several times during the period 1926 to 1948. *Randall Collection.*

Another example of the "Healthful Cookery by Mary Dunbar" pamphlet.

Waterless Cookery by Mary Dunbar

The 23-page Waterless Cookery booklet. *Byerly Collection.*

The Kitchen Calendar

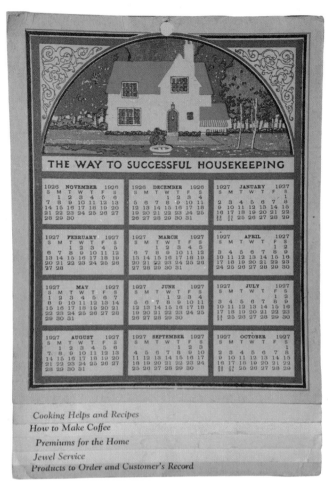

Issued in 1926 was the Kitchen Calendar booklet shown here. This 1926 calendar has a tan paper cover front, a place to keep the customer's records on the back, a collection of recipes inside, household suggestions, pictures of premiums available, and an editorial page. This calendar was repeated in 1927. There is no current information on the 1928 edition calendar. See the "Paper and Plastic" chapter. *Preo Collection.*

The 23-page Waterless Cookery booklet was offered to customers circa 1948 by Jewel Tea Co., Inc. Mary Dunbar mentioned in the opening page that the new Mary Dunbar Waterless Cooker would give customers many years of real service, just as it has to other enthusiastic owners.

The Mary Dunbar Cooker was specially designed for cooking a whole meal at one time by the healthful "Waterless" way. The booklet was prepared to guide the customer in its use as a whole meal cooker, and to give practical instructions for other uses such as canning and preserving. The recipes provided were tops in flavor, ease of preparation, and nutritional value. See the Waterless Cooker in the "Jewel Homemakers; Institute Kitchen" chapter.

Mrs. Leone Rutledge Carroll.

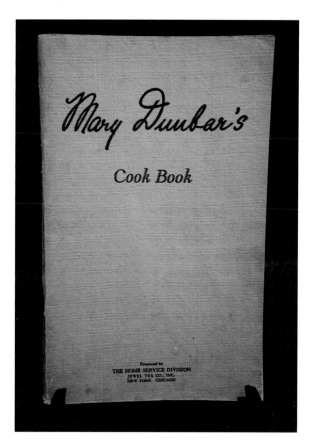

The first *Mary Dunbar's Cookbook* was published early in 1927. The copyright date appears on the inside. A copy of this cookbook, with its plain gray, embossed cover, was given free to each customer. *Author's Collection.*

Mrs. Hartson resigned in January 1927 due to ill health. At that time Jewel hired Mrs. Leone Rutledge Carroll, by far the best-known "Mary Dunbar. "

In 1924, Ruth Leone Rutledge B.S., Director of Domestic Science, RB Davis Co., Manufacturer of Davis Baking Powder, was the author of a publication "A Lesson Plan, On Cakes, Frosting and Fillings." (This is also the first time Ruth's first name was used in print.) This publication was prepared for Teachers, Demonstrators and Students of Foods and Cookery. A copy of this publication is in a private collection.

Mrs. Carroll was a graduate Home Economist and her association with Jewel was to last 17 years.

Coffee As a Flavoring

A 24-page booklet appeared during the 1926-1929 era, entitled "Coffee as a Flavoring Makes The Whole Meal Better With Jewel Best Coffee." The cover is orange, brown, and gold, and the booklet measures 4-7/8" x 6-3/4". This booklet is highly sought after by collectors. If you own this booklet I would like to hear from you.

A New Format

A different format of *Mary Dunbar's Cookbook* appeared in April 1930, after Jewel's move to its Barrington, Illinois headquarters.

It was noted in 1930 that a school binder would hold the "Mary Dunbar's Tested Recipes" which came in 8-page sections. The sections measured 7-3/16" x 10-7/16" and had a two-hole punch. 25,000 of these "Tested Recipes" were printed.

The Home Service Division was renamed "Jewel Homemaker's Institute" in July 1931, because of other companies with similar divisions and names.

At that time, all of the items, packaging, appliances, and publications tested and approved by Mary Dunbar received a "seal of approval" which had been designed for them.

The Jewel "seal of approval," 1931.

The Christmas Gift

All Jewel customers were given a Christmas gift in 1933 of *Mary Dunbar's New Cookbook,* which had been printed in November.

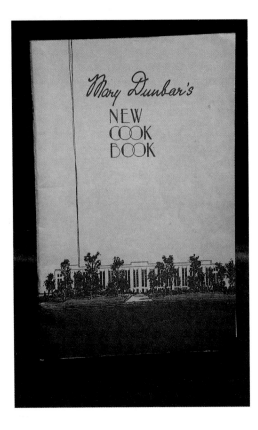

Mary Dunbar's New Cookbook, Christmas 1933, featuring the Barrington building. *Author's Collection.*

Mary Dunbar's Favorite Recipes, 1939. *Author's Collection.*

Favorite Recipes

Jewel had a million copies of the *Mary Dunbar's Favorite Recipes* printed in December 1936. The diagonal plaid brown and tan covered cookbook repeated many favorite recipes.

Mary Dunbar's Favorite Recipes, 1936. *Author's Collection.*

In June 1939, the cookbook was reprinted. This edition had a different cover, a golden basketweave on pale yellow. The book appears to be exactly the same inside as the 1936 edition. Half a million copies of this cookbook were printed.

The following announcement, "Jewel Cook Book Ready For New Customers," appeared in publication in "The New Jewel" from March 1939.

JEWEL COOK BOOK READY FOR NEW CUSTOMERS

A new edition of the Jewel cook book, *Mary Dunbar's Favorite Recipes,* has just come off the press. The new book is intended for new customers only. One-half million books were printed, and while this is a large quantity there are obviously not enough for distribution to present customers.

A few minor revisions were made in the contents of the popular cookbook, but there are no major changes and the number of pages is the same. One noticeable change in the new edition is the attractive cover. The new cover background is a picture of the reed matting which protects boxes of Jewel Tea in their trip to America from the Orient.

Managers of branches which have no copies of the old edition in stock may requisition the new book for new customer use. Every new customer should receive a copy of *Mary Dunbar's Favorite Recipes.* Use the new edition of the Jewel recipe book as an extra sales tool to get more new customers.

476 Tested Recipes

In April 1941, Jewel came out with the *476 Tested Recipes by Mary Dunbar* cookbook. While almost identical to the previous two editions, all the pictures had been re-photographed in order to eliminate dinnerware that was no longer sold. Half a million of these were printed. The cover featured a rolling pin design in yellow on a blue photo of Jewel products. No known editions were published during World War II.

476 Tested Recipes by Mary Dunbar, 1941. *Author's Collection.*

Post-War Endeavor

Circa 1945-1946 *The Jewel Cook Book* appeared as the first post-war endeavor. The cover had a bright yellow background with pictures of muffins and cake pieces. Numerous recipes had been eliminated and many favorites were repeated.

The Jewel Cook Book, 1945-1946. *Randall Collection.*

The Final Episode

In the 1947-1948 era the last cookbook was produced, also entitled *The Jewel Cook Book.*

The Jewel Cook Book, 1947-1948. *Author's Collection.*

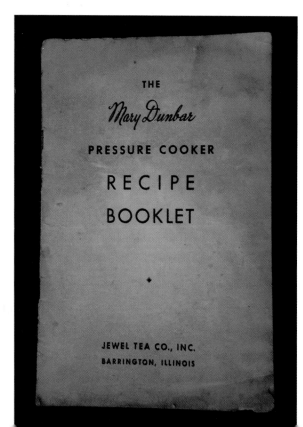

Seasonal Recipes Pamphlets

This seasonal recipes pamphlet measures approximately 4-1/2" long x 2-3/4" wide. The pamphlet is a three-fold that offered a selection of various recipes and pictured Jewel products, china, etc. Seasonal recipes pamphlets can be found in various colors and with different seasonal pictures on the front. Collectors believe this pamphlet may have been an insert in Jewel products, available during the 1920s. The back reads "Jewel Tea Co., Inc., New York-Chicago"; no date appears. *Author's Collection.*

The Mary Dunbar Pressure Cooker Cookbook

The Mary Dunbar Pressure Cooker Cookbook. Author's Collection.

It is believed that the *Mary Dunbar Pressure Cooker Cookbook* may have been offered with the pressure cooker. No date appears in the publication.

In October 1948, the new enlarged *Mary Dunbar Pressure Cooker Cookbook* was available to every Jewel customer who owned a Mary Dunbar Pressure Cooker. Any Jewel customer who had already sent in the postcard included with their Mary Dunbar Pressure Cooker received a free copy of this new cookbook after October 10, 1948. If they did not mail the postcard, but owned a Mary Dunbar Pressure Cooker, they could send a card in after that date. However, they could just write their request for the new *Mary Dunbar Pressure Cooker Cookbook* on a penny postcard, together with their name and address, and mail it to the Jewel Tea Co., Inc. in Barrington, Illinois; the free copy would be sent to them by mail. It was pointed out that "your Jewel Man will not have these cookbooks for distribution — please do not ask him to get one for you."

The new cookbook was full of recipes that helped a housewife get full value from her pressure cooker. See the discussion of the Mary Dunbar Pressure Cooker elsewhere in this book.

The booklet "21 Delicious Ways To Prepare Jewel Banana Nut Loaf Mix" was distributed by the Jewel In Home Shopping Service — Division of Jewel Companies, Inc. Barrington, Ill. The 8-page booklet offers twenty-one recipes for preparing Banana Nut Loaf Mix and is dated October 1976. *Author's Collection.*

The new Mary Dunbar Pressure Cooker Cookbook. *Private Collection.*

Numerous Jewel pamphlets and brochures containing various recipes can be located with some searching. Among them is this "Refreshing Iced Coffee and Tea" brochure. *Byerly Collection.*

The inside of this brochure, published in April 1940, offered various recipes. *Byerly Collection.*

This four-page brochure, "Oh! So Many Uses — Jewel Prepared Biscuit Flour," offered an assortment of recipes using Jewel biscuit flour. The brochure measures 5" x 7" and is dated July 1939, from the Jewel Tea Co., Inc. Jewel Park Barrington, Ill. *Randall Collection.*

An eight page booklet entitled "You will enjoy — Heat Flow Mary Dunbar Ovenware" included recipes and instructions for the Heat-Flow ovenware. Published in 1938, it measures approximately 5" long x 3" wide. The pictures and recipes in this booklet were only a suggestion of the many foods you could prepare in Heat-Flow ovenware.

Mary Dunbar's Trunk

During late 1926, Mary Dunbar or a Jewel representative would meet with salesmen and their wives to conduct classes and demonstrate the uses of Jewel products when cooking.

These classes were then offered to groups of customers, clubs, church groups, and societies throughout the country. From the beginning the cooking demonstrations were a spectacular event. When a demonstration was scheduled, Mary Dunbar gathered her cooking utensils together and packed them into a trunk, and headed out for the event. There she would give a demonstration, answer questions and then end the event by giving premium coupons as door prizes. After 1934 no information is available about these events.

This trunk shows thirteen drawers, which held an assortment of kitchen utensils. Each drawer is carefully labeled with its contents. It measures 38-1/2" high x 26" deep x 30-1/2" wide, and is very heavy. *Easley Collection.*

The Mary Dunbar trunk. Note the red lettering "JEWEL TEA CO., INC CHICAGO, ILL." on the side of the trunk. *Easley Collection.*

A close-up view of the drawers, showing leather snaps above each handle. The straps held each drawer in place during movement of the trunk. Note the metal frame that holds each label. *Easley Collection.*

Years after Mary Dunbar's demonstrations had stopped, this cooking trunk (with old utensils inside) was found in a storage area at the office building in Barrington, Illinois. The cooking trunk was thrown into a dumpster, but was later removed by a Jewel employee, Shirley Easley. *Easley Collection*

One of the larger drawers held an assortment of cooking pans and colander. *Easley Collection.*

This 1-1/2 qt. cooking pan is called the "Mirro," one of numerous pans Jewel offered. *Easley Collection.*

This drawer was lined with a soft material that is believed to have been a cushion for glassware. The measuring cup was found in this drawer along with what is believed to be Jewel's Best Coffee paper napkins. The measuring cup can be seen in various historical photographs found in the archives in Barrington, Illinois. *Easley Collection.*

This drawer held an assortment of utensils, lids, and pans. *Easley Collection.*

A historical Jewel promotional photograph showing the measuring cup.

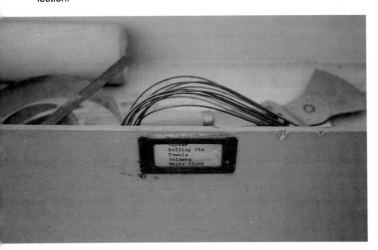

This drawer held a sifter, rolling pin, towels, and magic cloth. *Easley Collection.*

In another opened, heavily lined drawer, a green-handled hand beater was found. *Easley Collection.*

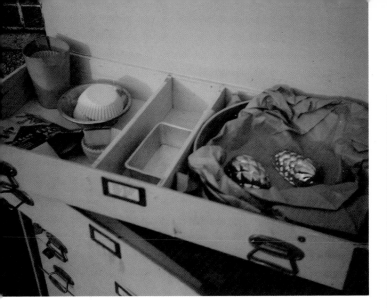

This drawer held an assortment of small loaf pans, large cake pans, paper cup cake wrappers, and jello molds. *Easley Collection.*

It is believed that many items that may have been stored in this trunk were lost when it was thrown into the dumpster. The trunk was not taken out in one unit but in several sections; some drawers were open, the contents of which may have been lost in the dumpster. These drawers may have held other kitchen items, which today are part of a landfill.

Leone "Mary Dunbar" Rutledge Carroll with her secretary (unknown). No date is given for this photograph. Note the modern, clean look of this office. *Barrington Archives.*

The Gallery

Mrs. Leone Rutledge Carroll is shown at her desk in Barrington, Illinois, taken August 30, 1933. Note this is also the same photograph that appeared in the Jewel cookbooks. *Barrington Archives.*

A late 1920s photograph of field representative Mrs. Julia J. Goddard. Mrs. Goddard is also seen in the chapter, "The Jewel Homemakers' Institute Kitchen." *Hedges Collection.*

I would appreciate hearing from anyone with information concerning any staff employee of the Jewel Homemakers' Institute Kitchen.

CHAPTER 6
THE JEWEL HOMEMAKERS' INSTITUTE KITCHEN

The kitchen or kitchenette is one of the most popular rooms in an American home. From high-tech chrome to rustic terra cotta designs, kitchens are the places where daily meals are prepared, either microwaved or home-cooked. They are the places where card games are won and lost, and where hearts are broken and mended.

It is the place many mothers conversed with their Jewel Tea salesmen while placing orders, receiving Jewel calendars, or receiving the latest Mary Dunbar cookbooks. Jewel provided numerous other utensils for the kitchen other than groceries, china, and linens. It is impossible to list or provide photographs of the many kitchen items offered or given away by Jewel. I can only provide those that were made available to me.

In many of Jewel's archive photographs, one can see many of the utensils and products being used in the Jewel Test Kitchen.

This photograph is dated August 29, 1935. (Left to right) Miss Mavis Galloway, Mary Dunbar, Mrs. Julia Goddard, and Mrs. Bierman. The photographs show many Jewel products, including Autumn Leaf china, a cake safe and the Mary Dunbar Waterless Cooker on the stove. At the far left, note the metal kitchen stool, without motif. This is basically the same stool that would later appear with the Autumn Leaf motif.

This photograph can be dated 1933 by the calendar behind Mrs. Julia Goddard, who is preparing to open canned goods. Mary Dunbar looks over the insert pans for the Mary Dunbar Waterless Cooker, as Miss Mavis Galloway prepares a pot of Jewel Blend Coffee. At the far right, house-keeper Mrs. Bierman cleans a pan. Note other items in the room.

This photograph has a date of December 19, 1935 and is believed to be Mavis Galloway who is critically examining the Mary Dunbar Cooker to detect flaws, errors, etc. Miss Galloway holds the Healthful Cookery Booklet. Note various Jewel products.

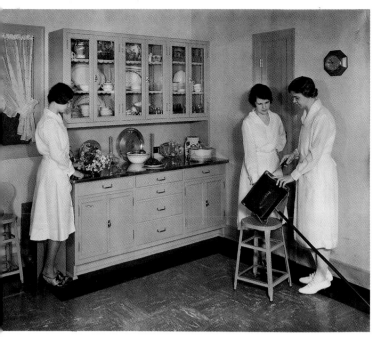

Mary Dunbar and two staff members prepare for a busy work day in the Institute Test Kitchen. Mary Dunbar, far right, makes an adjustment to a "Hygrade" sweeper. Photographed prior to 1933.

Jewel's Test Kitchen periodically underwent renovations. This is is evident in historical photographs found in the archives at Barrington, which had appeared in various Jewel News editions.

In 1940, Jewel issued an invitation into their kitchen. Mary Dunbar, Jewel Homemakers' Institute Director, extended the open request with the words, "Won't you come into my kitchen?"

Mary Dunbar with Miss Mavis Galloway and Mrs. Bierman. Mary Dunbar was respected as a judge of the hard cold facts, but she offered her readers a warm personal invitation to come and inspect the premises and have a cup of Jewel Coffee.

For the Homemakers' Institute, Jewel changed the old invitation to visit. The photographs explain why: the institute had moved into their completely new kitchen. At the far left in the photograph shown here, you can see the fold-away ironing board cabinet with a shelf for the iron. Next to that is a built-in metal desk. The staff had always said "the proof of the pudding is in the eating," and they allowed for that with a dinette nook for the staff to eat and enjoy the results of the recipe development and food testing. The nook of the dinette was located to the left of the enclosed ironing board cabinet.

The Lloyd furniture had the chromium-plated, metal tube foundations and green leather upholstery. The table top was green composition linoleum.

Mary Dunbar then introduced her staff again. Although everyone had been introduced before, she felt as though they were new people in their delightful new surroundings.

Mary Dunbar is seated at the demonstration table or work counter, to her left is Mavis Galloway measuring lids. Also pictured is Mrs. Julia Goddard, and at the far right, Mrs. Bierman. Miss Marian Kessel, another staff member, was not present when the photograph was taken. She was in Minnesota giving a demonstration.

Mary Dunbar received her Bachelor of Science degree from Milwaukee Downer College, and then taught college and high school chemistry and home economics. She was a baking expert for the United State Bureau of Chemistry in Washington, D. C., a commercial home economist in New York City, and a homemaker and businesswoman. Beginning in 1926-1927 she served as the Director of the Jewel Homemakers' Institute.

Miss Galloway earned her Bachelor of Science degree in Home Economics at Stout Institute in Menomonie, Wisconsin and was employed at Jewel for several years.

Mrs. Julia Goddard was known by thousands of Jewel customers who had met her when they attended her cooking school workshop. Mrs. Goddard received her home economics training at Simmons College in Boston, Massachusetts, and had served as president of her hometown women's club. She was advertising manager and social editor of a newspaper and was a part of the Homemakers' Institute staff since January 1928.

Jewel's loyal housekeeper, Mrs. Bierman, had been with Jewel since 1930. Mrs. Bierman appeared in numerous photographs in the Jewel News during her career with Jewel.

Miss Marian Kessel, another staff member, earned her Bachelor of Science degree from Indiana State Teachers' College, taught home economics, and had been with the department since 1935.

After being introduced to the Homemakers' Institute family, visitors were ask to inspect the new kitchen.

(Left to right) Mrs. Biernman, Mavis Galloway, Mary Dunbar and Julia Goddard appear in this kitchen photograph. You can see the general plan of the kitchen, which was really two kitchens in one. The left-hand side was equipped with a gas range and refrigerator, while the right-hand side was the electric kitchen. A general utility cabinet was located between the two ranges that contained the supplies which serviced either side of the kitchen. Overhead cabinets allowed space for those many things which they kept on hand for comparative work, but used frequently in the preparation of foods.

The cabinets throughout the new kitchen were by the St. Charles Company. They were enameled steel with chromium fixtures.

The counter services, except the hardwood work table, were of stainless steel. The floor was rubber linoleum tile. The walls were completely new and different, made of porcelain-enameled steel.

The electric kitchen included a Westinghouse refrigerator, dishwasher, and range. The glass cupboards display the Jewel tableware premiums, the location having been selected conveniently close to the dishwasher along with the electric towel dryer with individual racks which could be pulled out one at a time.

In an October 1947 issue of The Jewel News, a similar photograph appears much like the one shown here. The caption from that 1947 issue read,

> Shown in the picture was Jewel's test kitchen, a part of Homemakers Institute. Here, the recipes you find on pages of The Jewel News are developed, tested, and tasted by trained home economists, who are themselves homemakers. One feature of the kitchen is that it is equipped with both gas and electric ranges, so that recipes can be tested on both. Homemaker's Institute tests every product, every grocery item, every piece of merchandise sold to Jewel customers, under conditions similar to those in your own home. That is why Jewel can guarantee its quality merchandise with a promise of your money back with a smile if you are not satisfied.

The photograph gives you a general view on the opposite side of the kitchen. This was taken from the dinette and shows the demonstration table or work counter in the center of the room. This was a movable counter, and in addition to its use for general food preparation it served as a demonstration table when they had groups in the kitchen. The lower section was divided into two large parts where test items were kept; these were separate from their standard equipment, as long as they were being worked on or until they had been reported upon. One side had the premiums being tested and the other side had the grocery items that were being tested. Mary Dunbar, Mrs. Goddard, Mrs. Bierman and Mavis Galloway are once again busy in their kitchen; Mary Dunbar is passing a final judgment on a delicious new salad dressing.

A photograph similar to this one appeared in the October 1947 edition of The Jewel News, showing the Jewel test kitchen. Mrs. Julia Goddard and Mrs. Bierman can be seen here. Carefully note the Autumn Leaf china, Jewel products, and -- for those of you who are into cookie jars -- note the Shawnee "Smiley" cookie jar in the corner behind Mrs. Goddard.

Kitchen Aprons

·At one time kitchen aprons were as popular as home-made bread. They served as a protection to one's garment. Women worked in them, shopped in them, gardened and cooked in them.

Little is know about the Autumn Leaf patterned plastic bib apron. It is believed to have been offered during the time of the plastic bowl covers. This is uncertain and I found no reference in the Barrington Archives. One collector shared with me a copy of an advertisement that came with the Autumn Leaf plastic apron. It read "Coverall Fabric Apron Plastic Coated — Stain Resistant — No Laundering — Wipes Clean with a Damp Cloth — Floral Design — Will not chip or peel. Style No. (no number appeared) The Sunlite Mfg. Company—Milwaukee 4, Wis." A few of these aprons are in private collections. *Courtesy of Pomray Collection.*

WATERPROOF KITCHEN APRON

This rubberized apron is easily cleaned. It is waterproof and protects the clothes from water and grease. Indispensable in the laundry. Price $1.00 (Cash only). Our Item No. C–6010.

An original 1925 advertisement and caption from The Jewel News.

This apron was almost impossible to photograph in full length. The approximate measurements are 37" wide x 54" long. Here we have folded the apron and drawn the ties across. *Costanza Collection.*

This photograph shows a portion of the bib that can be seen to the left, under the folded apron. This is one of three known Autumn Leaf plastic bib aprons. *Costanza Collection.*

An advertisement for the above 10" long "JEWEL Food Chopper No. 4" premium appeared in 1919. The chopper had five grinders in different sizes for kitchen chores. Inside the handle appears "PAT 9-25-06. 2-24-14. 3-2-15." In 1919 this Chopper sold for $2.35. *Scott Collection.*

Food Choppers

**CLIMAX
FOOD CHOPPER**

Made by Landers, Frary and Clark, famous manufacturers of Connecticut. Competitive tests in our Home Service Division proved conclusively that this food chopper gave the most satisfactory results, was easiest to operate and to clean, and was in all respects an absolutely satisfactory piece of kitchen equipment. Price $2.25 (in P. S. C. or Cash). Our Item No. 734.

What a food chopper it was! This original advertisement and caption appeared in a 1926 Jewel News for the No. 5 Climax Food Chopper.

The Universal Food Chopper. Like the No. 5 Climax or the No. 4 Jewel, this Universal may have been a part of the Homemakers' Institute Test Kitchen before being offered to the Jewel customers. Made for Jewel Tea Co., Inc., Jewel Park Barrington, Ill. by Landers, Frary & Clark of New Britain, CT. It also chops all kinds of vegetables and fruits. *Byerly Collection.*

In 1938, in the "Idea Exchange," Mary Dunbar received a household suggestion. "The Jewel Onion Chopper is not only a chopper but a juicer as well. After chopping the onion put the board on top of the onion, replace chopper and press down," suggested a Jewel Customer in Jacksonville, Florida.

A Tearless Onion Chopper No. 45069 sold for 59¢ in 1946. A promotional photograph appeared in "The Jewel Shopper's News" on April 8, 1946.

A Tin Colander

In 1926 Jewel offered a tin colander that could be used for draining hot foods, such as Jewel macaroni, spaghetti, or noodles. Vegetables and fruit could be quickly cleaned in this very good grade tin colander. It had two sturdy handles for holding and the entire construction allowed for durability and service. Holes were arranged to allow for rapid washing. It was listed as Item No. S-1193 and sold for 25¢.

This Jewel Tea "Tearless" Onion Chopper, Item No. S-1584, may have been part of Jewel's test kitchen before being offered to customers. The container also served as a measuring cup. *Mercer Collection.*

Mary Dunbar Handymix

The popular, small, and lightweight Mary Dunbar Handymix was easy to use in any kitchen. Introduced in 1940, this new mixer performed tedious work. It was easy to operate, practical for whipping, mixing, beating and stirring. This was the mixer everyone had been wanting for a long time, one that anyone would want to use. It was listed as Item No. 856 and sold for only $4.95, including mixing bowl. The baked enamel finish looked good with any color scheme. *Randall Collection.*

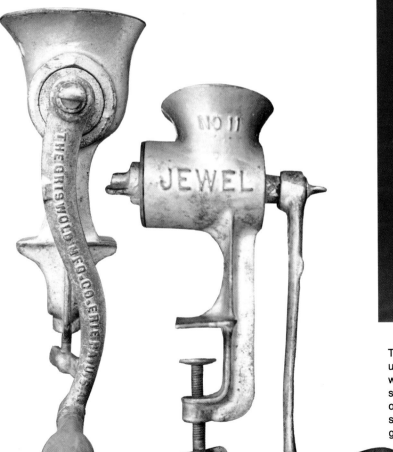

This 10" x 6" food grinder is marked "The Griswold Mfg. Co. Erie, Pa, USA" on the handle. On the reverse side, it is marked "No. 11 Jewel."

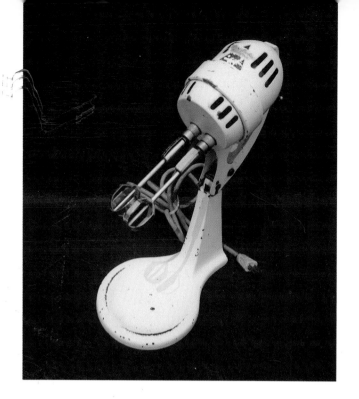

The original Handymix mixing bowl, 4-1/2" high with a 6" diameter. *Hedges Collection.*

In Vol. 18 No. 3 of The Jewel News in 1940, the following appeared: "In further evidence of the tremendous popularity of Jewel Premiums, the 1,000,000th Mary Dunbar Handymix has just been purchased."

The Mary Dunbar Handymix in the tilted position, which allowed for removing the unit and blades to be used elsewhere or cleaned. The Mary Dunbar Handymix had a paper decal label on the front of the unit. The label read, in part, "Mary Dunbar Handymix CHICAGO ELECTRIC MFG. CO.," and listed under that several patent numbers: 1,943,270, which indicates 1934, and 2,179,383, which indicates 1940. Design patent number D-121.124 also indicates 1940. *Byerly Collection.*

In 1972 Mary Dunbar Stand Mixer (X) was offered through the Spring and Summer Jewel Catalog. The mixer converts to portable by detaching the powerful 3-speed mixer from the stand. It has a handy thumb-top speed control, automatic beater ejector, and the tilt-back stand has a turntable base. Two glass bowls and a detachable cord were included, and it was offered in white only.

Item (Y) was a 3-speed Mary Dunbar Portable Mixer with the same fine features as the stand mix; no stand or bowls were included with this portable.

The 1972 Mary Dunbar Stand Mixer (X).

Toasters and Blenders

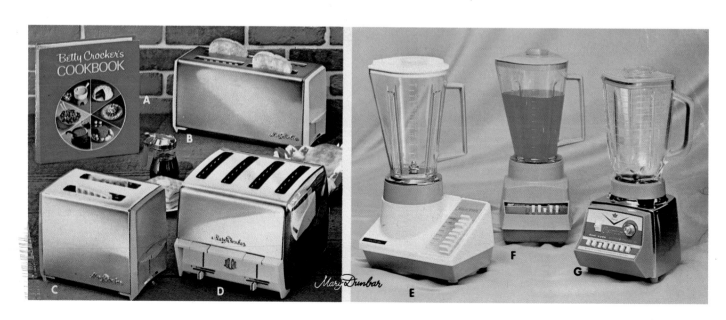

Jewel's Item A, a Betty Crocker cookbook.

Jewel offered a variety of toasters and blenders in the 1972 Jewel Home Shopping Service. Item (B & C) Mary Dunbar toasters came in either two-slice or four-slice, with a shade selector and a hinged crumb tray. They were chrome-plated with trim colors of Harvest Gold, Avocado, or White.

Item (D) The Mary Dunbar Deluxe four-slice toaster had independent controls. It toasted two slices without using as much wattage as the four-slice, and had a separate shade selector and hinged crumb trays. It came in a chrome finish with trim color choices of Harvest Gold, Avocado, or White.

Item (E) was a seven-speed Mary Dunbar Blender. Its 48-oz. container was easy to read with cup/ounce graduations. The 1-oz. measuring cap (cover) lets you add ingredients while the blender is in operation. It had a powerful motor with stainless steel cutting blades and a cord storage compartment.

Item (F) was the Shetland five-speed blender with six push-buttons. Item (G) was the Osterizer sixteen-speed "Pulse Matic" Blender.

The following appeared with the 1972 advertisement:

"Nationally advertised appliances will be repaired or replaced at no charge within the terms of the manufacturers warranties. Generally, this covers only electrical or mechanical defects in material or workmanship."

Mary Dunbar appliances were made with such care that they gave years of dependable service. If a Mary Dunbar appliance needed attention with the first year of service after purchase, it would be repaired at no charge by the nearest authorized station. This assumes normal use and reasonable care was given to the appliance. After twelve months the repair station would continue to care for Mary Dunbar appliances for a reasonable charge. The Branch or Distribution Center office supplied the customer with a list of repair stations.

The original advertisement and caption from a 1930 edition of The Jewel News, showing the Electric Toaster priced at $4.50. (Seems somewhat high-priced for 1930.)

ELECTRIC TOASTER $4.50

Toast, Crisp and Piping Hot

Golden brown toast quickly prepared right at the table. Convenient to use, efficient in performance. Manning, Bowman made. This item looks attractive on the table for any meal. Have you one in your home?
Item No. 770 . . . . $4.50

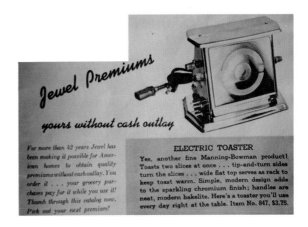

Jewel Premiums
yours without cash outlay

For more than 42 years Jewel has been making it possible for American homes to obtain quality premiums without cash outlay. You order it . . . your grocery purchases pay for it while you use it! Thumb through this catalog now. Pick out your next premium!

ELECTRIC TOASTER

Yes, another fine Manning-Bowman product! Toasts two slices at once . . . tip-and-turn sides turn the slices . . . wide flat top serves as rack to keep toast warm. Simple, modern design adds to the sparkling chromium finish; handles are neat, modern bakelite. Here's a toaster you'll use every day right at the table. Item No. 847, $3.75.

The Manning-Bowman Electric Toaster as it appeared in a 1940 Jewel Premium Catalog. The toaster browned two slices at once; the tip-and-turn sides turned the slices. The wide, flat top served as a rack to keep the toast warm. It had a modern design which added to the sparkled chromium finish. The handles were made of neat modern Bakelite. Listed as Item No. 847 in 1941.

Scales

The "IMPERIAL FAMILY SCALE Patented Oct. 25, 1898 & April 20, 1909 Other Patent Pending — 24 lbs. — Warranted." It is 9-1/2" high. *Randall Collection.*

A side view of the IMPERIAL FAMILY SCALE is shown above. The side reads, "JEWEL TEA CO. The largest exclusive Retail Tea and Coffee House in the World." *Randall Collection.*

The Hanson Scale

In 1926 Jewel urged each customer to "do your preserving with the aid of a Hanson Scale," and to be sure that you have your "pound for pound" measurement correct. The Hanson Scale weighs accurately by ounce up to 25 pounds and has an adjustable screw which permits weighing materials in their containers. It is made of gray enamel with strong, heavy steel, and has an easily read dial. Not only is it invaluable for correctly preserving and canning proportions, but saved the housewife money by helping her check her grocery orders. Listed as Item No. 758 and priced at $2.25.

A SCALE WORTH WHILE

Check Their Weight

HOUSEHOLD SCALE—PREMIUM

Every efficient housewife should have a scale and one that she can depend upon. This Hanson Scale speaks for itself. It is accurate, dependable and neat in appearance. Made of heavy steel and enameled apple green. The face is white with black letters, and a black hand, so easy reading is assured. Item No. 758 **$2 00**

(Cash or Jewel Profit Sharing Credits)

The Hanson Scale advertisement with original captions from a 1929 Jewel News.

Shown above is the "JEWEL FAMILY SCALE 24 Pounds By Oz. NOT LEGAL FOR USE IN TRADE. Pat. Date Dec. 27, 98 (1898), Mar. 14, 99 (1899), Mar. 28, 99 (1899) and June 23, 03 (1903), Pats. Pend'g." *Hedges Collection.*

In 1940 the Hanson Utility Scale appeared in a Jewel Premium Catalog. This scale made it easy to check market deliveries, or weigh ingredients for recipes. The Hanson was modern in appearance, and accurate in measurement. A variety of uses could be found for it in the home. Listed in 1940 as Item No. 809.

Pitchers

Catch that Ice!

No splashing (with resulting ice on the tablecloth) when a "lipped" beverage jug is used. Made of heavy pressed glass, with paneled sides. The lip extends over the top about one-third of distance, and prevents ice, lemon rind, or other floating material from slipping into the glass, or spilling on to the tablecloth. The capacity of this useful jug is 1½ quarts. Item No. C-6057. Price 50c.

A Utility Pitcher Indeed!

Your iced beverages, milk, or griddle batters may be conveniently handled in this easy-pouring, non-drip aluminum pitcher. Because of its highly polished finish, and graceful, well-proportioned lines, it may be used at the table. It is sturdy, although light in weight. Full capacity, nearly 3 quarts. Item No. 43. Price $1.25.

The heavy pressed glass pitcher and the aluminum pitcher appear with the original advertisement in a 1927 edition of The Jewel News.

A Rolling Pin

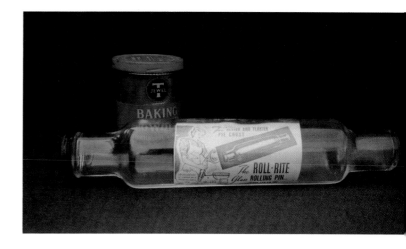

"The Roll-Rite Glass Rolling Pin. . . Jewel Tea Co., Inc. Jewel Park Barrington, Ill." *Author's Collection.*

Jewel Tea's Roll-Rite rolling pin included a brochure that listed various recipes and made suggestions about keeping dough chilled before baking, using a smooth, hard rolling surface, and always keeping sanitary — the rolling pin was easy to clean and endorsed by professional chefs. They instructed customers to fill it with cold water or cracked ice a few minutes before using. The Roll-Rite was tested and approved by Mary Dunbar Jewel Homemakers Institute.

A Jewel Griddle

Many Jewel pancakes may have been prepared on this Aluminum Griddle, backstamped "JEWEL T." The griddle has a diameter of 10-3/4", and measures 18-1/2" to the end of the handle; a hole is in the handle for easy hanging. *Hedges Collection.*

The Mary Dunbar Waterless Cooker

A Whole Meal Cooker!

Convenience and healthful cookery are combined in the Mary Dunbar Cooker. Of excellent quality aluminum is this 6-quart waterless cooker. The heavy steel base furnishes even and steady distribution of heat. Meat is seared a delicious, golden brown before the cover is placed; vegetables are cooked with the meat, and a steamed dessert may be placed on the rack. No clamps. Item No. 47. Price $4.25.

The original 1927 advertisement and caption for the Mary Dunbar Cooker. Note that this cooker had no clamps.

The Mary Dunbar Waterless Cooker was designed by the West Bend Aluminum Co. and patented especially for Jewel. This cooker has appeared in a variety of Jewel publications. It has a 6-quart capacity aluminum pot that was easy to handle and kept the steam from escaping if the heat was properly controlled.

A post-1927 advertisement for the Waterless Cooker included the base, cover, and a wire insert. The lid was equipped with two clamps that held the cover in place, and a safety valve that allowed the steam to escape. Priced at $4.25, this was offered as Item No. 49.

By using the Mary Dunbar Waterless Cooker, a housewife could save time, space, energy, and gas, and still prepare a healthy meal for her family.

The first Mary Dunbar Waterless Cooker booklet had a 1926 copyright date. A November 1927 Jewel News advertised the cooker as "The Whole Meal Prepared in One Pot, Over One Flame At One Time. "

During 1929, Item No. 49 changed to seven quarts and included a set of three pans selling for $5.25. A 10-quart cooker was then introduced as Item No. 52 and sold complete for $7.25.

During the shortage of metal during World War II, the cooker did not appear in a catalog. Later in the 1940s it reappeared and looked more modern. The 10-quart then sold for $5.75, while the 7-quart remained the same price.

In a 1949 Jewel's spring and summer catalog, the Mary Dunbar Waterless Cooker appeared and was still selling for the same price.

This 8-1/2" high Mary Dunbar COOKER has the patent number 1639093, which indicates the year 1927. In a 1929 advertisement, it is listed as a 10-quart cooker for large families or for cold pack canning. Jewel offered a cooker which particularly suits the needs of the very large family; or for any family it will prove a real help during canning season. It is deep enough to hold the 1-quart size jars, and large enough to process three jars at a time. Equipped with three 1-quart inset pans, this cooker is missing the base. *Randall Collection.*

These three 1-quart inset pans are from the Mary Dunbar COOKER that lists the patent number 1639093. The cooker appeared in numerous Jewel News issues and on the cover of "Healthful Cookery" by Mary Dunbar. *Randall Collection.*

The 7-qt with lid removed showing inserts and 10-qt. Mary Dunbar COOK-ERS. *Hedges Collection.*

The 10-qt. Mary Dunbar COOKER is shown above with three pans and a tray. The tray sits in the bottom of the cooker and the pans on top. This 10-qt. COOKER was perfect for large families. *Hedges Collection.*

The Jewel Pizza Cutter

A 7-3/4" stainless metal pizza cutter with a black wooden handle can be found. "JEWEL" is imprinted on the metal circular roller. The sticker on the original plastic bag reads "Distributed by Jewel Home Shopping Service Division of Jewel Companies, Inc., Barrington, IL 60010." The cutter is marked with the number 94-441. *This pizza cutter is in a private collection.*

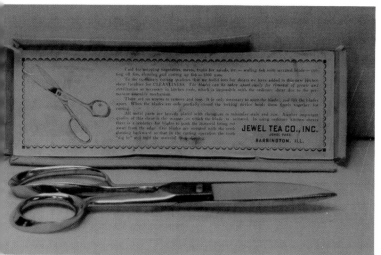

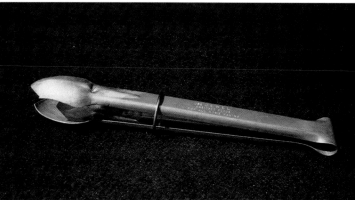

The 8-3/4" Jewel Kitchen Tongs, a grasping device usually consisting of two pieces joined at one end. These tongs are marked "Jewel Tea," with "Use JEWEL enriched flour for all home baking" printed on the handle. They are handy for ice, turning meats, handling hot noodles or spaghetti, and various other kitchen uses. *Hedges Collection.*

Jewel Kitchen Shears

These kitchen shears could be used for snipping meats, vegetables, fruits for salads, scaling fish with the serrated blade, cutting off fins, cleaning and cutting up fish—and a thousand other uses.

To the customary cutting qualities built into the shears were added features to enhance CLEANLINESS. The blades can be taken apart easily for removal of grease and for sterilization, which is impossible with ordinary shears due to the permanent assembly mechanism. There are no screws to remove or lose. It is only necessary to open the blade, and lift the blades apart. When the blades are only partially closed the locking device holds them firmly together for cutting. All metal parts are heavily plated with chromium to minimize stain and rust.

Another important quality of this shear is the manner in which the blade is serrated. In using ordinary kitchen shears there is a tendency for blades to push the materials being cut away from the edge. These blades are serrated with the teeth slanting backward so that in the cutting operation the teeth dig in and hold the material from slipping. The item was offered by JEWEL TEA CO., INC. Jewel Park Barrington, Ill.

The Jewel kitchen shears. *Weales Collection.*

The Pickle Fork

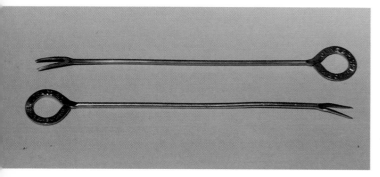

Presently nothing is known about the origins of this pickle fork. It measures 8" in length; on one side of the flat round head it reads, "Olive & Pickle Fork" and on the reverse side "Compliments of JEWEL TEA CO., INC." This pickle fork has also been found with a flat oval head. *Author's Collection.*

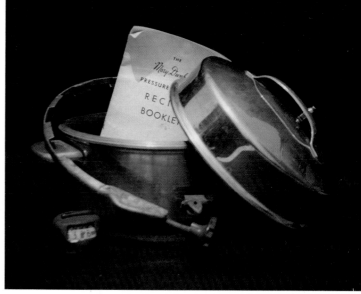

The Mary Dunbar Pressure Cooker opens to reveal parts and Pressure Cooker booklet. *Byerly Collection.*

The Mary Dunbar Pressure Cooker

The Mary Dunbar Pressure Cooker was guaranteed to be free from defects in material and workmanship and to perform properly before it was shipped from the factory. The above Pressure Cooker is marked on the bottom "Made Expressly for the Jewel Tea Co., Inc., Barrington, Illinois. Pat No. 1901699." The patent number dates the item to 1933. *Byerly Collection.*

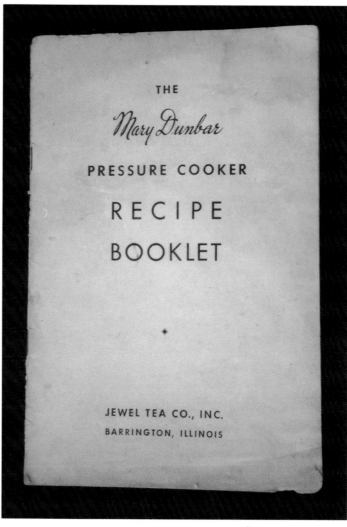

At "The Jewel Tea Co., Inc. " they were interested in making certain that the pressure cooker was in working order all the time. Very little service would be required because it had been designed and built to be sturdy.

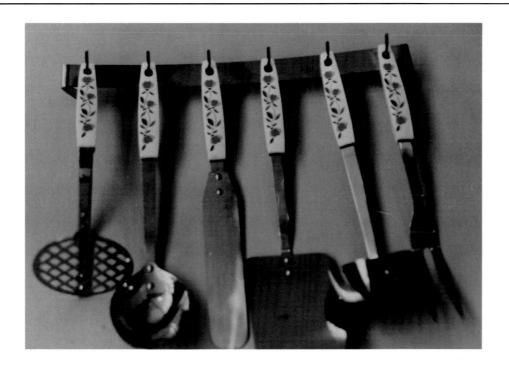

This seven-piece kitchen utensil set was a sample submitted to Jewel in the 1970s and after being rejected found its way into the Jewel employees' store. The set consisted of a 2-tine fork, ladle, turner, narrow spatula, basting spoon, masker and holder. Easley Collection.

Openers

Nowhere else but in a kitchen could you find this opener, in gold metal finish and plastic, which was designed with a special logo for the 75th Anniversary in 1974. The opener is approximately 4-1/4" long and it is believed that orange was the only color released for general distribution. An attached magnet at the back will hold the opener to a metal surface. *Author's Collection.*

Jewel rejected the wooden spice rack shown here. The white wooden holder with the Autumn Leaf decal across the back held 12 spice bottles. This sample rack was found in the Jewel employees' store. *Easley Collection.*

Magnetic Holders

Every kitchen refrigerator is decorated with the latest in children's art work, pet photographs, reminder notes, phone calls, bills, or notes to children. They all are held in place by the ever-famous magnetic note holders. Jewel In Home Shopping Service provided a Collectors' Series to decorate any steel surface; they were washable, and while they would not scratch the surface they were still powerful. The Collectors' Series included five holders, each with an illustration from Jewel's history: two different Jewel trucks, a wagon and horse, an Autumn Leaf cup and saucer, and a coffee grinder. They were distributed by Jewel Companies Inc., Barrington, Ill 60010. An assortment of magnetic holders can be found in the collecting world of Jewel, as well as a "Memo Center" board. This magnetic write-on/wipe-off message center board had permanently attached magnets that could turn a refrigerator into a message center. A built-in pen holder and pen were included. The original packaging reads "Jewel Home Shopping Service Jewel Park Barrington, Ill. 60010. #91-264."

The above 4-1/4" long bottle opener/can opener is marked on the front, "J.T.'s General Store" in orange. On the reverse side is a bottlecap sealer that snaps onto an open bottle. *Author's Collection.*

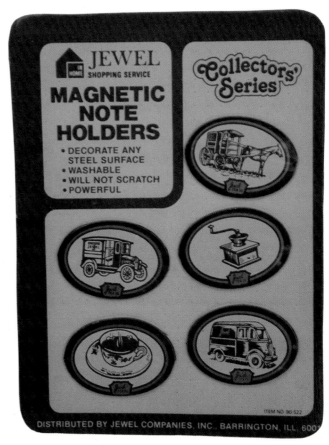

The Jewel Collectors' Series magnets. *Author's Collection.*

From the late 1980s, "You've Got a Friend In the Kitchen with the Power-Pal Magic Jar Opener." Made of genuine rubber the "Power-Pal" lets you open tightly-sealed jars, cans and bottles. Simply grip the part to be opened with the "Power-Pal" disc and turn. Also perfect to use as a coaster or a non-slip anchor. J.T.'s General Store "Power-Pal" was a real power gripper. *Byerly Collection.*

Tea Kettles

In 1933 a smartly modernistic teakettle appeared in The Jewel News, as practical as it was attractive. Made of heavy enamel, it carries the spout-filling feature and chromium-plated cover with a handsome black finial and a pleasing, soft green finish. This teakettle had a 4-quart capacity. It was listed as Item No. 390 and sold for $3.65. A paper label appears on one side, with the Jewel logo.

Below the logo the following appears: "STAINLESS LIFE-TIME ENAMEL-WARE / THE FINEST MADE." Below the wording the Mary Dunbar Seal of Approval appears. Recently one of these modernistic teakettles was located at a Michigan show. A portion of the original label was missing. No photograph was available.

CALLS YOU WHEN THE WATER BOILS!
—Listen for the Blue Bird's Happy Note

Here is one of the most useful household items seen in years

BLUE BIRD Singing Tea Kettle

No more kettle watching. Place this kettle on the stove when you get up in the morning and go about your dressing. When the water boils the kettle sings and you know the water is ready for your coffee or tea.

Saves Fuel—Saves Time—and MY! What a Convenience

After you have had this almost human tea kettle in your home you will wonder how you ever got along without it. Every homemaker who has tested it says, "I couldn't keep house without it."

Ideal As a Gift

For the bride—for the graduate—for the bridge party—Anyone of your friends will be delighted with it.

You may have this popular item by merely pinning a dollar bill to the coupon and sending it to:

Lake Products Company
Barrington, Ill.

It will be mailed to your home. Offer expires July 1, 1933.

Lake Products Company, Barrington, Ill.
For each $1.00 attached please send me one Blue Bird Singing Tea Kettle.

Name..
Street...
City...
R. F. D....................................State...............
Print your name and address.

Copper Blue Bird Singing Tea Kettle
Manufactured by the Aluminum Goods Manufacturing Company

2 quart capacity. Polished finish with lacquer protective coating. Blue enamelled hollow steel handle. Cast aluminum blue enamelled bird as a whistle. Plated on the inside.

A bird in the kitchen! You could have a "Happy Note" right in your kitchen with the above Blue Bird Singing Tea Kettle. Offered in The Jewel News, Vol. 11, No. 6 in 1933. *Hamilton Collection.*

Wall Cabinet

In 1932, Jewel offered a wall cabinet that was neat and attractive. The cabinet could be placed either in the bathroom, over the kitchen sink, or above the stove. Jewel promoted it as a handy place for storing the things you want within easy reach but kept out of sight. The wall cabinet was listed as Item No. C-6210 and was priced at $1.25.

The wall cabinet's original packaging reads "Item No. C-6210—ONE ONLY WALL CABINET." Also included with the unit was a booklet titled "Wall Cabinet for Kitchen or Bathroom." The booklet provided instructions for placement of the cabinet -- either over the sink for cleaning supplies, dish mop, cleanser, and chip soap or above the stove for spices, salt, hot pan holders, and lifters; or in the bathroom for cold creams, toothpaste, and other toilet articles.

Jewel's 1932 wall cabinet. *Hamilton Collection.*

The wall cabinet's beautiful decal. *Hamilton Collection.*

The coloring of the cabinet and beautiful decal blended with the color scheme of any kitchen or bathroom and added a note of beauty. The cabinet was hung securely against the wall by two wall screws and the screw-slits in the back of the cabinet. It was strong enough to hold cleaners, soap chips, etc. The glass finial located in front allowed for easy access to the specially constructed shelf inside that accommodated two soap dishes and supplies. The booklet has the seal, "Tested and Approved by Mary Dunbar Jewel Homemakers' Institute."

The little conveniences of modern equipment allowed for greater enjoyment and satisfaction in one's home. The Jewel premium line offered many opportunities to add pieces of modern equipment which one might otherwise not have been able to afford. It was one of Jewel's contributions to the happiness of the American home.

Every item in the Jewel premium lines was there because it had already proven its worth through use in Jewel's Homemakers' Institute Kitchen. It was only those items of unusual quality that gave greater satisfaction in use, that Mary Dunbar approved and recommended to Jewel customers.

Miscellaneous

An all-glass covered water bottle and a cookie jar from the mid-1940s. A multi-colored floral decal surrounds each piece; the foil sticker appearing on the cookie jar lid reads, "Jewel Holiday Candy Mix." *Lemons Collection.*

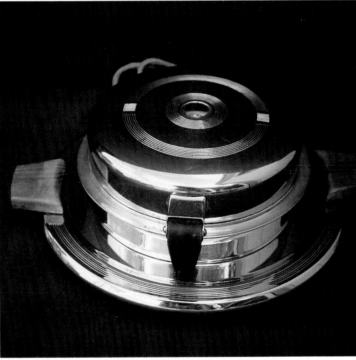

In 1940, the Manning Bowman Waffle Baker was dependable and long-lasting. Jewel listed the baker as Item No. 839, and sold it for $4.95. The baker has a chromium finish, with a strong plug, heat indicator, walnut handles, batter trough, and a cast aluminum grids. *Hamilton Collection.*

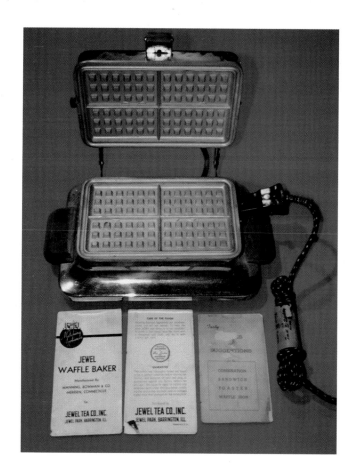

In August 1942, Jewel introduced a new whole-meal cooker made of heat-flow glassware and listed as No. 432. This new cooker was promoted with other pieces of Mary Dunbar glass ovenware. (See first book, *The Jewel Tea Company, Its History and Products*.) Made exclusively for Jewel customers, this cooker allowed homemakers to actually see their food cook. The glass cooker had its own metal base that was placed over medium heat. In the center of the lid is the famous Mary Dunbar seal.

Informative pamphlets accompanied the above Jewel Waffle Baker, manufactured by Manning, Bowman & Co. in Meriden, Connecticut for Jewel in Barrington, Illinois. The pamphlets offered "Suggestions for the Combination Sandwich Toaster Waffle Iron," ideas for the "Care of the Finish," and general instructions. This baker was "Tested and Approved by Mary Dunbar. *Barringer Collection.*

"Shakers from the Garden of Jewel" were distributed by the Jewel Co. from Barrington, marked "Made in Japan." Two shakers were included in the 9-1/4" x 9-1/4" carton shown here. *Lemons Collection.*

A handy booklet called "Whole-Meal Cookery Recipes and Instructions for the Heat-Flow Whole-Meal Cooker" by Mary Dunbar, Director, Jewel Homemakers' Institute, came with the 1942 whole-meal cooker. A 7" all-glass skillet marked "Heat-Flow Mary Dunbar Top Stove Ware Pat. USA" was available during this same period (photograph not available). *Author's Collection.*

Pyrex made cooking easier with this 1-1/2 quart casserole. Jewel listed it as Item No. 406, priced at $1.75, in 1927. The holder/frame was made by Manning, Bowman, and it listed as Item No. 769 for $1.75. Jewel also offered a pie plate and a utility tray (photograph not available). *Hamilton Collection.*

This casserole frame/holder appeared in a 1956 Jewel catalog. The 3-pint Hall Autumn Leaf casserole was given away free when a customer bought the chrome-plated frame/holder for $2.79. *Hamilton Collection.*

Item No. 753 is a nickel-plated cake and sandwich tray. This item appeared in a Jewel Premium Price List No. 35 (effective on and after July 5, 1925) for $2.00. The tray was beautifully designed, with a dainty filigree border, heavily plated with a silver luster polish, made by Manning, Bowman. The backstamp says "Manning Bowman." *Hamilton Collection.*

The attractive combination of the salad bowl and cake plate all in the same design made an attractive table. The cake plate was Item No. S-1440 and sold for 40¢; the salad bowl was Item No. C-6160 and sold for 85¢. A cake safe was also offered (photograph not available. See page 120 in *The Jewel Tea Company, It's History and Products*). These items appeared in 1933 and are believed to be the only items Jewel offered that were manufactured by the Homer Laughlin China Co. of Newell, West Virginia. *Hamilton Collection.*

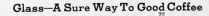

An original advertisement from 1942, for the Victory Silex No. 862 eight-cup coffee maker and the all-glass No. 449 dripper. This dripper is avidly sought by collectors. Two are known to exist in private collections.

The famous Manning Bowman Percolator was listed as Item No. 104 in the Jewel News 1923. It is backstamped with the famous "Jewel T Scale" logo. *Hamilton Collection.*

The Victory model Silex coffee maker, in an Old Sandwich design with a Silex electric warmer. *Hamilton Collection.*

Another teakettle. This kettle has a base diameter of 8-1/2", an opening of 5", and is 6-1/2" high (not including the handle). Note the different style and handle. This teakettle is marked with the "Jewel T Scale" logo enclosed in a square. *Hamilton Collection.*

This teakettle has a base diameter of 9", an opening of 4-3/4", and is approximately 6"/7" high (including final). It is marked with the "Jewel T Scale" freeform logo introduced in the late teens. *Hamilton Collection.*

Jewel announced the offer of the cream maker in a special 1934 issue of the Jewel News (with no assigned volume number). This "Club Aluminum Hammercraft Cream Maker" is shown with the original Jewel article. The cream maker was amazing, simple to use, and quick, and was useful in other ways as well. This maker has the original price tag of $4.99 inside, with complete directions for use. *Hamilton Collection.*

No. 21—LOX LID COMBINATION COOKER

Kettle holds six quarts. This cooker may be used in many combinations, such as a preserving kettle, soup kettle, meat boiler, double boiler, steamer, pot-roaster, collander or baking pan. Manufactured for Jewel by Aluminum Cookware Mfg. Co., Brooklyn, N. Y.

Price $3.00 (in P.S.C. or Cash)

The original advertisement for No. 21 Lox Lid Combination Cooker appeared in the Jewel News, 1925.

A 6-quart "Lox Lid Combination Cooker," manufactured for Jewel by Aluminum Cooking Mfg. Co. of Brooklyn, NY. The No. 21 Cooker appeared in the Jewel News 1925, sold for $3.00, and could be used in many combinations. It is backstamped as shown here. *Hamilton Collection.*

The No. 21 "Lox Lid Combination Cooker" shows timeless service and is missing the two insert pans. This cooker also appeared in a Jewel brochure entitled "Why 700,000 Housewives Buy THE JEWEL WAY." This brochure can be dated to April 1925. *Eisnaugle Collection.*

This Jewel 2-qt. freezer is 7-3/8" in diameter x 8-3/4" high. "Trade Steinfeld Mark New York" appears on the front. The freezer was available through Jewel during 1923-1924, and was discontinued sometime during 1925. *Hamilton Collection.*

This versatile 1-1/2 quart covered casserole (1935-1976) is shown for its variation of the decal's motif. It is not uncommon to find Jewel Hall Autumn Leaf pieces with variations, which do not change the price; variant pieces will sell for the same as those with the standard decal motif. *Eisnaugle Collection.*

The Hall China Autumn Leaf pie baker was introduced in 1937 and discontinued in 1976. The baker is 9-1/2" across and 1 3/4" deep. Listed in a Jewel Premium Catalog as Item No. 311, it was priced at 75¢ and advertised as ovenproof, with a smooth, non-porous surface and all-rounded edges. In 1952 the pie baker sold for $1.00 and was No. 5H108. Also shown is the reverse side of the pie baker. *Gibson Collection.*

CHAPTER 7
THE PERFECT TABLE

"If I were to entertain," many homemakers ask themselves, "how should I set my table?"

This was a query that was asked of The Jewel Lady so frequently that she became convinced that her customers would appreciate a short, simple article on the subject: *How to Set the Table for a Holiday Meal.* In her own dining room, Mary Dunbar set the perfect table.

BAVARIAN CUP, SAUCER AND DINNER PLATE

An old custom which is still practiced in many localities is to offer guests a cup of hot coffee with a plate of delicious cakes. The best dishes were always used. This cup, saucer and plate are attractive for serving your guests. Made of genuine imported Bavarian China. Decorated with a red rose and delicate green leaves. Manufactured by Heinrich & Co., Selb, Bavaria. Price—Cup and Saucer, 35c; Plate, 45c (in P. S. C. or Cash). Our Items No. 228– A and B, and No. 231.

A promotional photograph taken in the Jewel test kitchen in Barrington, Illinois, to be used for advertisements. The photograph shows the Ivanhoe pattern silverware, covered later in this chapter, and the imported china that appeared in a 1938 edition of The Jewel News. Many Jewel housewives may have set a table as picture perfect as shown in the photograph. Carefully note the linen tablecloth. Just above the cake, embroidered on the tablecloth appears the Jewel "T" logo. Where could this priceless tablecloth be today?

In 1925, Jewel offered a cup, saucer, and plate made of genuine imported Bavarian china decorated with a red rose and delicate green leaves. The original Jewel News advertisements with captions are shown here.

Imported Bavarian Rim Soup

Imported china, of the same beautiful design as the cup and saucer. Price $.45 each (in P. S. C. or Cash). Our Item No. 229.

In a 1926 Jewel News the Bavarian rim soup appeared, with original captions.

Imported Bavarian Berry Set

In 1926, Jewel offered this useful and harmonious seven-piece set with beautiful floral decorations. The set could be used for salads, fresh fruits, or cereal dishes in combination with any china on the dining table.

China Pitcher
New Rose Pattern

Every one has a need for a 5½-cup capacity pitcher. It is handy for milk or water. This one is of beautiful china with a dainty cluster of roses and foliage on either side and a gold edge. Has an easy pouring lip and a comfortable handle. Price 60c. Our Item No. S-1148.

China Salad Bowl
New Rose Pattern

Time can't always be taken to fix individual salads. Instead, line a dish with lettuce leaves and fill up the bowl with the salad. A pretty bowl sets off the salad and this Rose china one is most attractive with its narrow escalloped edge and sloping sides. It has a capacity of 6 cups so is very useful for fruit, salads or creamed vegetables. Price 65c. Our Item No. S-1149.

A Bavarian china plate has been reversed to shown the Jewel scale logo. *Pomroy Collection.*

During 1926, two additional New Rose pattern pieces appeared: the China Rose pattern pitcher and a new China Rose pattern salad bowl. The ads for them appear here with original captions.

From a 1926 Jewel News, the original advertisement and original captions for the New Rose pattern.

18-Pc. Breakfast Set—New Rose Pattern

A good looking breakfast set of cups, saucers and plates, all of fine domestic china. Has a pleasing rose design with a neat gold border. It is just the thing for a small breakfast set. May be used for afternoon or evening parties, or to "fill in" with the main set. Price $3.95. Our Item No. N-5022.

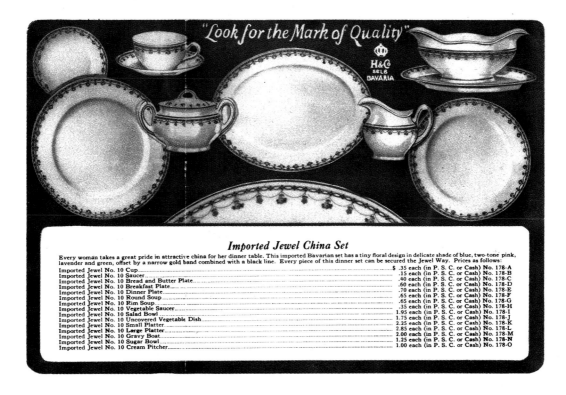

"Look for the Mark of Quality"

H&Co
SGL&
BAVARIA

Imported Jewel China Set

Every woman takes a great pride in attractive china for her dinner table. This imported Bavarian set has a tiny floral design in delicate shade of blue, two-tone pink, lavender and green, offset by a narrow gold band combined with a black line. Every piece of this dinner set can be secured the Jewel Way. Prices as follows:

Imported Jewel No. 10 Cup	$ .35 each (in P. S. C. or Cash)	No. 178-A
Imported Jewel No. 10 Saucer	.15 each (in P. S. C. or Cash)	No. 178-B
Imported Jewel No. 10 Bread and Butter Plate	.40 each (in P. S. C. or Cash)	No. 178-C
Imported Jewel No. 10 Breakfast Plate	.60 each (in P. S. C. or Cash)	No. 178-D
Imported Jewel No. 10 Dinner Plate	.70 each (in P. S. C. or Cash)	No. 178-E
Imported Jewel No. 10 Round Soup	.65 each (in P. S. C. or Cash)	No. 178-F
Imported Jewel No. 10 Rim Soup	.65 each (in P. S. C. or Cash)	No. 178-G
Imported Jewel No. 10 Vegetable Saucer	.35 each (in P. S. C. or Cash)	No. 178-H
Imported Jewel No. 10 Salad Bowl	1.95 each (in P. S. C. or Cash)	No. 178-I
Imported Jewel No. 10 Uncovered Vegetable Dish	1.75 each (in P. S. C. or Cash)	No. 178-J
Imported Jewel No. 10 Small Platter	2.25 each (in P. S. C. or Cash)	No. 178-K
Imported Jewel No. 10 Large Platter	2.85 each (in P. S. C. or Cash)	No. 178-L
Imported Jewel No. 10 Gravy Boat	2.00 each (in P. S. C. or Cash)	No. 178-M
Imported Jewel No. 10 Sugar Bowl	1.25 each (in P. S. C. or Cash)	No. 178-N
Imported Jewel No. 10 Cream Pitcher	1.00 each (in P. S. C. or Cash)	No. 178-O

The China of China advertisement appeared in a 1926 Jewel News. This imported Bavarian Jewel china carried the mark of quality.

Nothing pleased the American housewife more than to cover her mahogany table with the finest tablecoth. Linens became victims of daily use and abuse, resulting in the high prices found by today's collectors. Linens that have been stained, cut, torn, patched, or badly faded list below the high prices for those in perfect condition.

Jewel offered customers a variety of tablecoths and bed linens over the years. It would be impossible to list or photograph each item.

Old kitchen, bed, and table linens that have been stored for a long period of time should be soaked in water for at least twelve hours. This rehydrates the fibers and lossens any dirt or leftover soap.

Item No. C-6011, cotton towels from 1925 that sold for 70¢ a pair.

Well-woven cotton is ideal for glass towels, for it is lintless and leaves glassware sparkling. In 1925, Jewel offered cotton towels that were woven with a linen-like finish. The borders were fast colors, and the more they were laundered, the softer and more absorbent they became. Listed as Item No. C-6011, a pair sold for 70¢ in cash only.

In 1941, Jewel suggested Wildwood china on a lace tablecloth for the perfect table setting. The cloth was in natural linen color, and could be used for numerous meals without laundering. It folded without wrinkling or mussing; spots could be sponged off without leaving water marks. It was easy to dry, and could be pressed or finished with stretchers. It was truly a tablecloth that would last. A tablecloth dressed up any table, and even made meals taste better. The stunning cloth could be paid for with premium credits.

The Wildwood pattern was indeed, beautiful. The floral design is colorful but delicate, suitable for any occasion. A 16-piece Starter Set was priced at $2.95, and open stock pieces were individually priced.

A more detailed view of the border and motif on the 16" square napkin. *Byerly Collection.*

The 48" x 48" woven banded luncheon cloth, often referred to as a "Go-With," remains another mystery with collectors. Banded in shades of brown, orange, rust, and gold, it is believed to have been available at the same period as the banded tumblers shown elsewhere in this chapter. It has been brought to my attention that there is a set of four napkins that match this cloth in a private collection. *Hamilton Collection.*

In 1937, the above 56" x 81" muslin tablecloth was introduced with a set of smartly matched 16" square napkins, in the design and colors of the Hall chinaware. This set was discontinued by 1942. *Byerly Collection.*

Tablecloths

Few Autumn Leaf pattern tablecloths in the aqua, purple, and yellow color scheme have been located. Very little is know about them, and no photograph available. The cloth has bands of aqua, purple, and yellow that appear around the edge, with the Autumn Leaf motif above the band. Like the banded luncheon cloth, this tablecloth is a mystery.

Similarly, little is known of the 56" x 68" muslin tablecloth in the blue, red, and teal/green color scheme. . A band of blue and red appears around the edge of the cloth, with the Autumn Leaf motif above the bands. The motif appears in colors of red, yellow, and teal/green. It is unknown if other sizes of this tablecloth were offered.

The blue, red, & teal/green tablecloth, 56" x 68". *Costanza Collection.*

It is wise to carefully check plastic-coated tablecloths for any sign of damage. The loss of color, brilliance is the first damage noticed by collectors. Signs of cigarette damage are also important. Remember that plastic-coated tablecloths resist stains and water, but not heat!

In 1950 Jewel offered two sizes of plastic-coated tablecloths. One was 54" x 54" and the other was 54" x 72". Both plastic cloths had the all-over Autumn motif. In 1950 Jewel advertised them as Hall "Autumn" Plastic Tablecloths. The lovely cotton fabric tablecloth has a plastic-coated surface that resists stains and water. Hall "Autumn" pattern tablecloth matches Jewel's "Autumn" Dinnerware. *Byerly Collection.*

The above cotton sailcloth Autumn tablecloth appeared in 1955. Offered in two sizes (54" x 54" and 54" x 72"), the design featured a gold stripe below the motif. By late 1958 these sailcloth tablecloths were discontinued. See original advertisement within this chapter. *Author's Collection.*

This Burlington Cotton Crash tablecloth, 54" x 70", was offered in Jewel Summer 1949. Two hemmed and two salvaged edges, woven of strong cotton yarns in a homespun texture. Choice of three color combinations on natural cotton background: brown predominating with yellow and orange; blue predominating with red and yellow; or green predominating with orange and yellow. (The green tablecloth was shown in color on page 3 of this catalog.) Priced at $2.98. *Lemons Collection.*

Jewel Curt Towels

Jewel Curt Towels were produced from 1957 to 1959 and served a number of purposes. Curt Towels were made of blended cotton, rayon, and linen, an ideal blend for dishtowels; their softness and absorbency made wiping with them easy. They were pre-shrunk, could be laundered, and they ironed easily. The floral design was in washfast dye.

By inserting a curtain rod in the wide hem of the 20" x 35" Autumn Leaf dish towel, a housewife could make the towel into a curtain. Two towels made a pair of decorative curtains, with a single narrow gold band traveling down the sides of each curtain. At the bottom there is approximately 1-3/4" wide band of gold, and above that a narrow band of orange. At the base are three leaves and two large motifs. A clock appears in the middle, and four cups and saucers are on each curtain. In the middle between the cups and saucers are two plates.

There are two known Autumn Pattern Fatigue Mats in a private collection today. If you should have a fatigue mat, I would like to hear from you.

A folded Jewel Curt Towel. *Byerly Collection.*

These 16" x 33" cotton towels matched your "Autumn Leaf" dinnerware and other linens. Offered in 1956, discontinued in late 1957. *Author's Collection.*

The clock design in the middle of the Curt Towel. *Byerly Collection.*

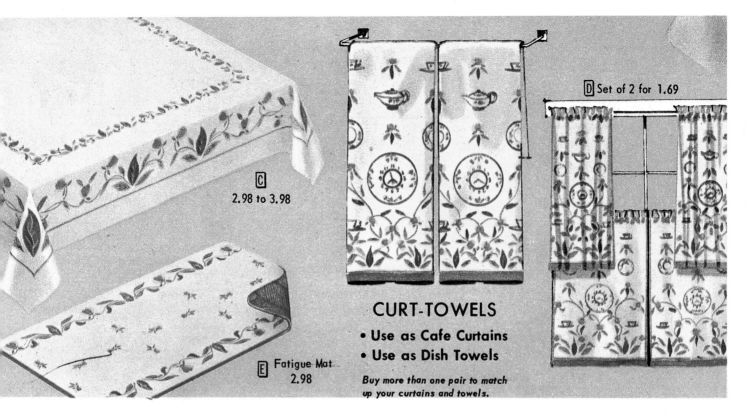

C
2.98 to 3.98

CURT-TOWELS
- Use as Cafe Curtains
- Use as Dish Towels

Buy more than one pair to match up your curtains and towels.

E Fatigue Mat
2.98

D Set of 2 for 1.69

An original advertisement from the Jewel Home Shopping Service Spring and Summer 1958 Catalog, promoting the "Autumn" Pattern Luncheon Cloth (C), hand-screen printed to match Jewel china, along with ovenware and curt towels (D). "Long-wearing, fine-woven cotton sailcloth that washes and irons easily, washfast multicolor. Offered in sizes 54" x 54" for $2.98 and 54" x 72" for $3.98. Also shown above (E) new Autumn Pattern Fatigue Mat, a sponge rubber mat that provides wonderful comfort for all standing chores! The mat was covered with a new DuPont Mylar synthetic fabric that sheds dirt and wipes clean. The mat was non-skid safety material with a multicolor floral design. The only size offered was 18" x 30", sold for $2.98."

The Anniversary Sale Special

The modernistic Anniversary Sale Special Luncheon Cloth first appeared in The Jewel News, Vol. 14, No. 7, in 1936, with only a limited quantity available of this special value. Jewel promoted this cloth as gaily colored and yet not noisy. It laundered well and gave a cheery note to the breakfast nook. Listed as item numbers S1672 and S1673, it sold for 75 cents. A picture of the cloth also appeared in a promotional with other Jewel products and premiums, but no mention of it was made in this promotional. While I have been unable to find one of these cloths, a photograph of one with the original packaging appears in *The Collector's Encyclopedia of Hall China* by Margaret and Kenn Whitmyer. I find no record of this cloth appearing after 1936, and remember that Jewel had only a *limited* quantity available!

Ivanhoe Silverware

One of the most attractive silverware patterns offered by Jewel was called Ivanhoe. This silverware dates to the 1930s. By the late 1940s it appeared on the discontinued list.

Ivanhoe silverware appeared in various promotional photographs in Jewel publications.

In 1939 Ivanhoe was listed as a Jewel exclusive pattern, and they offered six each of teaspoons, tablespoons, dinner forks, dinner knives, soup spoons, and dessert spoons. Sold individually were butter spreaders, a sugar shell, butter knife, meat fork and berry spoon. As a Jewel Tea premium, prices ranged from $2.00 per set of teaspoons to $5.00 per set of dinner knives. Ivanhoe was never offered as a complete set until 1946.

The brochure accompanying a set of Ivanhoe iced tea spoons states "Made by the famous International Silver Co., only makers of original Rogers silverplate in Jewel's exclusive Ivanhoe pattern."

In 1938, it was brought to the attention of Jewel employees that even though Jewel was vitally interested in silverware, they had no conception of what actually went into the making of the finest quality silver-plated flatware. A fundamental requirement of good salesmanship was to know the product they were selling.

Prospective buyers of silverware were interested, first, in the beauty of the product. Cheap dinnerware can serve its purpose in the eating of a meal almost as well as the most expensive sterling silver. The sale of expensive, quality silverware had its roots in pride of ownership, appreciation of beauty, and the desire of every housewife. Jewel salesmen had first to create a desire in each customer for good silverware as a thing of beauty. They had to conjure up a picture of a lovely table setting in her home, and build up the pleasure received from a smart and distinctive silver service.

Ivanhoe was a lovely modern design of simple orna-mentation, made exclusively for Jewel. The pattern was popular and with proper presentation the service had plenty of "eye-appeal." After a salesman created the desire for Ivanhoe, he had to call upon his knowledge of the prod-uct. The customer had to be convinced that Ivanhoe was a fine quality silver, sure to give dependable service.

Ivanhoe is stamped "WM. ROGERS MFG. CO.," one of the famous Original Rogers Silverplate brands. It is made by International Silver Company, the world's largest sil-versmiths company. Any piece not giving satisfaction was replaced without charge. Staple pieces (those most often used) had an extra heavy deposit of pure silver, reinforced plate, at the point where the most wear would occur. This insured long life and enduring beauty.

One spoon of Ivanhoe ware went through 25 major manufacturing operations, not counting much preliminary work and dozens of important minor handlings. The entire process is impossible to explain. Ivanhoe embodied the finest in raw materials, in modern machinery and scientific research, and in craftsmanship.

In 1946 customers had a chance to complete their Ivanhoe silverplate set. Seven pieces of Ivanhoe silverplate were on sale from the friendly Jewel man. The prices were in sets of six.

Those customers who had an incomplete set of the Ivanhoe pattern could buy what they needed, because there was some question as to when Jewel would have this pattern available again. Jewel believed that it was wise to buy extra sets of these pieces to supplement whatever other silver they might have.

Autumn Flatware

In 1958 Jewel offered silver-plated Autumn flatware service, made by the International Silver Company. This flatware was offered in a 24-piece service for six, and a 50-piece service for eight. Open stock was avail-able to customers. *Lemons Collection.*

In 1960-1968, this set of stainless steel tableware was a Jewel exclusive, made by the world's finest silversmiths, International Silver Co. It was perfect in detail, matchless in balance and design. The American house-wife could acquire beautiful stainless steel to match her Autumn China and bakeware. Its lovely, slender, sculptured lines are wrought with su-perb craftsmanship. Knives have mirror-finish blades. *Lemons Collec-tion.*

Jewel's Autumn motif flatware is growing in popularity among collectors and becoming quite expensive. Only those pieces in mint condition are sought by collectors. Flatware that is heavily damaged or tarnished is often passed over. It is wise to keep flatware in a silver chest of your selection. Tossing flatware together is detrimental.

Jewel pointed out that customers had waited for four years when they offered a 26-piece set of attractive flat-ware in 1946. In April of that year, the friendly Jewel man had the set available, under the time payment plan if a customer wished. This flatware, with red plastic handles, would be for use in the kitchen, for everyday use, or would make a perfect gift for the bride.

The mirror-polished bowls, blades, tines were as beau-tiful as jeweler's silver, and would remain bright for a life-time. There was no plating to wear off. The set would not tarnish or rust because it was made of stainless steel. To keep it clean and bright only soap and water were required.

The original advertisement from Jewel Home Shopping Service Spring and Summer 1958 Catalog. Among items offered were (A) "Autumn" Silverplate exclusive at Jewel, along with (B) Imperial Cape Cod stain-less steel. Finlandia (C) by International Silver Co. was a style that re-flected casual elegance in modern living. Also offered were (D) Kingston Pattern by Imperial and (E) Malibu Pattern by Imperial with a bambo-like handle of WondaWood. A mahogany-finished Hardwood Chest (F) was tarnish-free to keep silverware gleaming bright without polishing.

A AUTUMN

B CAPE COD

C FINLANDIA

D KINGSTON

E MALIBU

F Hardwood Chest
keeps Service for 12!

ALL SHOWN
ACTUAL SIZE

Glasswares

Sherbet, Iced Tea, Goblet and Water Sets
These four sets of glassware are etched in the favorite Apple Blossom design. The tall, graceful stems of the sherbet and goblet sets will please the most fastidious hostess. Slender iced tea glasses are very popular for refreshing beverages of all kinds. Every woman knows that fruits, ices or ice creams and many other cold desserts are most attractively served in sherbet glasses. All of this glassware has a clear, sparkling luster.
Sherbet (set of six) $2.40 (in P. S. C. or Cash) No. 426
Iced Tea (set of six) $2.40 (in P. S. C. or Cash) No. 427
Goblet (set of six) $2.70 (in P. S. C. or Cash) No. 428
Water (set of six and water pitcher) $3.25 (in P. S. C. or Cash) No. 436

A 1926 Jewel News advertisement for the Apple Blossom design sherbet, iced tea, goblet, and water sets.

Jewel's set of two-tone glassware for iced beverages, as advertised in The Jewel News in July 1927.

These banded tumblers are basically the same as the 5-1/2" (14 oz) frosted Autumn Leaf. The date is unknown, there are four painted Autumn-color stripes encircling the tumbler: (bottom to top) brown, orange, rust, and gold. Each stripe measures approximately 5/16" wide, with the bottom stripe beginning 5/16" from the bottom. There is 1/8" between stripes. The bottom is clear and signed Libbey. *Hamilton Collection.*

In July 1927, The Jewel News told readers that iced beverages would become more tempting when served in attractive two-tone glassware offered by Jewel. Homemakers might choose a 9-glass capacity beverage jug with a set of six matching 5-1/8" tall glasses. This water or beverage set made serving a pleasure.

Frozen desserts could be served in a two-tone green and clear crystal ware.

For a more formal look a housewife could select a set of six "goblets" (Item No. 439) in green and crystal that were gracefully tall (6-2/3") and well-balanced. They would add real beauty to any dinner china and a elegant touch to any table.

An emerald green base could capture the afternoon sun and cast a luminous energy, while the diagonally-ridged optic of the tops could capture the sparkle of the ice and liquid, spreading it about the table. *Author's Collection.*

Introduced in 1975, these clear tumblers with the Autumn Leaf pattern were made by Brockway Company of Clarksburg, West Virginia. They were offered in three different sizes: 16 oz., shown here, 13 oz., and 9 oz., also shown here. They were discontinued in 1976. Brockway glassware is not as common as the frosted glassware; some hunting may well be required. *Byerly Collection.*

The Autumn Leaf motif glassware is a popular item among collectors of the famous pattern. The 14 ounce Jewel frosted tumbler by Libbey were introduced in 1940. The tumbler is 5-1/2" high and is commonly found quite reasonably priced. Jewel's Spring and Summer catalog from 1949 listed these 5-1/2" glasses as "Autumn" Pattern Frosted Tumblers. The set would add a touch of summer to any table scene. The "Autumn" pattern, so popular in dinnerware and ovenware, is duplicated on them in the colorful autumn tones of brown and orange. They are proportioned to sit firmly and to eliminate water-spilling accidents. Carefully molded, smoothly finished. Listed as Item No. 5J24, 14 oz. size. *Author's Collection.*

In 1958 you could have the exclusive Autumn Pattern tumblers. They were beautiful, in the 10 oz. size. These glasses had an all-over Autumn pattern in 22K gold, an etched frost motif, and Safedge gold rims to defy chipping. They were of distinctive shape, and had extra-heavy bottoms. A classic elegance, designed for perfect harmony with Autumn china and silverware. Listed as Item No. 5J58.

The 3-3/4" high frosted tumbler was introduced in 1950. This 9 ounce tumbler is more difficult to locate than the 14 ounce. *Author's Collection.*

By 1960, you could add the 15 oz. "Autumn" Libbey tumblers (shown here with the 10 oz. tumbler), listed as Item No. 5J71. *Byerly Collection.*

In 1960 the 6-1/2 oz. Footed Sherbet was listed as Item No. 5J70. Also available was the 10-1/2 oz. Footed Goblet, listed as Item No. 5J69. By 1961 the 22K glassware has been discontinued. *Byerly Collection.*

This glassware and stemware can be somewhat hard to locate. It is popular among collectors and becoming quite expensive.

This photograph was taken in Jewel's text kitchen in Barrington, Illinois during the late 1930s for promotional purposes. I have been unable to locate information concerning the beverage pitcher and glasses. Without a doubt any housewife could set the perfect table with assistance from the Jewel Lady, Mary Dunbar, or a friendly Jewel man. *Barrington Archives.*

More Tableware

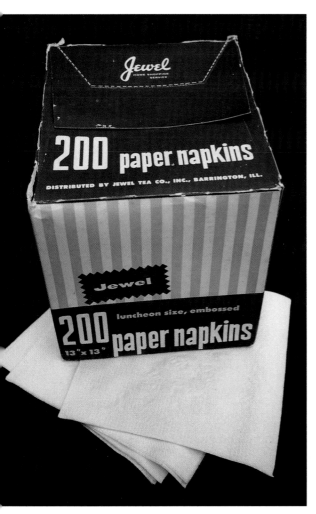

This carton held two hundred Jewel Home Shopping Service luncheon size (13" x 13") embossed paper napkins. Distributed by Jewel Tea Co., Inc., Barrington, Ill. *Author's Collection*

The No. 230 imported Bavarian china berry set. This fine china set featured beautiful workmanship, appearing in the Jewel News in August 1924. These pieces may be older than 1924. Note the large "J" in the mark. This logo can be found on pieces of Bavarian china. *Hamilton Collection.*

During the mid-1940s, this set of nesting mixing bowls in the "Blue Floral" pattern was produced for the Jewel Tea Company. The set included a 6-1/4" bowl, a 7-3/4" bowl and a 9" bowl. Also available was a 2-quart covered casserole (photograph not available). *Hamilton Collection.*

85

In the May 1928 issue of The Jewel News, Vol. 6 No. 4, this imported floral rose Bavarian cup and saucer was promoted as a "Man's Size" cup, with a capacity of 10 ounces. The cup was listed as Item No. 233-A and sold for 20¢. The saucer was Item No. 233-B and sold for 10¢. The cup is backstamped "BAVARIA #776" and the saucer is marked only "BAVARIA." *Hamilton Collection.*

This china is of the highest grade and decorated with a floral design in two-toned pink, blue, lavender, and green. A fine black line is entwined in the narrow gold border. This imported "Palace" Bavarian China was promoted in The Jewel News of August 1926 and may be older.

The "Palace" cup and saucer. The cup sold for 35¢ and the saucer for 15¢. *Hamilton Collection.*

In February 1928, the above Bavarian ware "Man-sized Cup" was a new Jewel premium. A set of six cups and saucers sold for $1.50; Jewel had reduced them from the original price of $1.80. The modest green fleur-de-lis pattern combined nicely with any china pattern and would not craze. The cup was listed as Item No. 232-A and the saucer was Item No. 232-B. This "Man-sized" cup and saucer are backstamped "BAVARIA." *Hamilton Collection.*

Two "Palace" dinner plates. Note the "J" in the laurel wealth backstamp on the reversed plate. *Author's Collection.*

The "Palace" sugar and creamer. In 1926 the sugar sold for $1.25 and the creamer sold for $1.00. *Hamilton Collection.*

The small "Palace" platter was listed as item 178-K and sold for $2.24 in 1926. *Author's Collection.*

The Bavarian fruit bowl appeared in The Jewel News, Vol 3. No. 8 in August 1925, and in Vol 3. No. 12 in December 1925. The backstamp is the large "J" surrounded by the laurel wreath. *Hamilton Collection.*

In August 1942, Jewel offered the "Morning Glory" pattern No. 550. Produced exclusively for the Jewel Tea Company by the Hall China Company. Each piece is backstamped in gold "HALL'S SUPERIOR QUALITY KITCHENWARE" with the "Tested and Approved by Mary Dunbar Jewel Homemakers Institute" in a gold circle. The straight-sided set consists of a 4-1/4", 5", 61/4", 7-3/4" and a 9". This set has the original paper labels in the center of each bowl. Each bowl has a cadet blue exterior and white interior with the morning glory motif that consists of tiny pink and blue blooms with green leaf intertwined on a hi-white glazed body. A direction booklet was provided with this set. *Author's Collection*

Shown at left, the "Morning Glory" pattern Aladdin teapot. *Hamilton Collection.*

CHAPTER 8
PREPARING THE BRIDE'S HOME

From the very beginning, Jewel had an interest in the American home—from fresh roasted coffee to the finest in china, clocks, dinnerware, tableware, cookware, kitchenware, and later a complete line of apparel. Jewel could provide almost anything for the home. Simply inquire of your route salesman!

Equipping a new bride's home was a concern of The Jewel Tea Company and of Mary Dunbar. Jewel could provide numerous items as appropriate gifts for any bride's shower, an anniversary, or other occasion.

The bride was the center of attention when conversation of a forthcoming wedding took place. In 1946, there was nothing that could start interesting conversation more easily than the discussion of a wedding. What silverware pattern had the bride chosen? Where will they live? What kind of a shower should be given? Who was the lucky man?

Jewel believed an unusual shower theme for a bride who has a home or apartment all ready to move into would be pantry shelf supplies. The new bride isn't sure what she needs for a well-stocked cupboard, ready for almost any emergency. Jewel could help her start off on the right foot by giving a "Jewel Grocery Shower." Jewel suggested the following staples: coffee, tea, cocoa, spaghetti, noodles, and marcaroni. Also useful are fully prepared mixes: gingerbread, devil's food cake, spice cake, griddle cake mix, and biscuit mix. Pudding mixes were also handy, including: Pud-N-Pie, butterscotch, or chocolate. The new bride would also need baking supplies: baking powder, vanilla, cake flour, and extracts. Jewel also suggested mustard and steak sauces.

A new bride could use cleaning supplies, such as Jewel cleanser, scouring pads, granulated soap, starch, bowl cleaner, drain cleaner, bluing, stove cleaner, floor and furniture polish.

A guest to a bridal shower could accumulate quite an extensive assortment of gifts at very low cost, and fill a new bridal pantry.

Jewel knew that any bride would be grateful for any Jewel product or premiums given as gifts. She would find them economical to use and prepare — important considerations for any new bride.

Jewel suggested that on the visit of a friendly Jewel man you should order a complete supply of pantry shelf items as a gift for the new bride.

In 1928, a June bride would have been delighted with the Vernon pattern in silverware. The design was simple, yet distinctive, and would make a well appointed table. Jewel suggested that the customer order early for delivery in time for a June wedding. The Oneida Community Par Plate had a 20-year guarantee.

Jewel suggested an ideal gift for the bride would have been a set of Haviland China.

This unknown bride appeared in a 1938 Jewel News that was promoting "Ivanhoe" silverware. Could this radiant bride have also been a faithful Jewel shopper?

See the first volume for a discussion of Haviland. Also see "The Perfect Table" chapter for other appropriate wedding gifts.

When Jewel began offering its vast array of products and household items, a new bride listened. Prices were affordable when money was hard to come by. Most new brides took charge of the household finances and learned to budget. Each of them paid the bills, prepared the meals, did the sewing, laundry and cleaned the house. She cared for the children and looked after the needs of her new household. She built her home into a place of safe refuge for herself, her working husband, and the children.

From the very beginning Jewel provided the most perfect gift for any new bride. The reasonable prices of Jewel products allowed a new bride an assortment of useful gifts. Let's allow Jewel to suggest a prefect gift!

HANDKER-CHIEFS—Dainty squares, lace edged, and of delicate pastel shades are these imported Swiss Handkerchiefs. They are durable, despite their sheer appearance. Price $1.25, box of three. (Cash only). Our Item No. 6019.

In 1925 the perfect gift for a young bride (or any other woman) might have been the dainty lace "Swiss Handker-Chiefs," shown here in an original 1925 Jewel News advertisement.

In 1925, Jewel offered dainty lace handkerchiefs, a perfect gift for the new bride. Did you know that 21 years later Jewel would reject 60,000 ladies handkerchiefs? Rejections like this didn't happen often, but the material situation of 1946 made it necessary a few times.

Two items promoted in a September issue of The Jewel News were a pin-up lamp and a ladies' handkerchief, featured to be on sale beginning September 23, 1946.

Both items were withdrawn after The Jewel News had gone to press. It seems that the suppliers could not get materials necessary to make good quality merchandise, and Jewel refused to provide merchandise that was not of good quality. Sixty thousand handkerchiefs were delivered to the Jewel plant in Barrington, Illinois, but upon inspection and comparison with the original sample, Jewel found they were made of inferior quality material and showed poor workmanship. They did not come near to Jewel's specifications of quality merchandise. The whole sixty thousand were returned to the supplier. Careful inspection and quality specifications like these made Jewel a better place to trade!

Jewel makes no other mention of the Pin-Up Lamp.

Cosmetics

Cosmetics are a big concern of today's woman, much as they were in 1926. Jewel provided a wide variety of quality cosmetics, many of which were good gift ideas for the new bride. During the 1940s, Velvetouch became the leading facial cream for all complexion types, and the well-groomed woman no longer considered make-up an afterthought. Powders, shampoos, and soap were provided for that bride-to-be, or for the family in general. Any bride and groom could look and feel perfect on their wedding day, with Jewel Products.

VELVETOUCH
"PROTECTS AND HEALS"
fine for sunburn windburn

DELIGHTFUL

Is the feeling of this soothing, healing, jelly-like skin lotion. If your face is sunburned, or wind burned, or if you've been swimming and are "blistery," apply a light coating of Velvetouch and feel that soft, cooling, delightful sensation which almost instantaneously follows.

Velvetouch is a delightful and necessary toilet preparation for the delicate skin of women and children. A man has to use it just once after shaving to become a staunch advocate and a continuous patron. He knows that it leaves his skin with a soothed feeling that is delightful.

Jar—Price $.25 (P. S. C. $.05).

Order it from Your Jewel Man

ALCO-GRAVURE, INC. ?

Dentaglow Tooth Paste—Keep your teeth healthy and clean with a fine, smooth cleansing cream, free from abrasives. Dentaglow is all of these. It will in no way harm the enamel and will leave a pleasing fragrance to the breath. Put up in an attractive tube of convenient size, handy for use two or three times a day. Tube, Price, $.25— (P. S. C. $.05).

If the bride of 1926 had that perfect, delicate-looking skin on her wedding day, she may have used Jewel Velvetouch, a small gift from a friend or purchased from a friendly Jewel Man. Velvetouch protects and heals; it was even good as the groom's aftershave. An original 1926 advertisement appears here.

Perfume—Lilas Divine, a blend of choice perfumes, is neatly packaged in a sealed glass stoppered bottle, and an expensive box. None of the essence can escape before it reaches you. Choose it as your own distinctive perfume. Bottle, Price $1.00—(P. S. C. $.15).

On their wedding day, the lucky couple's breath had to be perfect, and she must smell like fresh flowers. Jewel provided the perfect selection in Dentaglow Tooth Paste and Perfume Lilas Divine, as shown in this original 1926 advertisement.

Talcum Powder

Is delicately perfumed and mildly medicated. Sprinkle it on the body after bathing to cool the skin. It has many uses: after shaving, for prickly heat, chapped hands, sachet, inside of gloves, dry shampoo. Especially good for the tiny baby. Protect him from heat with Amado, Price $.25—(P. S. C. $.05).

Velvetouch

Soothe sunburned or windburned skin with Jewel Velvetouch. It is a daintily scented skin lotion, with a blend of five delightful odors, in which jasmine predominates. Men, too, like it after shaving. Jar, Price $.25— (P. S. C. $.05).

Liquid Shampoo

Keep your hair glossy, silky and clean in hot weather with Jewel Liquid Shampoo. It lathers quickly, cleans rapidly and is easily thoroughly rinsed. It is an absolutely pure shampoo. Bottle, Price $.50—(P. S. C. $.10).

Toilet Articles

Toilet Soaps

Pure Jewel—A sensitive skin requires a neutral soap. Pure Jewel is composed of scientifically neutralized pure ingredients, faintly scented. It is suited to the fastidious for a general toilet soap. 3 cakes in carton, Price $.30 — (P. S. C. $.05).

From The Jewel News, 1926.

In the late 1930s, this photograph was taken of Mary Dunbar, her assistant (believed to be Marvis Galloway), and the photographer. A selection of Jewel beauty products were being photographed for a promotional advertisement. Carefully examine the historical photograph; you may have one of the numerous items appearing. *Barrington Archives.*

Ladies' Umbrella

A serviceable umbrella, made of good quality gloria, called "Amisilk." It has ten strong ribs and can be secured in either deep silk-like purple or blue. The daintily carved handle is set off with an ambered tip and has a silk loop for easy carrying. This is an exceptional value at $3.25. Our Item No. C-6018.

Jewel provided protection from the elements on any bride's most jubilant day. This ladies' umbrella was offered in a Jewel News in 1926; it was perfect for any event.

Three Piece Pantry Set

Keep the pantry shelves neat by having food in sanitary containers. This white painted set of bread box, sugar box, and flour box will be great conveniences to the homemaker. The bread box has ventilating holes to keep the bread sweet and free from mold. The sugar box has a 10-lb. capacity, and the flour box 15-lb. They can all be quickly and easily cleaned. Price $2.15. Our Item No. 768.

This original advertisement appeared in a 1926 Jewel News. What a perfect gift this three-piece pantry set would have made!

Enjoy Sunny Cheer Through This Lovely Lace Curtain

Grace and dignity given to the window, without shutting out the cheery sunlight! A panel curtain that is cream colored, of a characteristic soft texture, and an even square mesh. It has a dainty, floral, all-over pattern. It is 2½ yards long, 40 inches wide, with a 3½-inch fringe. Is used one to a window; if window is wide it hangs with dignity, and if window is narrow it falls in graceful folds. Made of imported Egyptian and South American yarns. It is delivered spotlessly clean in a transparent envelope. It will give good service because it launders beautifully. Price $3.40. Our Item No. 288.

Brighten the Home

Treat Your Eyes Kindly

A "homey" atmosphere is given to your living room or hall by this graceful table lamp. It has a heavy, burnished bronze metal base, with a neatly decorated stem. The colorful rose and tan shade has a black and gold edge, and a floral spray on one side. This shade is 10½ inches by 6¼ inches in bottom dimensions and 7¼ inches tall. The lamp stands 16½ inches over-all, and has 6 feet of insulated cord. Price $4.45. Our Item No. 767.

An original advertisement and captions for lace curtains and a graceful table lamp. This advertisement appeared in The Jewel News during the late 1920s.

In 1938 Mary Dunbar gathered together a variety of Jewel Premiums for a promotional display that any bride would have been pleased with.

She started first in the kitchen, with the three sizes of the Hall China mixing bowls. Mary Dunbar believed they were nice enough bowls for serving, and since they were ovenware, they could be used for baking. She felt they would serve every need of a new bride for a long time to come.

Next she suggested the Club Aluminum Ware Covered Skillet. Used as a chicken fryer or shallow Dutch Oven, they could be used to prepare tougher cuts of meat which required long, slow cooking to become deliciously tender. The Covered Skillet would serve a lifetime.

A new bride must have one large cooking pot, and the suggestion was The Mary Dunbar Waterless Cooker. Not only does it serve as a kettle but is, at the same time, a whole meal cooker. This offers the bride the opportunity to really cook economically. Here was a life-time piece which could save time, trouble, and expense.

Hot Weather Tricks

In 1929, Mary Dunbar offered some "Hot Weather Tricks." On hot summer days, the heat from the oven could make the kitchen a less comfortable place to work in no time. Mary Dunbar had learned a few tricks that helped her to keep the kitchen cool while still actually accomplishing some baking. She passed these secrets on to her customers and readers.

The principal tool involved was the Mary Dunbar Waterless Cooker. Instead of using it as a waterless cooker, she used it as a miniature oven on top of the stove. The base went over the flame as usual, and for most things the rack sat directly on the base. The kettle part of the cooker was set down over the base, forming a tightly closed up 'oven.' Mary Dunbar pointed out that a very low flame was needed. This kept the heat from filling the kitchen, and still allowed you to prepare a complete meal.

The Waterless Cooker is also covered in the "Jewel Homemakers' Institute Kitchen" chapter.

Making Coffee

Most brides must learn the correct procedure in coffee making, for it was essential.

Mary Dunbar selected various coffee services. First she spoke of the Hall China teapot.

Since the new bride's family is small and because every Jewel Premium was built to be of extra service, the teapot is built so that it may carry the four-cup Dripper—making it also a small drip coffee maker. The piece is decorated in the attractive autumn colors which match the creamer, sugar, and tray of the larger coffee service.

Oven Glassware

Every new bride liked to have certain pieces in oven glassware.

Mary Dunbar selected the oblong baker for loaf cakes, puddings, or biscuits, or a jell mold. The pie plate was the large standard size and the casserole serves a double purpose since the cover is flat and makes a small pie plate.

Then you have in the saucepan set the three sizes most likely to be needed year in and year out. Furthermore, they are graduated for your convenience in measuring as well as cooking.

So there you are — a complete and permanent set of equipment and all from the Jewel Premium line — a set which can be built without additional cash outlay through the purchase of Jewel Groceries. All of the items she suggest could be earned in less than a year.

For the perfect wedding or anniversary gift, or just for setting the perfect table, the "VANITY FAIR" cake platter and 6 matching cake plates were a perfect idea. From the 1930s, the set includes a 10-1/4" cake platter, measuring 11-1/4" from tab handle to tab handle. The matching cake plates are 6-1/4" in diameter.

This set was given to the present owner's mother as a gift from another family member. The rims are done in a swirled gold trim, while the center is decorated with a circle of flowers in blue, rose, yellow, green and gold. Each piece has a backstamp that reads "VANITY FAIR Made in U. S. A. WARRANTED 22KT. GOLD Approved by MARY DUNBAR" with the notation "Q-1." The backstamp measures 1-1/2" wide and 7/8" high. *Kinder Collection.*

Clocks

Jewel often pointed out when selecting a gift for a wedding, anniversary, to remember that you are honoring both husband and wife. The most appropriate gifts were those for the home, or something both may share and enjoy.

Ansonia Alarm Clock

You can depend on an Ansonia to arouse you on time. It is 4¼ inches tall and 3½ inches wide. It is neat appearing with its case of seamless metal and brushed gold effect finish. This is easily kept bright and shiny. Will run 30 hours without winding. A most attractive clock in the bed room, kitchen or dining room. Price, $2.50. Our Item No. 762.

In 1925 Jewel advertised this Ansonia Alarm Clock.

In 1956 the Hall 9-1/2" China Autumn Pattern Electric Clock appeared. The clock could be hung on the wall, or (using the attached wire stand) rested on a shelf or flat surface. It was self-starting, with a red sweep second hand, glass crystal, and semi-porcelain body. The decoration was brown and orange floral on a cream-colored background with a gold edge line. With Master Crafters movement. "HALL" is stamped on its face. Listed as Item No. 11D831 and sold for $7.98. *Rolls Antiques.*

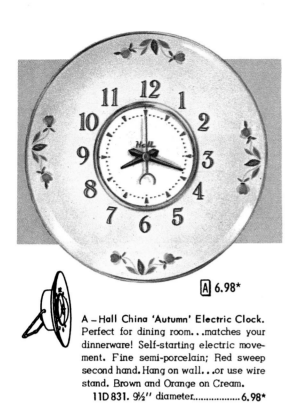

A – Hall China 'Autumn' Electric Clock. Perfect for dining room...matches your dinnerware! Self-starting electric movement. Fine semi-porcelain; Red sweep second hand. Hang on wall...or use wire stand. Brown and Orange on Cream.

11D 831. 9½'' diameter................. 6.98*

[A] 6.98*

This Autumn Leaf Clock is the work of a private individual, who has created this lovely piece from a 10" dinner plate. Numerous clocks have been created from various Autumn Leaf plates and the flat cake plate. Beware of individuals telling you these are the real thing. *Private Collection.*

An original advertisement from the Jewel Home Shopping Service's Spring and Summer 1958 Catalog.

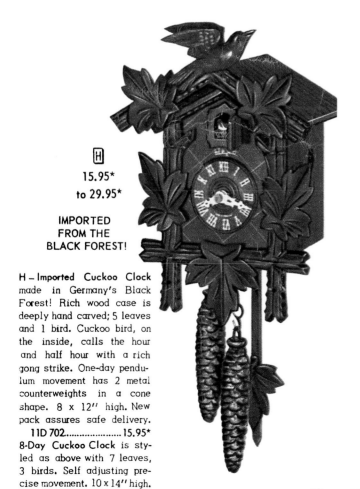

[H]
15.95*
to 29.95*

IMPORTED
FROM THE
BLACK FOREST!

H – Imported Cuckoo Clock made in Germany's Black Forest! Rich wood case is deeply hand carved; 5 leaves and 1 bird. Cuckoo bird, on the inside, calls the hour and half hour with a rich gong strike. One-day pendulum movement has 2 metal counterweights in a cone shape. 8 x 12'' high. New pack assures safe delivery.

11D 702.................... 15.95*
8-Day Cuckoo Clock is styled as above with 7 leaves, 3 birds. Self adjusting precise movement. 10 x 14'' high.
11T 864.................... 29.95*

J.T.'s General Store Clock was a sales incentive. The slogan "Serving American Families Since 1899" appeared on the face with a variety of Jewel vehicles. It is believed that no more than 200 of these clocks were awarded no earlier than May 1982 and no later than 1984. *Byerly Collection.*

Imported from the Black Forest—what a perfect wedding gift this cuckoo clock would have been. This original advertisement and caption appeared in 1958.

Even though this 9-1/2" Autumn Leaf clock was a salesman's award, it would nonetheless have made a perfect gift. The clock is more rare than the Hall Autumn Leaf clock, and is battery operated. Its backstamp is covered by the mechanism. *Byerly Collection.*

Introduced in 1975-1976, this wooden and glass tray might be hard to find, since they were made only for a short time. A wooden and glass serving tray has been located with an original paper label that reads: "Oil Paint On Glass Made in USA. " This tray is often referred to as a "reversed painted tray," as the painting is done on the reverse side of the glass. These trays are often found in poor condition; water that had seeped between the glass and the back caused the paint to shrivel up and pull away from the glass. This condition affects the price considerably. *Byerly Collection.*

Anniversaries

Anniversary parties for the first 15 years are usually informal and are given for a few close friends. Beginning with the 20th anniversary, the parties are more formal and dignified. Instead of small, intimate groups, larger gatherings are more appropriate. Large teas, receptions, and dinners with flowers and decorations are suitable to these occasions.

Occasionally Jewel provided the following list of anniversary gift reminders to customers:

> 1st — Paper
> 2nd — Cotton or Straw
> 3rd — Leather or Candy
> 4th — Books
> 5th — Wood
> 6th — Iron
> 7th — Copper, Brass or Flowers
> 8th — Bronze or Electrical Appliances
> 9th — Pottery
> 10th — Tin or Aluminum
> 11th — Steel
> 12th — Silk or Linen
> 13th — Lace
> 14th — Ivory
> 15th — Crystal
> 20th — China
> 25th — Silver
> 30th — Pearl
> 35th — Coral or Jade
> 40th — Ruby
> 45th — Sapphire
> 50th — Gold
> 55th — Emerald
> 60th — Diamond

Jewel Blankets

PART WOOL BLANKET $4.75

Cool Breezes Need Not Chill

The refreshing cool breezes of fall nights need not chill the sleeper with a fluffy, soft, part wool, Nashua blanket conveniently kept at the foot of the bed. Size 66 x 80. Choice of four pleasing color schemes: blue, rose, lavender, and tan.
Item No. 315 . . . . **$4.75**

One possible wedding gift in 1926 was Jewel's excellent medium-weight cotton blanket. They were well woven in an attractive plaid pattern, and were made in pairs of single blankets for easy laundering. The edges were stitched to prevent unraveling. They were 64" x 76" and useful on any size bed. Listed as Item No. N-5024, reasonably priced at $3.75 a pair.

Such a large selection of blankets were offered by Jewel that it would be impossible to list them all. It would not be until 1979 that Jewel offered the Autumn Leaf motif blankets. The Autumn Leaf blankets were offered in three sizes: twin, full, and king/queen size. They were offered in two different colors: earth tones (the normal Autumn Leaf colors), and more pastel tones (blue and lavender shades).

The blankets were expensive when they were first offered, and disappeared from the catalog by 1980. The twin size was 66" x 90" and sold for $22.99; full size was 80" x 90" and sold for $29.99; and king/queen was 108" x 90" and sold for $46.99. Today, these are the most sought-after blankets of the Jewel line. Those in original condition and packaging demand extravagant prices in the current market.

It is wise to carefully examine an Autumn Leaf blanket completely. Check for burn marks, moth-holes, simple repair signs, and torn sections, and check the overall appearance of the blanket for discoloration. If it is in the original packaging, remove the blanket and make a thorough examination. You may be surprised what is hidden in the folds of a blanket, or under the cover of original packaging. If the packaging is sealed and the owner prefers that you not open it, then it is your decision in the matter. Many collectors prefer original packaging. Use your better judgment in this matter.

The majority of the blankets had a gold paper label over one corner inside the plastic covering, reading:

> VELLUX BLANKET BY MARTEX. Velvety Soft, it will look fresh and new even after 50 washings. Completely machine washable and dryable. Cozy warmth without weight. Will not pill or mat, shrink or stretch out of shape. 100% nylon face on an insulting base exclusive of ornamentation.

The blankets themselves have a cloth tab which reads on one side: "Martex Vellux Blanket." On the other side it has the washing instructions, the patent numbers, and the address "West Point Pepperell, West Point, Georgia 31833."

Fine, True-Tone Radios and Record Players

1 – Arvin Transistor Radio fits in hand, pocket or purse...clips on belt or it'll stand alone! 5 transistors have high output; thumb-knob tuning; automatic volume control. AM and Civil Defense frequencies. Operates on 9-volt battery (not included). Turquoise unbreakable plastic. Wt: 1 lb.
11D 822. 6½ x 3 x 2" deep.............44.95

2 – Trav-ler Table Radio. 5 tubes including rectifier. Alnico PM dynamic speaker; built-in antenna; full vision tuning dial. Complete AM coverage. Plastic case; color as shown. 110-120 volts, AC or DC.
11D 730. 9½ x 6 x 6¼" deep...........23.95

3 – Trav-ler 3-Way Portable. Plenty of power for out-of-the-way areas! 5-tubes including rectifier...super-sensitive antenna plus 4" dynamic speaker. Thumb wheel tuning. Automatic volume control, no blasting or fading. Green plastic case. 105-125 volts. AC, DC or battery (not included).
11D 806. 9½ x 7¼ x 3¼" deep........29.95

4 – Arvin Clock Radio wakes you gently... lulls you to sleep! 5-tubes including rectifier; automatic on-off switch and alarm set, plus 1100 watt appliance outlet and clock timer! Loop antenna; Alnico 'V' PM speaker; and Civil Defense frequency too! Charcoal plastic case. AC, 105-120 v.
11D 823. 5½ x 12 x 5½"deep..........36.95

5 – G.E. Clock-Radio lulls you to sleep... wakes you to music! 60-minute automatic slumber switch; appliance outlet; phono-jack; Snooz-Alarm gives you an extra '40 winks'. 5-tubes including rectifier; powerful speaker. Dial beam spotlights each number selected. Luminous clock dial; sweep second hand. Pink plastic case. 105-120 v.
11D 783. AC-DC. 13 x 6¾ x 6½"deep..39.95

6 – Manual 4-Speed Phonola plays all size records. Duo-fi model, 2-tube amplifier including rectifier; 2 balanced tone 4" speakers. Volume and tone control; crystal cartridge; turnover Sapphire needles. Built-in adapter for 45 RPM's. Color as shown. Simulated leatherette case. 110-120 v., AC.
11D 726. 11 x 12 x 7½" deep.......... 29.95

7 – Phonola 4-Speed Automatic. Crystal cartridge has turnover Sapphire needles. Plays 16, 33, 45 and 78 RPM's, all sizes. Automatic shut-off; 2-tube amplifier including rectifier; two 4" speakers. Automatic 45 spindle adapter. Color as shown. Leatherette case. 110-120 volts, AC only.
11D 728. 14 x 16 x 8½" deep..........59.95

8 – Phonola Hi-Fi Two-Speaker Automatic. 4-speed changer has 45 spindle adapter... plays all sizes! Automatic shut-off; long life ceramic cartridge; turnover Sapphire needles. Hi-Fi amplifier has 3-tubes including rectifier. 6" woofer speaker for bass, 5¼" tweeter for best highs. Color as shown. Leatherette case. 110-120 v., AC.
11D 729. 18½ x 15 x 8½" deep........79.95

1 44.95
2 23.95
3 29.95
All radios and record players are U.L. approved
4 36.95
5 39.95
6 29.95
7 59.95
8 HIGH FIDELITY 79.95
59

A Versatile New Decorator Look in Home Fashion

The Rich "Petit Point" Print

• Multicolor Print with choice of Harmonizing solid colors...all in Everglaze Polished Cotton!

1 – Petit Point Quilted Coverlet...quilted with plump dacron for washability! Sturdy cotton backing. Tailored with scalloped edges on 3 sides, double side welts. Everglaze polished cotton in "petit point" multicolor print as shown.
6D 699. Twin: 63 x 103"............................ 12.98
6D 700. Full: 76 x 103"............................ 12.98
Petit Point Quilted Pillow Sham...quilted with plump dacron! Corded and ruffled...Everglaze polished cotton. Each: 20 x 26" plus 3" ruffle.
6D 705. Multicolor print shown.........Each 3.98

2 – Solid Color Dust Ruffle is made with a muslin top that fits between spring and mattress. Deep ruffle has a 17-inch drop. Colors: Pink, Blue, or Yellow to harmonize with Multicolor.
6D 701. Twin size. State color....................5.98
6D 702. Full size. State color....................5.98

3 – Petit Point Boudoir Lamp. An enchanting miniature reproduction of the china pitcher and bowl Grandma used to treasure! Ceramic base; on-off switch. 12" diameter Lumarith shade is edged with a froth of White nylon ruffles...matching petit point polished cotton overskirt removes for washing! Color: Multicolor as shown.
6F 870. 17" high, U.L. appr.......................9.98

4 – Petit Point Draperies are styled with full triple pinch pleats, buckram lined headings to retain shape and symmetrical pleating. Washable polished cotton boasts an Everglaze finish. Four pinch pleats on each side; 1½-inch side hems; 3-inch bottom hems. Hang them with solid color cafe curtains (item 5) for privacy and bedroom beauty. *Width listed below is per pair*, after pleating. See How to Measure for Draperies, page 71. Color: Multicolor on White ground as shown.
6D 703. Size: 40 x 84 inches...............Pair 6.98

5 – Solid Color Cafes have smartly scalloped tops; bright brass rings are spaced for even draping. 2-inch bottom hems. In polished cotton with the famous Everglaze finish. Fully washable. Colors: Blue, Pink or Yellow. State color.
6D 704. Size per pair: 64 x 36"...........Pr. 3.98

6 – Petit Point Percale Sheets. Pacific's 180 percale sheets have a screen printed border across top in print matching ensemble! 4-inch top hems, 1-inch bottom hems. Multicolor on White.
6D 870. Twin: 72 x 108".......................Each 4.49
6D 871. Full: 81 x 108".......................Each 4.98
Matching Pillow Cases. All-over Multicolor print.
6D 872. Size: 42 x 38½.......................Pair 2.59

Jewel Tea Co., Inc.

Matching garment bag described on page 84
Harmonizing blanket described on page 91

These original advertisements and captions appeared in a Jewel Home Shopping Service Spring and Summer 1958 Catalog. Jewel could decorate the home *and* bring music to the ears.

The Autumn Leaf design was scattered all over the Autumn Leaf blanket. Sprays of nine buds, two buds, and one bud seem to go in all directions. The binding was not satin but a plain version of the same vellux material used for the rest of the blanket. *Byerly Collection.*

To commemorate the 60th anniversary of the Autumn Leaf Pattern in 1993, J.T.'s General Store produced a 100% cotton, limited edition Autumn Leaf Afghan, made in the U.S.A. Approximately 50" wide x 70" long, this commemorative afghan could be purchased through a J.T. Merchandise Service (J.T.'s General Store) representative. The afghan displays a variety of Autumn Leaf that represents good old-fashioned service. *Byerly Collection.*

In the center of this unusual metal hot water bottle it says "Jewel Hot Water Bottle - Guaranteed 5 Years." It has been brought to my attention that this bottle was not used to relieve pain in aching muscles; it was used to warm beds and feet on cold nights. A metal clasp-like clip located at the side can be pulled out away from the container. It was never a good idea to put hot or warm metal directly onto your body. If someone was suffering from aching joints, usually a bottle of this type would be wrapped with a piece of flannel. I am told that this bottle could be also used as a Thermos bottle, for keeping liquids at almost their original temperature. *Scott Collection.*

The hot water bottle shows the metal clasp pulled out in order to raise the container. The metal stopper says "A. Schaders & Son, Inc. N. Y. Pat. Mar. 27. 06 & Oct. 27. 08," and also "Australia - Austria - France - Germany - GT Britain - Japan - Also Pat. in Russia." The hot water bottle had a cloth covering. Its association with Jewel Tea is uncertain. *Scott Collection.*

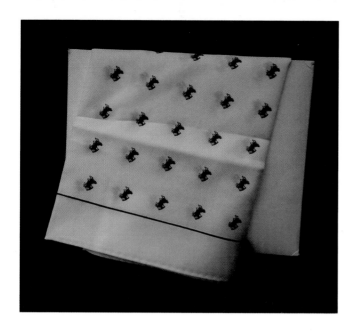

A lovely ladies' scarf, a prefect gift for any sweetheart. A small Jewel horse and wagon motif appears on the scarf. *Schwartz Collection.*

Eastman Hawkeye Camera

It's an Eastman! A handy sized camera—the picture is actual size and measures $2\frac{1}{4}$x$3\frac{1}{4}$". The camera measures $5\frac{1}{2}$x$4\frac{1}{4}$x3". Price $2.50. Our Item No. N-5023.

During the late 1920s, Jewel offered this Eastman™ Hawkeye Camera. This is an original advertisement and captions. The perfect camera for wedding photographs.

A popular ladies head scarf, displaying a rendition of a popular historical photograph that also appears on a parson table. *Randall Collection.*

Jewel promoted this "Blue Enamel Oval Roaster" for large family gatherings, or for the church social supper. The original advertisement and captions are from the late 1920s.

Blue Enamel Oval Roaster

Save the delicious flavor of your meat by cooking it in a dependable enamel roaster. This one is well-constructed, oval shape, handle at both ends, on top and lower sections. Will serve the large family for preparing meat, fowl or game; or will bake the beans for the church supper. Price $2.15. Our Item No. 386.

97

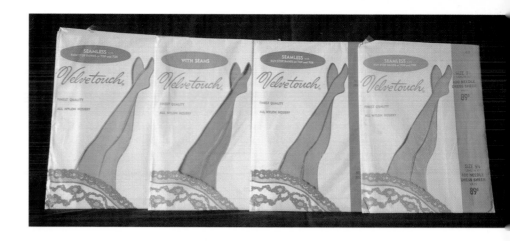

Four packages of Velvetouch all-nylon hosiery (three seamless, one with seams). A Jewel guarantee accompanied each package and each is marked "JEWEL TEA CO., INC . MELROSE PARK, ILL." *Hamilton Collection.*

During Christmas 1951, Jewel offered the above Sessions Electric Clock, beautifully hand-decorated china, trimmed in 24-karat gold with a gold-color bezel. It measures approximately 7-1/2" wide and stands 11" high. Jewel listed it as Item No. 6G445-c and sold it for $13.92. *Hamilton Collection.*

The Sessions Planter Clock was offered during Christmas 1951. It featured 24-karat gold trim, easy-to-read roman numerals, and a self-starting electric movement. It had ample room on either side of the clock face for potted plants. The clock measures approximately 11-3/4" wide and stands 6-1/2" high. Jewel listed it as Item No. 6G44-c and sold it for $16.38. *Hamilton Collection.*

The reverse side of a covered container of "Sara Carnation Dusting Powder." The opalescent "Moonstone" container held eight ounces of powder. The paper label reads "Distributed by Jewel Tea Co., Jewel Park Barrington, Ill." This is from Jewel's cosmetic line of the 1930s. *Hamilton Collection.*

CHAPTER 9
UNUSUAL ITEMS

Many collectors of the famous Autumn Leaf pattern search for *any* item related to the famous Jewel Tea Company, with either the name Jewel or the famous Mary Dunbar name. This is often referred to as 'cross-over' collecting. A number of collectors with whom I have spoken offered photographs from their private collections of these unusual pieces.

Many of these pieces ended up in the Jewel employee's store in Barrington, Illinois. It has often been said that every once in a while the buyer would clear out the sample room and dispose of the sample items. I have included any available dates for these items, but those whose dates are impossible to ascertain at this time are shown for your enjoyment in random order. Most of these exceptional pieces never appeared in promotional advertisements and records cannot be located.

In other chapters of this book you will come across other unusual items. It is best to read each chapter carefully for the expectional items.

I was unable to locate photographs or owners of many of the pieces shown in this chapter. I would appreciate hearing from anyone that might have any of the following pieces in their private collection.

The rhythmic line of the batter bowl handle is shown above. *Hamilton Collection.*

The flare of the batter bowl spout; note the beautifully applied gold detail. *Hamilton Collection.*

Believed to have been a promotional piece at one time, this batter bowl is one of the most sought-after Hall Autumn Leaf pieces, the hardest to find, and extremely expensive. The bowl is 5-1/2" high, diameter is 7-1/4", measuring 10-1/4" from spout to handle. *Hamilton Collection.*

Looking into the batter bowl, we notice that it is not perfectly circular. *Hamilton Collection.*

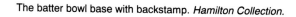

The batter bowl base with backstamp. *Hamilton Collection.*

One item which is most unusual and extremely hard to find is a "Shirred Egg Dish". The egg dish was used to bake eggs with crumbs. This exceptionally unusual dish is 8-3/4" in diameter and 10-1/2" across with tab handles. It is unknown where this exceptional piece is today.

This Autumn Leaf condiment set is believed to be circa 1940 and was a design submitted to Hall only to be rejected. *Hamilton Collection.*

At one time in a lady's pantry there sat a beautiful Hall Autumn Leaf fluted vase, shown here. It is said that the fluted vase held the owner's cleaning pads! Next to the fluted vase is a two-cup size individual Boston teapot. Very few of these teapots are in circulation. During the 1950s they were made for executive management in the Barrington office. Very little is known about these exceptional pieces. *Private Collection.*

This condiment dish, showing lid, bowl, and underplate, is the only one of its kind known to exist today. *Hamilton Collection.*

The only known frosted water bottle/jug, approximately 7" tall and 5" wide at the base. No other information is known at the present time concerning this exceptional piece. It is shown with the 5-1/2" frosted tumbler. *Private Collection.*

These beautiful custard pieces are an exceptional find. Note the variation of sizes and decals; the container on the left is larger than the custard piece on the right. Measurements are 2-1/4" high and 4-1/4" in diameter. The only marking appearing on the bottom is "274/751"; this number is in gold. *Private Collection.*

Shown above is a set of four beautifully frosted sherbet glasses that are believed to have been made by Libbey. They are approximately 5-1/4" tall. These sherbets have a twisted stem and the Autumn Leaf pattern around each top section; they measure 3-1/2" in diameter. The set was purchased through an antique dealer whose aunt was employed with Libbey and retired in 1974. *Casey Collection.*

The above mustard canister measures 2-3/4" high x 2-1/2" in diameter, and has the Mary Dunbar back-stamp. This is a one-of-a-kind piece. *Private Collection.*

Offered in 1939, these 2" miniature ruffled shakers were too small to be practical, and were soon replaced with the regular ruffled shakers shown in the center. Note the difference between the decal on the miniature shaker and that on the larger (2-3/8") shaker. *Fausset Collection.*

This lampshade is machine-sewn, including the side seams and bottom ruffle. The top and bottom are hand-sewn into a cardboard material. The shade clips onto the lightbulb. The Autumn Leaf pattern lamp shade is 6-1/2" high x 4-7/8" wide at the top, and 8" wide at the bottom. *Long Collection.*

The 2-1/2" tall candleholders are believed to have been purchased in the Jewel employee's store by a former cafeteria worker. *Easley Collection.*

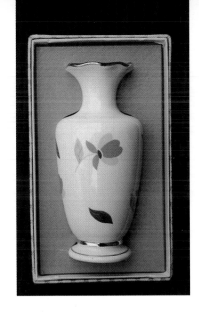

Little information is available about this bud vase. Note that the decal on the unboxed example is smaller than that on the vase originally offered, shown here in its original box. Variation in size is also a factor: the unboxed vase is 6" high, while the boxed vase is 5-3/4" high. Both were offered in 1940. *Easley Collection.*

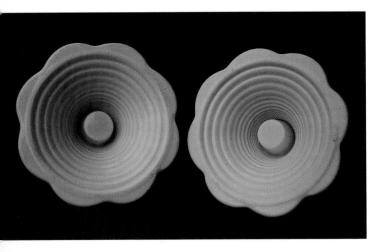

The bottom of the candleholders. Everson Hall from the Hall China Company believes these were made by Hall China. *Easley Collection.*

Only one known pair of "Medallion" shakers is in existence, but the whereabouts of the shakers is unknown at this time. If you should happen to have this set, please contact me.

This exceptionally beautiful Autumn Leaf canister set includes containers for tea, coffee, and sugar. Note the variation in the decals. The coffee canister at the far left has gold trim around the neck, and the lid is taller. The other canisters do not have the trim. All three have the Gold Hall backstamp. An additional Black Hall stamp appears on the sugar and tea canisters. It is believed there may be a flour canister also; possibly two different sets were made. *Private Collection.*

This is the only known candleholder with this shape; 4" tall. *Hamilton Collection.*

The bottom of the candleholder; the base is 3-5/16" in diameter. Note this is not marked. *Hamilton Collection.*

Nothing is known about this 11-1/4" tall, unmarked Autumn Leaf vase, an exceptional one-of-a-kind piece. Some collectors believe this may have been a lamp base, but it is only hearsay! Note single leaf near the top, also shown in detail. *Hamilton Collection.*

These beautiful Autumn Leaf pieces shown include a sample cup, a saucer, and a large plate. They were submitted to Jewel by the Mikasa China Co., only to be rejected. There was also a Mikasa Autumn Leaf teapot submitted and rejected. The whereabouts of this teapot is unknown. *Easley Collection.*

This St. Denis cup and saucer set, which displays a Jewel logo, is believed to be a one-of-a-kind item. This is one of my favorite pieces. *Easley Collection.*

103

The "Jewel Coffee Champ" cup and saucer. *Easley Collection.*

This St. Denis coffee cup and saucer set is marked "Group Coffee Champ January 1956." *Easley Collection.*

(Left to right) An Autumn Leaf demitasse cup and saucer. Note how small the saucer is; this set is marked "Mary Dunbar." Note the exceptional Autumn Leaf coaster next to the regular breakfast cup and saucer. The demitasse cup, saucer, and coaster are believed to be one-of-a-kind. *Easley Collection.*

(Left to right) An Autumn Leaf Thermo Mug, a Thermo Tumbler, and a 1981 Father's Day mug (see the "For Men Only" chapter). *Easley Collection.*

The Zephyr is one of the most exceptional butter dishes ever discovered. Presently only three are known to exist. The butter dish measures 4" high x 7-1/8" long x approximately 4-3/8" wide. *Poppemiller Collection.*

This butter dish does have the proper backstamp. *Hamilton Collection.*

The second of three known Zephyr butter dishes. Note the slight rise to the finial. *Hamilton Collection.*

This style of butter dish is from a Hall line of refrigeratorware produced in the late 1930s. This line included two sizes of water bottles with china stoppers, the butter dish, and a rectangular leftover, primarily in Chinese Red. Could there possibly be another Autumn Leaf Motif piece somewhere?

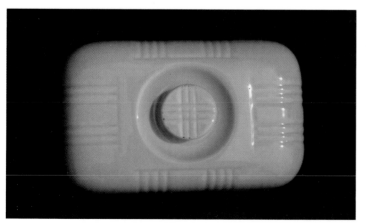

The top of the Zephyr butter dish cover. This butter dish is also referred to as "Bingo" style. *Hamilton Collection.*

This tray has the Mary Dunbar gold backstamp. This unusual tray measures 5-3/8" in diameter and 7-3/8" across at the handles. Private Collection.

This exceptional one-of-a-kind vase measures 8" high; unmarked. While many collectors believe this was not manufactured by Hall China, I have recently been told that it is *definitely* a Hall piece. You be the judge! *Hamilton Collection.*

A view down into vase. *Hamilton Collection.*

A rare 10" Autumn Leaf oval "Fort Pitt" baker, one of only three known to exist. This baker holds 2 pints; the gold is worn but the decals are bright and vivid. Notice the backstamp of this exceptional piece. Even though this piece shows gold wear, it is otherwise in exceptional condition, and will still demand an extraordinary price. *Gibson Collection.*

This unusual 14" platter has two backstamps. The first is a double circle with the word "JEWEL" inside, with an unusual pattern of lines below the wording. This backstamp is pink. Above the double circle appears "THE DUCHESS" with the word "ENGLAND" and the company name enclosed in a laurel wreath. The company name cannot be made out. "THE DUCH-ESS" may be the name of the pattern of china. The platter is trimmed in gold with tiny pink and blue flowers and green leaves. In the center the flowers are repeated. At present it is uncertain if this platter has any connection to the historical Jewel Tea Co. *Author's Collection.*

A covered candy jar believed to be an one-of-a-kind experimental piece was submitted to Jewel and later rejected. I was not able to located this candy jar.

It is believed the Autumn Leaf "Morning Set" was never put into production. This set includes a sugar with lid, creamer and teapot. Few of these sets have been found.

Recently I was informed of the discovery of a covered, rectangular center section to a three piece "Sears Leftover" set with the Autumn Leaf motif. I understand this piece has the Hall "Mary Dunbar Approved" backstamp.

It is wise to consult *The Autumn Leaf Story* by Jo Cunningham to see a color photograph of three Autumn Leaf sample items that were never sold. The pieces include a bud vase, a small footed bowl with tab handles, and a small round tray. Their present whereabouts are unknown.

A one-of-a-kind 3-5/8" Libbey frosted glass. The outside top diameter measures 3-1/8" and the base diameter measures 2-3/4". This glass is marked on the bottom with the Libbey "L" mark. *Hamilton Collection.*

Beautiful 6" bread and butter plates, backstamped "Sovereign Potters, Canada" under the illustration of a maple leaf. These plates have no connection with the historical Jewel Tea Co., and are the product of another company that produced the famous decal/motif. Note the bold and vivid coloring of the motif. If you should have further information on this company I would appreciate hearing from you. *Bredengerd Collection.*

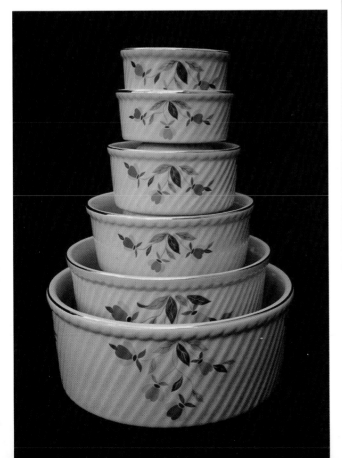

These six Autumn Leaf French Bakers include a rare 1-pint. From top to bottom, they are as follows: the top baker is the commonly found 10-ounce; next is No. 499, also a l0-ounce. The rare 1-pint, No. 501, is third; the 2-pint baker is fourth; the common 3-pint baker is fifth. On the bottom is a club (N.A.L.C.C.) 3-quart sample baker not produced. Also shown is the backstamp for the rare 1-pint No. 501 baker. At present this is the only baker of this size ever located, date uncertain. The 2-pint and the l0-ounce No. 499 can be somewhat hard to find. *Hamilton Collection.*

A "Wildfire" jug. This pattern was made by Hall exclusively for The Great American Tea Company and dates from the 1950s as a premium. On close examination of the backstamp, one would be surprised to discover the famous "TESTED AND APPROVED BY Mary Dunbar HOMEMAK-ERS INSTITUTE SUPERIOR QUALITY KITCHENWARE". The motif consists of tiny pink roses and a garland of green leaves intertwined with a pale blue ribbon, on a high-white glazed body with a 22K gold trim. This is the first piece of this pattern with the famous Jewel backstamp. *Author's Collection.*

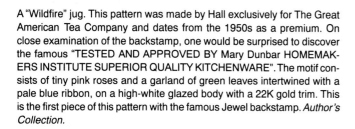

Two versions of the "JEWEL - BEATER - MIXER WHIPPER & FREEZER." These unusual items date to the early Jewel years and never appeared in an issue of The Jewel News. The one without the metal handle is believed to be the earlier version, marked "MANF BY JUERGENS - BROS. MINNEAPOLIS, MINN." The mixer with the metal handle is believed to be a later version and is marked "MANF BY CRAVITY TWINE BOX CO. CLEVELAND, OHIO." On the back of each mixer are measurements for "FLOUR in lbs., SUGAR in lbs., and LIQUID in qt. to pint." Presently four of these "JEWEL - BEATER - MIXER - WHIPPER & FREEZER" pieces are known to be in private collections. Be prepared; they can be extremely expensive. *Hamilton Collection.*

CHAPTER 10

SALEM CHINA

Many collectors of the Hall Autumn Leaf pattern also search for a pattern made by the Salem China Company of Salem, Ohio. Collectors often refer to this pattern as a 'Go-Along' (the term was coined by collectors to refer to a variety of products whose styles and colors were obviously made to accessories dinnerware). This aspect of collecting is very popular with many. Don't be fooled—it isn't Jewel Tea. Still, it looks great with Jewel Tea China.

The Salem China Company

In 1898, the Salem China Company was founded in Salem, Ohio by Dan Cronin, John McNichol, and Biddam Smith (who has been associated with the Standard Pottery Company in East Liverpool, Ohio). By 1918 the Salem China Company was in need of considerable capital to continue operations.

At the same time, F.A. Sebring was searching for a location for his son, Frank Jr., who was returning from the war. In 1918 F.A. Sebring was given an option on the Salem plant, and in August the company was taken over. Floyd McKee was asked to join the operation until Sebring's son was home. Mr. McKee retired in 1950 and became Chairman of the Board. In 1950, J. Harrison Keller was appointed President and General Manager.

Salem China Company is no longer in operation.

The Mandarin 10" china dinner plate by Salem, with no backstamp. *Author's Collection.*

Not all pieces of the Salem China line have a backstamp, and the small gold numbers vary. "Mandarin" appears only on the china line. Little information is known about the introduction and discontinuation dates of these pieces. Speculation is mid-1960s.

The 7" Mandarin luncheon or dessert plate by Salem is marked "MANDARIN©/ Salem® / OVENPROOF" with the number 66, possibly indicating the year 1966 (though this is only speculation). *Author's Collection.*

Salem's Mandarin 6" china bread and butter plate has no backstamp. *Author's Collection.*

Salem's Mandarin 9" round vegetable bowl. It is backstamped like the other pieces, but had two stars next to the number 67. *Author's Collection.*

Salem's Mandarin China 6" saucer has no backstamp. It is unknown if the coffee cup has the decal or is solid white. If anyone should have a coffee cup in this pattern, I would appreciate hearing from you. *Author's Collection.*

Salem's tab-handled Mandarin vegetable bowl. Marked as usual, but with a star before the number 66. The bowl measures 9" from tab handle to tab handle. *Author's Collection.*

Salem's Mandarin China 5-1/4" fruit bowl. There is no backstamp on these fruit bowls. *Author's Collection.*

Salem's 13" tab-handled Mandarin chop plate, backstamped, with the number 65. *Author's Collection.*

A Salem mug measuring 5-1/2" tall. *Author's Collection.*

A large Salem tumbler, 5-1/2" tall. *Author's Collection.*

Salem's 9-1/2" tall glass beverage pitcher displays the fall coloring of autumn leaves. Salem glassware is well marked. Look closely for "© Salem" marked near the base of the motif. *Author's Collection.*

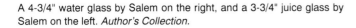

A 4-3/4" water glass by Salem on the right, and a 3-3/4" juice glass by Salem on the left. *Author's Collection.*

Recently I saw a beautiful "Mandarin" Salem China open-handled pitcher. It stood approximately 10" tall, and had a brown interior and white surface with the same motif that appears on the Salem glassware and china. Because it is so expensive, I did not examine it for a stamp, but I have been told that it *is* marked on the bottom. No photograph is available of this piece.

Salem's 7" covered candy dish has the pattern only on its base; the lid is clear. *Author's Collection.*

This piece by Salem, 5" high with a 6" diameter, is referred to as an open ice bucket. *Author's Collection.*

An 8" juice container with a yellow plastic cap lid. The numbers 6 and 12 appear on the bottom. The plastic lid has been seen in various colors. *Author's Collection.*

112

CHAPTER 11

MELMAC PLASTIC DINNERWARE

Jewel introduced their Melmac plastic dinnerware in 1959 and discontinued it by 1962. The Jewel catalog described this line as a new, exclusive "Autumn" pattern in Melmac plastic that stacks and handles easily; "It resists chipping, cracking and fading. It is unharmed by boiling water or fruit acids. A spray of Autumn Leaf decorates the flatware." It was dishwasher safe and the color was unharmed by the use of strong detergents.

Autumn Leaf Melmac is highly collectible and seems to be steadily climbing in popularity and in price. As it was available for such a short period, Melmac is not easily acquired, and may take sometime to find.

Offered as a 16-piece starter set (four cups, four decorated saucers, four fruit dishes, and four 10" decorated dinner plates), the set was listed as Item No. B-5C 1A. In 1960 the regular value price of $21.04 was offered, an increase from the original $15.95. A 45-piece service for eight, Item No. B-5C 45A, was regularly priced at $68.78, an increase from its original $49.95.

Open stock offered a 6" saucer at $1.19, a 7" salad plate at $1.49;, a 10" dinner plate for $2.59, and a 14" platter for $4.69.

Lifetime Melmac plastic dinnerware was offered in the New Autumn Pattern, or in a choice of rainbow, white or three solid colors.

In 1961 the "Autumn" pattern Melmac was shown in the catalog with stainless steel tableware by International Silver Co., along with the 22K gold Autumn pattern glassware.

A Melmac coffee cup saucer. The matching cup is solid white with no pattern. *Byerly Collection.*

The Melmac 10" dinner plate. *Byerly Collection.*

The 7" Melmac salad (or bread and butter) plate. *Byerly Collection.*

A 14" Melmac platter. *Byerly Collection.*

A Melmac 14" platter, a 10" dinner plate, a cup (solid white) and saucer, a covered sugar (solid white), a 7" salad plate, and a fruit bowl (solid white). In Jewel's Fall/Winter 1963 catalog list of discontinued stock, only the 10" Melmac dinner plates were available, for $1.99 each. *Byerly Collection.*

Shown for variation of decal on saucer. *Byerly Collection.*

If anyone owns pieces or has a complete set of the Autumn Leaf Melmac in their collection, I would appreciate hearing from you.

CHAPTER 12

PAPER & PLASTIC

Do you classify yourself as a paper collector? Do you find yourself at a booth in a local antique show or flea market patiently searching through cartons of paper items? If so, you know that this is one of the most time-consuming aspects of Jewel collecting; it can be nerve-wracking, and sometimes costly. The collection of Jewel booklets, pamphlets and brochures shown here took time to assemble; this applies to other paper memorabilia shown elsewhere in this publication. I suggest you check out local paper shows in your area. Most of those dealers are knowledgable with their merchandise. Recently the desire to have a collection of Jewel paper memorabilia has escalated.

It may be wise to add copies of The Jewel News Premium catalog, The Jewel News, or a Jewel Home Shopping Service catalog to your Jewel collection. They offer a wealth of information.

Are Your Paper Products In Danger?

Many collectors of paper products—issues of the Jewel News, calendars, catalogues, cookbooks, pamphlets, and brochures—do not realize that their paper collectibles could be in danger. Collectors of such items should become aware of the enemies of paper. Seek professional advice in preserving your Jewel paper memorabilia.

It is not wise to place your valuable paper items in plastic storage bags. If moisture develops inside the bag, your valuable paper may become worthless.

Acid burn can occur from wood, wood pulp mats, backings, and cardboard. Ultraviolet light causes colors and inks to fade. Infrared light accelerates aging, causing brittleness and discoloration. Permanent mounts (including drymounting, wetmounting, and most glues and tapes) cause permanent and irreversible damage. Improper framing causes and encourages all of the above. No matter how good your framed piece looks, what matters most is out of sight, inside the frame.

The greatest danger to your paper items are the insects that feed on them. The older the paper, the greater the risk.

It is wise to consult a professional in paper to retain the value of such items. Paper collectibles retain their greatest value in pristine condition. Anything that happens to change the condition of the item reduces its value.

Protect your investment, and avoid the enemies of paper. Consult only those who use only the finest materials and methods, which are used or endorsed by all conservation authorities such as the Library of Congress, the National Archives, the American Institute of Conservation, and the Professional Picture Framers' Association.

Be prepared: this can be quite costly.

Shelf Paper and Placemats

Autumn Leaf shelf paper is a popular paper item among collectors. Introduced in 1945, Jewel's shelf paper was offered in 9-foot long strips, measuring 9-1/4" wide. The Autumn Leaf motif was applied only on the edges.

By 1956 a plastic shelf paper 13" wide with a motif all over the paper was offered. This was sold for only one year. If you should have this 1956 shelf paper in your collection I would appreciate hearing from you.

Jewel shelf paper c. 1945, with the Autumn Leaf motif along the edges. 9 feet long, 9-1/4" wide. *Author's Collection.*

Little is known about the Autumn Leaf placemats that appeared in a 1940s premium catalog. The placemats measure 11" x 16-1/4". *Cross Collection.*

Premium Catalogs

Jewel Premium Catalogs are favorite paper items among collectors in today's market. They are available, but may take some searching for.

Note the scallop forming the ornamental edge on the above "Autumn Leaf Placemat" and the bold coloring of the motif. *Hedges Collection.*

The 1941 catalog offered the housewife 31 pages of various Hall China Autumn Leaf pieces, Jewel products, linens, crystal, and silverware. Jewel premiums were so economical! *Fausset Collection.*

Jewel Tea Calendars

The Jewel Tea Company gave their yearly calendars to established customers. On the reverse side of various calendars was the customer's record and receipts for cash paid. Customers were instructed to keep this card, for it protected them against misunderstanding.

The reverse side of the calendar provided spaces for the customer's name, street and number, route number, town, and state. The route man initialed the card, dated it, indicated the balance of groceries and premiums, groceries delivered, Profit Sharing Credits (P.S.C.), and cash paid. Below the record appeared a list of Jewel products and usually a Jewel advertisement.

Most Jewel calendars were done by an artist by the name of Dillon. The original paintings were kept by Jewel and hung in various rooms of the Barrington, Illinois office. The whereabouts of the original paintings are unknown at present. There were also other artists who did Jewel's calendar paintings.

This Jewel calendar is dated 1928 on the back. *Hamilton Collection.*

This 1926-1927 calendar housecard provided a 12-month calendar (from July 1926 through June 1927) on the front, along with the slogan "The Way to Successful Housekeeping." The housecard provided space at the back for the salesman to post a record of purchases, credits, and dues for his customers. The inside contained various pages of cooking hints, recipes, directions for how to make coffee, premiums, and general information. This style of calendar housecard is believed to have been provided to customers for a couple of years. *Preo Collection.*

The signature of Jewel's president Maurice Karker appeared on this 1929 Jewel calendar. *Hamilton Collection.*

117

An angelic child graces the cover of Jewel's 1930 calendar. *Hedges Collection.*

In 1931 this lovely lady appeared on the cover of Jewel calendar. *Hedges Collection.*

"I Got You Grandpa" is the title of this 1933 calendar. *Easley Collection.*

A mother and her beautiful child appear together on the cover of Jewel's 1932 calendar. *Hamilton Collection.*

This 1934 Jewel calendar is titled "Happy Days." *Hedges Collection.*

This 1935 Jewel calendar is titled "Playmates." *Hedges Collection.*

This complete 1936 Jewel calendar is titled "Flying High." *Hedges Collection.*

Dillon's 1937 rendition of "Going To Town" is missing the first three months. The calendar is approximately 7-3/4" wide by 12-3/4" high. Calendars with missing months bring a fraction of the price of those in mint condition. *Author's Collection.*

This 1938 Jewel calendar is titled "The Flying Cloud." *Weales Collection.*

The Country Cousin

"The Country Cousin" was selected for the title of this 1939 Jewel Tea Co., Inc. calendar. *Easley Collection.*

M.D. Penney, a national authority on calendars and lithographic advertising, stated that "if ever there was a medium of advertising or merchandising that fulfills all the requirements, it's the calendar."

Since the new, revised, and beautiful 1939 calendar housecard was distributed to Jewel customers, every route salesman should review Mr. Penney's five positive elements of advertising:

1) There was a real customer demand for calendars, both because of their utility value and because their artistic quality made them fine decorations each year.

2) Calendars were perfect for advertising at the 'point of use'. The calendar registers the Jewel name constantly in the customers' homes, where they made their purchases.

3) No competitive advertising reached the customers on Jewel's calendars.

4) No single magazine, newspaper, or radio ad presented itself to the customers day after day for one full year like calendars did.

5) The Jewel calendar was a valuable goodwill builder because customers appreciated the usefulness of Jewel calendars, their attractiveness as decorations, and their value as account records.

The 1939 calendar was delivered to all branches for distribution to customers during the last two weeks of the year's thirteenth sales period. Route salesmen was glad to know that 38% more space had been provided for their customers' records on this new house card. Posting was made easier and more accurate.

Another feature was the space for a record of premiums delivered. This enabled the salesman to show the name or number of a premium as a regular part of the posting, so that he would know at a glance all the premiums delivered during the current year. With this information, practical and helpful suggestions could be made to customers.

Jewel customers liked the appealing, colorful illustrations of the 1939 calendar. The calendar was hung advantageously in homes, where the beauty and the Jewel name was seen throughout the year.

This 1941 Jewel Calendar is titled "Little Scamps." *Easley Collection.*

Dillon selected the title "Buddies" for his 1940 calendar painting. *Easley Collection.*

Dillon titled his 1943 Jewel calendar "First Day At School." *Easley Collection.*

Dillon titled his 1942 Jewel calendar "Time To Play." *Hedges Collection.*

An arrangement of gladiolas and a baby picture was used for the cover of this 1944 calendar. *Easley Collection.*

This 1947 calendar cover, showing a winter scene, is signed "Olsen '44" and is untitled. One side lists the first six months and the reverse side lists the last six months. The July-December side pictures a housewife among her flowers as a Jewel Tea truck appears in the background. Between the two cardboard pages, on their reverse sides, were the customer's records and receipts for cash paid. The calendar measures 6" x 8". *Author's Collection.*

The inside section of a 1946 Jewel calendar. This actual photograph appears on the back side of the last page of this calendar, along with a general letter to Jewel customers from President Lunding. This calendar was accidentally torn while being photographed. *Hamilton Collection.*

Not available is a 1948 Jewel calendar. I understand that it is a two-page cardboard item with six months on the front and six months on the back. The picture on the front section is from the original 1933 calendar "I Got You Grandpa." On the back, Jewel's printed statement is wrong. Jewel stated the picture titled "Happy Days" that appeared was from the original 1944 Jewel calendar. It should have read from their *1934* calendar.

This Jewel Home Service 1950 calendar booklet measures 6" x 8" and displays numerous Jewel Tea products and tins. The reverse side shows laundry and cleaning products. Inside was located the customer's record and receipt for cash. *Author's Collection.*

This 1976 Jewel In Home Shopping Service calendar paid tribute to the United States of America. Historical information could be found behind the cover. On the reverse side of each month a recipe and helpful hints for the household were printed. The calendar measures 8-1/4" x 15". *Author's Collection.*

This Jewel In Home Shopping Service calendar for 1977 displays a colorful period-dressed housewife preparing her favorite Jewel dish. A Jewel product can be seen surrounded by various baking items. Across the back appears the word "JEWEL." The calendar measures 8-1/4" x 15", the inside cover describes "Dairy Foods: Natural and Instant." There are instructions for "Making More Room" and how to use the calendar page, along with other useful information, on the pad back. A selection of recipes is also offered. This same colorful calendar picture can be found on recipe cards from the same period. *Author's Collection.*

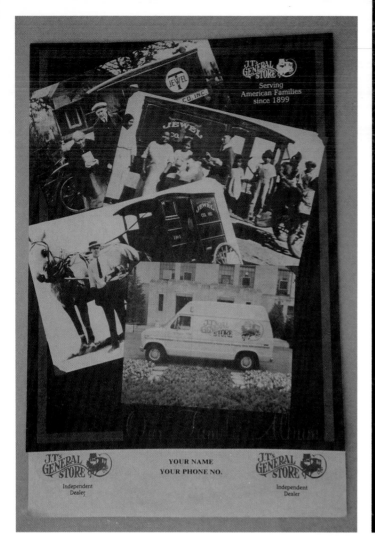

"Our Family Album" is the title of the J.T.'s General Store 1988 calendar. The 8" x 12" calendar displays four historical Jewel photographs: the famous Granny Hartney photograph, a 1923 routeman named G.B. Jackson who had made calls on an Indian reservation, a Jewel salesman with his horse and wagon, and a 1980s J.T's General Store van. The slogan "Everything in General—and a Whole Lot More, 1899-1988" appears at the beginning of January. At the end of the calendar there is a list of available grocery products. *Author's Collection.*

"Serving American Families Since 1899." The above cover of the J.T.'s General Store calendar from 1989 was courtesy of Thomas Sullivan, J.T. Dealer. The inside cover lists a large selection of J.T. products. At the base of each month is a perforated money-saving coupon for the purchase of a product; all coupons expired 1/31/89. The calendar is approximately 8-1/2" x 15-1/4". *Author's Collection.*

J.T.'s General Store presented the historical calendar (at left) in 1990. Before opening the 1990 calendar a brief history of the company, entitled "How Jewel Tea Became J.T.'s General Store," was given. Opening the calendar, you meet the founders Frank Skiff and Frank Ross of the Jewel Tea Company, along with a brief history. Historical photographs appeared on each page. On the last page, a list of grocery items available through your J.T.'s General Store Independent Dealer was provided for your convenience.
The J.T.'s General Store 1993 calendar (at right) is a repeat of the 1990. *Both calendars, Author's Collection.*

The Jewel News

Among the most fragile paper items relating to Jewel are editions of The Jewel News, a publication for customers which began in 1923. Many editions found from the 1920s are fast becoming fragile and brittle. It is important to seek the assistance of a professional in caring for them. Be aware that professional help in restoring these old documents can be quite costly.

An original section of The Jewel News after Jewel moved to Barrington.

The Jewel News—1925

Original cover page from a four-fold edition (September 1925) of The Jewel News, Vol. 3. No. 9, "Benjamin Franklin." *Author's Collection.*

Original cover page of a four-fold edition (November 1925) of The Jewel News, Vol. 3. No. 11, "Bringing Home The Turkey." *Author's Collection.*

Original cover page of the four-folded edition (March 1926) of The Jewel News, Vol. 4. No. 3, "Getting All That's Coming To Him." *Author's Collection.*

Original cover page of the April 1926 four-fold edition of The Jewel News, Vol. 4. No. 4, "It Won't Hurt A Bit.". *Author's Collection.* four fold?

The following article appeared in the March 1926 issue of The Jewel News:

No Longer a Leaflet — A Magazine!

Aren't you surprised at how I've grown? Last month I was only a leaflet — and now I am a magazine! You folks read me I know, for hundreds wrote in and told me how much they enjoyed my view of things. Somehow, though, I never felt quite grown up, and I knew I'd never meet your expectations 'til I did.

So here I am now, your new Jewel News — with more and more articles written each month for you.

This issue is just a sample of what every issue will be. Some of America's best know authorities on children and the home have written articles for my pages. Our own United States Government has prepared a special series of 12 articles on

"Your Children." Mary Dunbar, your Jewel Lady, will have two whole pages every month. Her suggestions will help you in preparing and varying the 1,095 meals you have to plan every year. And besides this, I will have a selection of articles, one for every month — by prominent women writers — including contributions by McCall's and the Modern Priscilla Magazines.

This issue marks another milestone in my progress. I was a leaflet, doing what I could to be of help and service to you in your home. And now that I'm grown up and can be of even greater service, I am especially proud. Proud of the Jewel Tea Co., Inc., and of the greater opportunity they have given me. Proud to say to you 600,000 readers —

"No Longer a Leaflet — a Magazine!"

The June 1926 edition of The Jewel News, Vol. 4. No. 6, "Speak," four fold, was not available.

The August 1926 four-fold edition of The Jewel News, Vol. 4. No. 8, "Fixing It For Daddy." *Author's Collection.*

Original cover of the July 1926 four-fold edition of The Jewel News, Vol. 4. No. 7. *Author's Collection.*

The September 1926 four-fold edition of The Jewel News, Vol. 4. No. 9, "Old Friends and New." *Author's Collection.*

Original cover page of the April 1927 four-fold edition of The Jewel News, Vol. 5. No. 4, "Singing." *Author's Collection.*

Original cover page of the October 1926 four-fold edition of The Jewel News, Vol. 4. No. 10, "Baking Day." *Author's Collection.*

Original cover page of the June 1927 four-fold edition of The Jewel News, Vol. 5. No. 6. *Author's Collection.*

The July 1927 edition of The Jewel News, Vol. 5. No. 7, "The End Of A Perfect Day," stapled 8 pages. Painting from photo ©Anne Shriber, NY. *Author's Collection.*

The October 1927 edition of The Jewel News, Vol. 5. No. 10, stapled 8 pages. *Author's Collection.*

The September 1927 edition of The Jewel News, Vol. 5 No. 9, stapled 8 pages, with colored cover photograph. *Author's Collection.*

The November 1927 edition of The Jewel News, Vol. 5 No. 11, stapled 8 pages, with colored cover. *Author's Collection.*

Not available is an 8-page special Thanksgiving edition, Vol. 5 No. 12, from 1927. Its cover photograph was done by H. Armstrong Roberts.

The December 1927 edition of The Jewel News, Vol. 5 No. 13, "Our Christmas Baby," stapled 8 pages. *Author's Collection.*

The Jewel News—1928

The March 1928 edition of The Jewel News, Vol. 6. No. 2, "Just A Breath of Spring From Way Down South," stapled 8 pages. *Author's Collection.*

The May 1928 edition of The Jewel News Vol. 6. No. 4, stapled 8 pages. *Author's Collection.*

The April 1928 edition of The Jewel News, Vol. 6. No. 3, photograph by H. Armstrong Roberts, stapled 8 pages. *Author's Collection.*

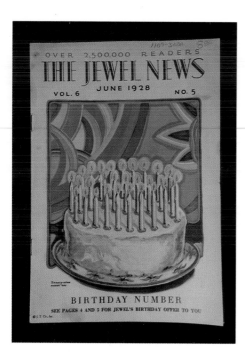

The June 1928 edition of The Jewel News, Vol. 6 No. 5. *Hedges Collection.*

The July 1928 edition of The Jewel News, Vol. 6 No. 6, "All Eyes Toward Washington," stapled 8 pages. *Author's Collection.*

The August 1928 edition of The Jewel News, Vol. 6. No. 7, photograph by H. Armstrong Roberts, stapled 8 pages. *Author's Collection.*

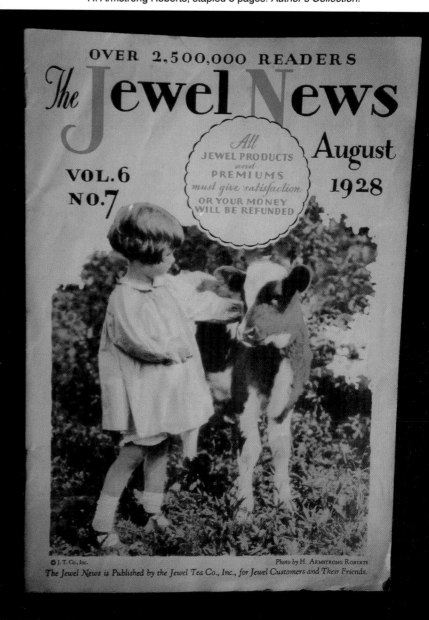

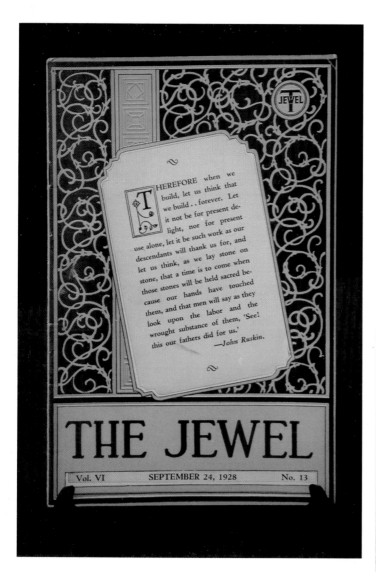

The September 1928 edition of The Jewel News, Vol. 6. No. 8, "Off To School" photograph by H. Armstrong Roberts, stapled 8 pages. *Hedges Collection.*

The October 1928 edition of The Jewel News, Vol. 6 No. 9, "Hallowe'en" painted by Dan Stark, stapled 8 pages. *Author's Collection.*

The 1928 Thanksgiving Issue of The Jewel News, Vol. 6, No. 11, photograph by Ewing Galloway, stapled 8 pages. *Author's Collection.*

The November 1928 edition of The Jewel News, Vol. 6. No. 10, photograph by H. Armstrong Roberts, stapled 8 pages. *Author's Collection.*

The 1928 Christmas Issue of The Jewel News, Vol. 6. No. 12, "Snowballs of Happiness" photograph by Ewing Galloway, stapled 8 pages. *Author's Collection.*

The Jewel News — 1929

The January 1929 edition of The Jewel News, Vol. 7. No. 1, "Start Young 1929 Right With Jewel Baking Powder," stapled 8 pages. *Author's Collection.*

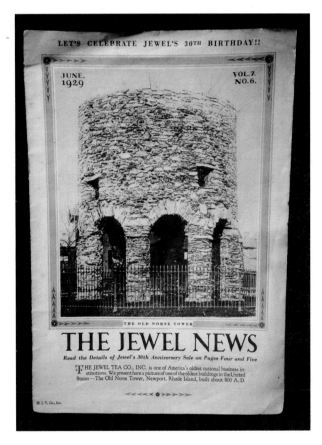

The June 1929 edition of The Jewel News, Vol. 7. No. 6, "The Old Norse Tower," stapled 8 pages. On pages four and five you could read details of Jewel's 30th Anniversary Sale. *Author's Collection.*

The March 1929 edition of The Jewel News, Vol. 7. No. 3, photograph by H. Armstrong Roberts, stapled 8 pages. *Author's Collection.*

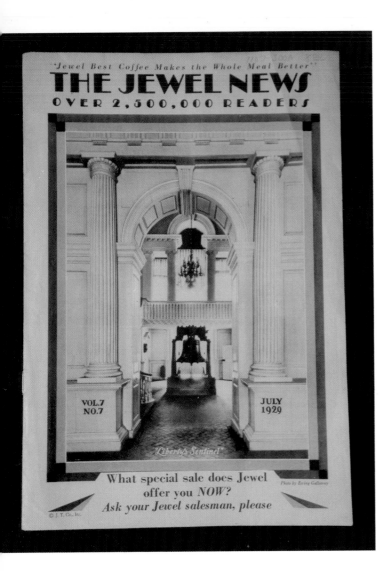

The August 1929 edition of The Jewel News, Vol. 7. No. 8, "A Stranger In Her Garden," initialed G.F.H., stapled 8 pages. *Author's Collection.*

The July 1929 edition of The Jewel News, Vol. 7 No. 7. *Hedges Collection.*

The September 1929 edition of The Jewel News, Vol. 7. No. 9, stapled 8 pages. *Author's Collection.*

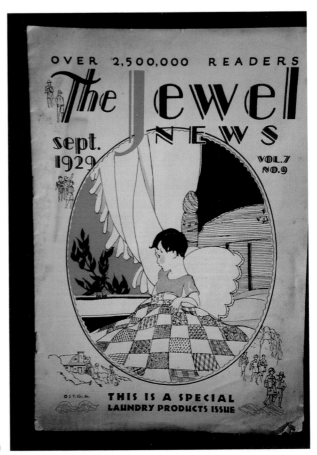

"Jewel Best Coffee Makes the Whole Meal Better"

The Jewel News

VOL. 7
No. 10

oct. 1929

OVER 2,500,000 READERS

READ WHAT PROFESSOR CHENEY OF NEW YORK UNIVERSITY SAYS ABOUT CO'

© J. T. Co. Inc.

The October 1929 edition of The Jewel News, Vol. 7. No. 10. *Author's Collection.*

The November 1929 edition of The Jewel News, Vol. 7. No. 11, stapled 8 pages. *Author's Collection.*

The Jewel News — 1930

The February 1930 edition of The Jewel News, Vol. 8 No. 2, celebrated great birthdays. *Hedges Collection.*

The January 1930 edition of The Jewel News, Vol. 8. No. 1, "The Coffee Kids," stapled 8 pages. *Author's Collection.*

The Jewel News stapled 8 pages Vol. 8. No. 3 March 1930, shown above. *Author's Collection.*

The Jewel News four fold Vol. 8. No. 4 April 1930, shown above. *Author's Collection.*

The June 1930 edition of The Jewel News, Vol. 8. No. 6, celebrated the 31st Anniversary, stapled 8 pages . *Author's Collection.*

The Jewel News "Special Mother's Day Number" stapled 8 pages Vol. 8. No. 5 May 1930, shown above. *Author's Collection.*

The August 1930 edition of The Jewel News, Vol. 8. No. 8, "Facing the Dangers of an Icy 'World' — Rear-Admiral Richard E. Byrd U.S.N.," stapled 8 pages. See the "20th Century Pioneer" chapter. *Author's Collection.*

The July 1930 edition of The Jewel News, Vol. 8. No. 7, stapled 8 pages. *Author's Collection.*

The original cover page of the four-fold September 1930 edition of The Jewel News, Vol. 8. No. 9, "Happy Days Are Here Again." *Author's Collection.*

The October 1930 edition of The Jewel News, Vol. 8. No. 10, stapled 8 pages. *Author's Collection.*

The 1930 Thanksgiving Special Issue of The Jewel News, Vol. 8. No. 12, stapled 8 pages. *Hedges Collection.*

The entrance to the Jewel building in Barrington appears on the November 1930 edition of The Jewel News, Vol. 8 No. 11, Special Photograph Number. *Hedges Collection.*

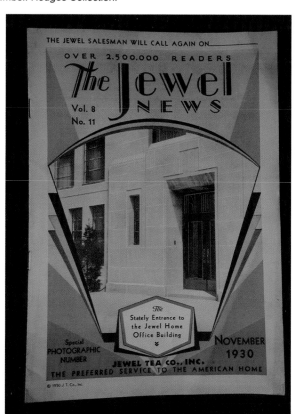

The 1930 Christmas Issue of The Jewel News, Vol. 8. No. 13, stapled 8 pages. *Weales Collection.*

The Jewel News — 1931

1931, The Jewel News, Vol. 9 No. 2. *Hedges Collection.*

1931, The Jewel News, Vol. 9 No. 1. *Author's Collection.*

"Make 1931 A Year of Plenty." The Jewel News, Vol. 9 No. 3. *Hedges Collection.*

"Spring is just around the corner" appears on The Jewel
News, Vol. 9 No. 4, from 1931. *Hedges Collection.*

"Dress Up Your Table for Christmas Dinner with Ivanhoe
Silverware" appears on the cover of The Jewel News,
Vol. 9 No. 13, from 1931. *Hedges Collection.*

Copies of Jewel News for 1932-
1934 and many issues from 1935
were not available. I would appreciate hearing from anyone with original copies of these in their collection.

The Jewel News—1935

A 1935 edition of The Jewel News, Vol. 13 No. 5. *Hedges Collection.*

A 1935 edition of The Jewel News, Vol. 13 No. 8. *Hedges Collection.*

The Jewel News—1936

A 1936 edition of The Jewel News, Vol. 14 No. 1. *Hedges Collection.*

The Jewel News—1937

A 1937 edition of The Jewel News, Vol. 15 No. 12. *Hedges Collection.*

A 1937 edition of The Jewel News Premium Catalog, Vol. 15 No. 11. *Hedges Collection.*

The Jewel News—1938

A 1938 edition of The Jewel News, Vol. 16 No. 3. *Hedges Collection.*

A 1938 edition of the Jewel News Premium Catalogue, Vol. 16 No. 2. *Hedges Collection.*

"A Service to Four Million Readers," a 1938 edition of The Jewel News, Vol. 16 No. 4. *Hedges Collection.*

An 1938 edition of The Jewel News, Vol. 16 No. 9. *Hedges Collection.*

A 1938 edition of The Jewel News, Vol. 16 No. 11. *Hedges Collection.*

A 1938 edition of The Jewel News, Vol. 16 No. 10. Note the Autumn Leaf china displayed in center of this issue. *Hedges Collection.*

"A Happy Thanksgiving." A 1938 edition of The Jewel News,
Vol. 16 No. 12. *Hedges Collection.*

"Merry Christmas to all — Your Jewel Man." A 1938 edition
of The Jewel News, Vol. 16 No. 13. *Hedges Collection.*

The Jewel News—1939

A 1939 edition of The Jewel News, Vol. 17 No. 1. *Hedges Collection.*

A 1939 edition of The Jewel News, Vol. 17 No. 3. *Hedges Collection.*

A 1939 edition of The Jewel News, Vol. 17 No. 2. *Hedges Collection.*

A 1939 edition of The Jewel News, Vol. 17 No. 6. *Hedges Collection.*

A 1939 edition of The Jewel News, Vol. 17 No. 4. Note the photograph in the center of this issue; the original black and white photograph appears in the first volume, *The Jewel Tea Company, Its History and Products,* in the "World War II" chapter. *Hedges Collection.*

A 1939 edition of The Jewel News, Vol. 17 No. 7. *Hedges Collection.*

"School Days." A 1939 edition of The Jewel News, Vol. 17 No. 9. *Hedges Collection.*

The Idea Exchange was a monumental part of The Jewel News; here is an original section. Household hints were sent to Mary Dunbar, and each month the best ideas were published, and $1 was paid to the readers who had contributed them. Note the promotional advertisement for Jewel U-No-Me in the center.

A 1939 edition of The Jewel News, Vol. 17 No. 10. *Hedges Collection.*

IDEA EXCHANGE

Send your original household hints to Mary Dunbar. The best, most practical group from each month's contributions will be published. Rules must be complied with.

RULES FOR THE CONTEST

1. $1.00 will be paid for each idea published in The Jewel News. *2. Recipes are not accepted as ideas. 3. Send only one idea for each contest. 4. A new contest opens with the distribution of each issue of* The Jewel News. *5. Do not expect letters of acknowledgment. 6. The submission of an idea carries with it the right of publication.*

Whenever I have leftover egg yolks I drop them in rapidly boiling salted water and poach them until they are hard. They can be used in salads or sandwiches. Mrs. Wm. D. Thomas, 17 W. Richardville St., Logansport, Ind.

Any one of the Hall Bowls can be used as the top part of a double boiler. I use the smallest to make seven minute frosting—it sets solidly and does not skid or tip as a pan would. Mrs. C. M. Newell, 86 N. Main St., Greenville, Pa.

A smooth cotton covered pan holder pinned to your ironing board provides exactly the right padding in a convenient form for ironing bits of embroidery, initials on linen, or collars, cuffs, pockets or any difficult places. Mrs. Lola Mason, 1023 Linden, Chariton, Iowa.

Rub Sara Cleansing Cream into the hands before blacking the stove or handling anything that will blacken the hands. When you wash your hands the black will come off easily and out of the pores of the skin. Mrs. Kenneth Grimes, 607 S. 12th St., Rocky Ford, Colo.

When hanging clothes out-of-doors, the children's play wagon can be used to save many steps and much back bending. Place the basket of clothes and pins in the wagon and pull it along as you go. Mrs. Carl

Seyfferle, 714 Steele Ave., Dayton, Ohio.

I use the Hall Custard Cups for the children's ice cream dishes. The cups are serviceable and do not break easily. Mrs. Thomas W. Price, Jr., N. Hamilton St., Leaksville, N. C.

A brush skims jellies perfectly and wastes no juice. Mrs. A. M. Mathisen, 422 E. Oxford St., Duluth, Minn.

★ Jewel U-No-Me is ideal for cleaning thermos bottles. Use a solution of one tablespoon U-No-Me, one tablespoon soap flakes, and warm water to fill the bottle. Leave over night. When you rinse the bottle you will find it fresh and sparkling. Gloria Sorenson, 7144 Portland Ave., So., Minneapolis, Minn.

The Jewel Onion Chopper is not only a chopper but a juicer as well. After chopping the onion put the board on top of the onion, replace chopper and press down. Mrs. H. A. Harris, 1023 Sylvan Court, Jacksonville, Fla.

When I entertained recently at a pantry shower I suggested that my friends bring Jewel groceries as gifts. The bride-to-be was delighted with her Jewel Pantry. Mrs. E. B. Vanskike, 1810 47th, Galveston, Texas.

Wash Jewel Extract bottles and put new labels on them for use in the medicine cabinet. Mrs. Eric Osthling, Mounted Route No. 7, Ellwood City, Pa.

Trace the design of any article of the Hall China Ware with onion skin paper (the bread box is the easiest to trace from), transfer with carbon paper onto plain curtain material, and embroider with same colors as in design. Make a border around the curtains with tape in brown, orange, and yellow. These curtains will match your Hall China Ware and complete your kitchen ensemble. Mrs. Clyde Pribble, Hudson, Wis.

A grand spicy cake filling is made by adding one packet of Jewel Mincemeat, cut, to seven-minute icing or a boiled white icing. Syble M. Bicknell, 36 Churchill Ave., Palo Alto, Calif.

As a convenience when traveling, seal enough Jewel Daintiflakes in an envelope to wash one pair of hose. Mrs. Nina Butchler, 3716 Ave. 0 ½, Galveston, Texas.

The Jewel News—1940

Coffee Cheers You Up! A 1940 edition of The Jewel News, Vol. 18 No. 4. *Hedges Collection.*

A 1940 edition of The Jewel News, Vol. 18 No. 1. *Hedges Collection.*

A 1940 edition of The Jewel News, Vol. 18 No. 5. *Hedges Collection.*

A 1940 edition of The Jewel News, Vol. 18 No. 10. *Hedges Collection.*

Santa and Jewel! A 1940 edition of The Jewel News, Vol. 18 No. 13. *Hedges Collection.*

A 1940 edition of The Jewel News, Vol. 18 No. 12. Note the Autumn Leaf china pieces in the lower righthand corner. *Hedges Collection.*

The Jewel News - 1941

Florida, California, and Pennsylvania appear on a 1941 edition of The Jewel News, Vol. 19 No. 1. *Hedges Collection.*

"Mary Dunbar Says." A 1941 edition of The Jewel News, Vol. 19 No. 10. *Hedges Collection.*

The Jewel News - 1942

A 1942 edition of The Jewel News, Vol. 20 No. 1. *Hedges Collection.*

A 1942 edition of The Jewel News, Vol. 20 No. 2. *Hedges Collection.*

Now just one more bite! A 1942 edition of The Jewel News, Vol. 20 No. 3. *Hedges Collection.*

A 1942 edition of The Jewel News,, Vol. 20 No. 5. *Hedges Collection.*

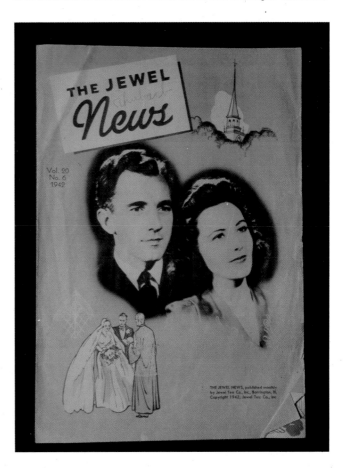

A 1942 edition of The Jewel News, Vol. 20 No. 4. *Hedges Collection.*

Could they be preparing for a June wedding? A 1942 edition of The Jewel News, Vol. 20 No. 6. *Hedges Collection.*

The Jewel News—1946

In 1946, a Jewel customer from Wichita, Kansas received $1 from the company for her good idea. The customer suggested, "To keep your new Jewel News for future reference, use a loose leaf note book. Punch holes for the rings to go through. They fit the note book nicely."

Caught Again! The Jewel News Shopper's issue from March 25, 1946. *Easley Collection.*

The Jewel News Shopper's issue from March 11, 1946. Note the holes punched in the margins. *Easley Collection.*

The Jewel News Shopper's issue from April 8, 1946. *Easley Collection.*

160

"Recipes of the States" began in The Jewel News issue from April 22, 1946. *Easley Collection.*

"Sugar Savers in this issue!" The Jewel News from May 20, 1946. *Easley Collection.*

Recipes compiled by the Ladies of the Congressional Club continued in The Jewel News from May 6, 1946. *Easley Collection.*

The Jewel News from July 29 to August 10, 1946, an 8-page leaflet. *Hancock Collection.*

"Cool Off with Cool Jewel Iced Coffee!" The Jewel News from August 26, 1946. *Easley Collection.*

"Wake Up and Live!" The Jewel News from August 12, 1946. *Easley Collection.*

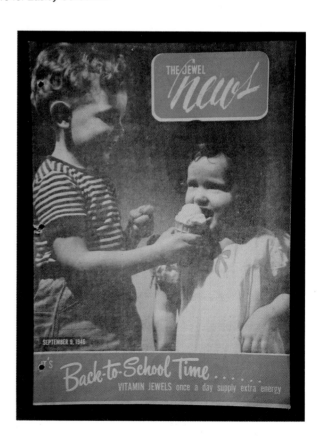

"Back-to-School Time..." The Jewel News issue from September 9, 1946. *Easley Collection.*

The October 7, 1946 issue of The Jewel News suggested "Do Your Christmas shopping Early!" *Easley Collection.*

The Jewel News from November 4 to 16, 1946, an 8-page leaflet. *Easley Collection.*

The Jewel News issue from October 21, 1946. *Easley Collection.*

The Jewel News Shopper's from November 18 to 30, 1946. The front cover was devoted to telling the story of America's Finest Coffee sold at the price of ordinary blends! *Easley Collection.*

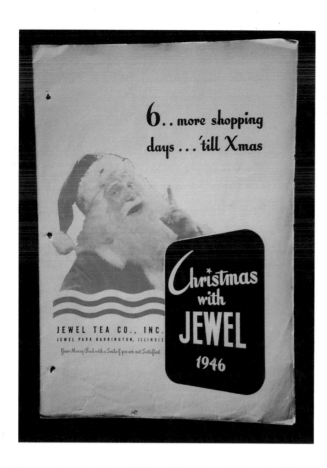

"6...more shopping days...till Xmas." Christmas with Jewel in 1946. *Easley Collection.*

Instruction for making the "Singing Choir Boys" were given in The Jewel News from December 16, 1946. *Easley Collection.*

Jewel customers had "1 more shopping day till Xmas." The Jewel News edition from December 2, 1946. *Easley Collection.*

Someone did some figuring on the cover of this issue of The Jewel News. The December 30, 1946 edition listed Annual Clearance. *Easley Collection.*

The Jewel News—1947

The January 13, 1947 edition of The Jewel News, Vol. 1, No. 2, an 8-page leaflet. *Hancock Collection.*

The February 10-22, 1947 edition of The Jewel News, Vol. 2, No. 2, an 8-page leaflet. *Hancock Collection.*

The March 10-April 5, 1947 edition of The Jewel News, Vol. 3, a 16-page leaflet. The cover illustration was done by Marge Opitz. *Hancock Collection.*

The April 7, 1947 edition of The Jewel News, Vol. 4. *Hancock Collection.*

"Vacation Days." The August 1947 edition, Vol. 8. *Hancock Collection.*

The June 2-28 edition of The Jewel News, Vol. 6, a 16-page leaflet. *Hancock Collection.*

Note the laurel wreath logo on the above edition of The Jewel News, Vol. 11 from October 20, 1947. *Hancock Collection.*

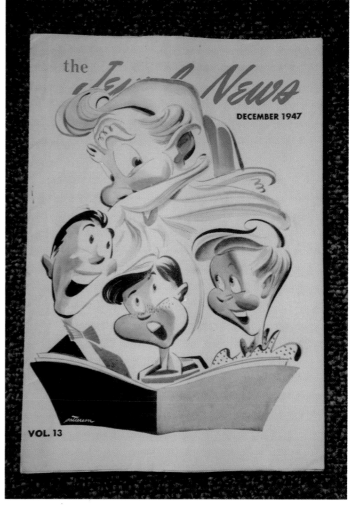

The December 15, 1947 edition of The Jewel News, Vol. 13, a 16-page leaflet. The cover illustration was done by Roy Patterson. *Hancock Collection.*

Marge Opitz and her artist husband, Roy Patterson, were both contributors to The Jewel News. Marge specialized in drawing covers for sports magazines. Roy Patterson's illustrations have appeared in The Jewel News since December 1946.

The Jewel News—1948

The February 9-March 6, 1948 edition of The Jewel News, No. 2, a 16-page leaflet. *Hancock Collection.*

The January 1948 edition of The Jewel News, No. 1, a 16-page leaflet. *Hancock Collection.*

The March 8-April 3, 1948 edition of The Jewel News, No. 3, a 16-page leaflet. *Hancock Collection.*

The April 5-May 1, 1948 edition of The Jewel News, No. 4, a 16-page leaflet. *Hancock Collection.*

The May 3-29, 1948 edition of The Jewel News, No. 5, a 16-page leaflet. *Hancock Collection.*

The July 26-August 21, 1948 edition of The Jewel News, No. 8, a 16-page leaflet. *Hancock Collection.*

The August 23-September 18, 1948 edition of The Jewel News, No. 9, a 16-page leaflet. *Hancock Collection.*

The October 18-November 13, 1948 edition of The Jewel News, No. 11, a 16-page leaflet. *Hancock Collection.*

The September 20-October 16 , 1948 edition of The Jewel News "Autumn Issue," No. 10, a 16-page leaflet. *Hancock Collection.*

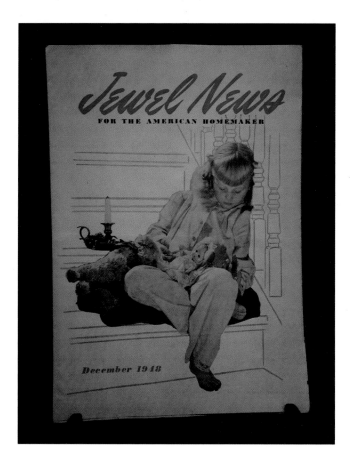

The Jewel News, No. 13, a 16-page leaflet from December 13, 1948 to January 8, 1949. *Hancock Collection.*

The Jewel News distributed from December 13, 1948 to January 8, 1949 was the last issue; after this, it was discontinued.

Jewel Catalogs

In March 1949, the Jewel Man gave his customers a new 32-page catalog showing Jewel's complete line of housewares, dinnerwares, aluminum cookware, kitchen utensils and equipment, blankets, bedspreads, lamps, rugs, and many other items.

The 32-page catalog was a guide to careful buying. Any housewife could plan what she wanted to order from her Jewel Man for a period of several months. All housewares shown was described fully so that everyone knew exactly what they were buying.

There was also a page of recipes prepared by Mary Dunbar, and helpful household hints (like how to care for your aluminum, how to get the most use from the pressure pan, or how to keep blankets, rugs, and bedspreads in the best condition). The pattern service was also continued.

Customers received a new Jewel catalog at least three times a year. Jewel suggested keeping the catalog handy in a safe place for future reference.

I can show you only those catalog issues I had access to. If you should have issues not pictured I would appreciate hearing from you. If you are unable to locate original Jewel Home Shopping Service catalogs, you can invest in a copy of Shirley Easley's Jewel Home Shopping 1949-1982 Catalog Reprints (see the Appendix for information).

Shopping with Jewel, Summer 1949. *Author's Collection.*

Jewel Home Shopping Service, Spring and Summer 1952. *Byerly Collection.*

Jewel Home Shopping Service, Fall and Winter 1954. *Byerly Collection.*

Jewel Home Shopping Service, 1953. *Byerly Collection.*

Jewel Home Shopping Service Woman's Catalog, Fall and Winter 1961. *Byerly Collection.*

Jewel Home Shopping Service Christmas Gift Book, 1962. *Byerly Collection.*

Jewel Fall and Winter Catalog, 1964. *Byerly Collection.*

Jewel Spring and Summer Catalog, 1964. *Byerly Collection.*

Jewel Christmas Catalog, 1964. *Byerly Collection.*

Jewel Home Shopping Service, Spring and Summer 1970. *Byerly Collection.*

Jewel Home Shopping Service, Fall and Winter 1969.' *Byerly Collection.*

Jewel In Home Shopping Service, Christmas 1970. *Byerly Collection.*

Jewel Spring and Summer 1971 Catalog. *Byerly Collection.*

Jewel Spring and Summer 1972 Catalog. *Byerly Collection.*

Jewel In Home Shopping Service catalog, Christmas 1971. *Byerly Collection.*

Jewel In Home Shopping Service catalog, Spring and Summer 1973. *Byerly Collection.*

Playing Cards

Little information is known about the original Jewel Tea Playing cards.

A collection of Autumn Leaf playing cards. In 1943 Jewel introduced two sets of playing cards, shown on the left and right: a pinochle set and a regular set. A 75th anniversary set is shown in the center, along with a J.T.'s General Store deck. *Pomroy Collection.*

A closer view of the Autumn Leaf set. *Byerly Collection.*

The Declaration of Independence

Jewel History

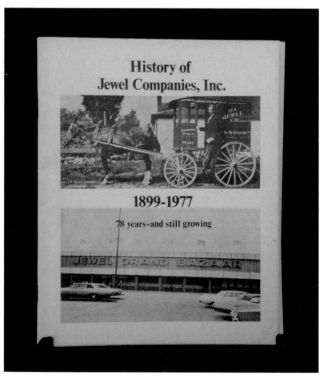

A booklet (for schoolchildren) on "The Declaration of Independence." The envelope that contained the 16-page booklet says "Here's Your Copy of 'The Declaration of Independence — A Story—With Compliments of Your Friendly Neighborhood Jewel Food Store," ©1947. The envelope also contained a sheet of stamps showing men who had signed the Declaration. The stamps could be placed within the booklet. This publication is in mint condition, and none of the stamps have ever been put into place. *Hamilton Collection.*

A 24-page paper booklet entitled "History of Jewel Companies, Inc., 1899-1977—78 years and still growing." This publication contained a general history and historical Jewel photographs. *Hamilton Collection.*

The Autumn Leaf Story

The first publication ever on Autumn Leaf is *The Autumn Leaf Story* by Jo Cunningham. No longer in print, this 48-page publication is highly sought-after by collectors of the pattern. *Author's Collection.*

1949-1982 Jewel Catalog Reprints

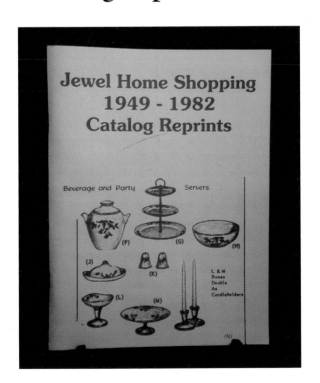

Other Jewel Paper Products

"Coffee Facts for You (A Text on Coffee and Jewel Coffees) JEWEL TEA CO., INC. NEW YORK CHICAGO," copyright 1927. This pamphlet is approximately 5" x 6-3/4" and was prepared primarily for the Products section of the Salesman's Manual. *Hamilton Collection*

For every Jewel collector who does not have access to original Jewel Home Shopping catalogs, this reprint is a worthy acquisition. It was assembled by former Jewel employee Shirley Easley. See the appendix for further information. *Author's Collection.*

"What You Should Know About Tea," published and copyrighted January 10, 1928 by "JEWEL TEA CO. Five North Wabash Ave., Chicago." Approximately 5" x 6-3/4", this 51-page pamphlet gives an account of tea. *Hamilton Collection.*

The above 16-page "Sales Course" booklet is approximately 6-7/8" x 4-7/8". The booklet is based on "What Influences The Housewife To Buy From The Jewel Salesman." No date given, JEWEL TEA CO. INC. New York Chicago. *Hamilton Collection.*

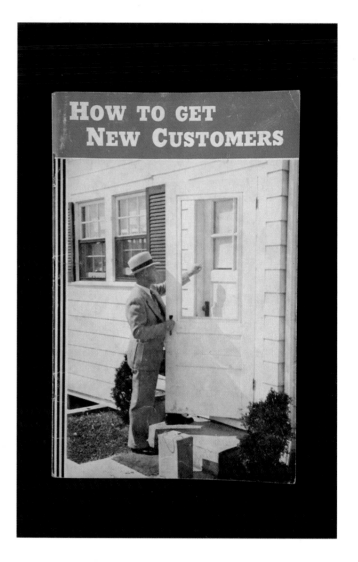

"How To Get New Customers," copyright 1936 JEWEL TEA CO., INC. JEWEL PARK, BARRINGTON, ILL. Approximately 5-1/2" x 8-1/4", this 48-page booklet discussed an encounter between a Jewel salesmen and Mrs. Brown, and pictured various premiums. *Hamilton Collection.*

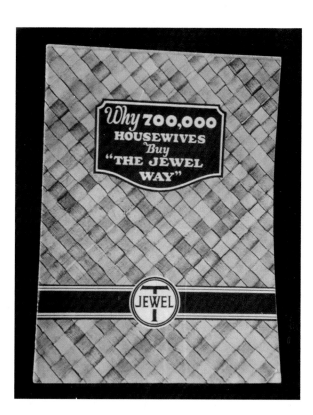

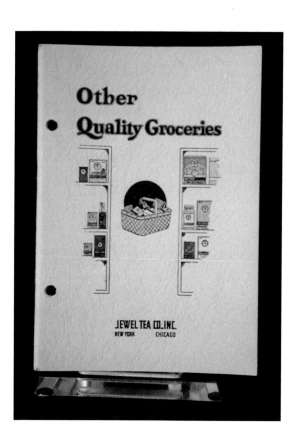

"Why 700,000 Housewives Buy 'The Jewel Way' from 1925 covered various Jewel products and quality premiums. It pictured the New York Harbor, where Jewel had the world's largest coffee roasting and packaging equipment, and the Chicago plant where many Jewel products were manufactured. It measures 5-1/2" x 7-1/2". *Hamilton Collection.*

"Copyright, April 1929 Jewel Tea Co., Inc. New York Chicago" appears on the inside cover of this "Other Quality Groceries" booklet. This 54-page publication carried articles on cocoa, shredded coconut, vanilla and lemon extracts, baking powder, Jewel-Jell, peanut butter, graham crackers, butter crackers, mayonnaise, spices, and cornstarch. The booklet is 4-7/8" x 6-7/8" and has numerous photographs. *Hamilton Collection.*

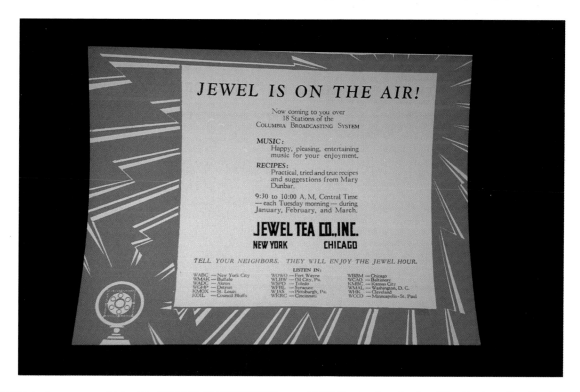

A 7-7/8" x 5-7/8" single page pamphlet entitled "JEWEL IS ON THE AIR!" At the bottom are listed eighteen stations. The reverse side reads "THE STANDARD OF COFFEE EXCELLENCE — That special shade of flavor which coffee lovers like best is THERE — in Jewel Best Coffee. And at slightly lower prices the Jewel Tea Co., Inc. offers the Jewel Special and Jewel Cup Blends, both of them high-grade, quality coffees. JEWEL BEST, THE COFFEE THAT MAKES THE WHOLE MEAL BETTER." *Hamilton Collection.*

The pamphlet "You'll find the key to Health Cookery inside" is a single page 9" x 5-1/2". No date appears on this colorful publication. *Hamilton Collection.*

The reverse side of the "key to Health Cookery" pamphlet.

180

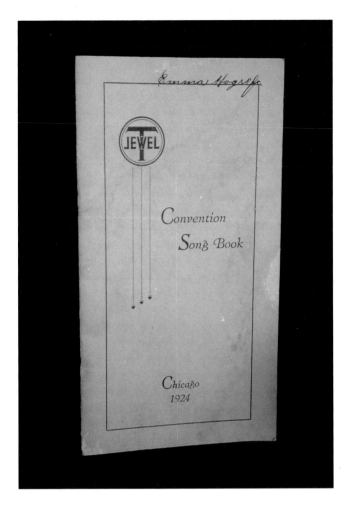

The inside of the "Jewel Coffee" advertisement: "All Jewel Groceries are Tested and Approved by Mary Dunbar."

The "Chicago 1924 Convention Song Book," measuring 4" x 7-1/2" with eighteen songs. On the back it say says "All the More in '24." *Hamilton Collection.*

The front and back view of a cardboard advertisement promoting Jewel products. "JEWEL TEA CO. INC JEWEL PARK BARRINGTON, ILLINOIS" appears on the cover of this "Jewel Coffee" advertisement; on the back Jewel premiums appeared. The back also states: "Here are a few of the many premiums you may own. Jewel premiums are yours at no extra cost because credits on regular deliveries of Jewel coffee and other groceries automatically pay for them while you use them." *Long Collection.*

A 4-7/8" x 6-7/8" booklet entitled "Jewel Cereal Products," by JEWEL TEA CO., INC. NEW YORK CHICAGO. This booklet listed "Helpful Information about Jewel Cereal Products" and covered rice, Tastiflakes, Quick Oats, macaroni, spaghetti, and egg noodles. Numerous pictures of cereal, Haviland China, and Jewel personnel are featured. *Hamilton Collection.*

Plastic Covers

Introduced during the 1950s, plastic covers were popular among American housewives. They kept foods fresh and prevented intermingling of refrigerator odors. They were offered in a handy plastic bag, listed as Item No. 4F177, and sold for $1.00.

Seven elastic-edge, washable plastic covers decorated with the "Autumn Leaf" pattern and handy storage bag. *Weales Collection.*

A closer view of the handy plastic bag that held the seven covers. *Author's Collection.*

A plastic cover placed over a bowl in order to keep the contents fresh in the refrigerator. *Byerly Collection.*

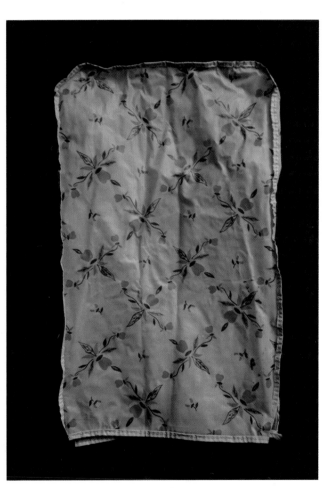

This plastic food-mixer cover fits all standard mixers, providing protection from dust and keeping the mixer sparkling clean. Made of easy-to-clean washable plastic with bound edges, in the Autumn pattern. The cover measured 15" x 8-1/2" x 8-1/2". Listed as Item No. 4F183 and sold for $1.00. *Author's Collection.*

Offered during the same period was a plastic toaster cover, to keep the toaster clean and dust-free. It fits any 2-slice toaster, measuring 10-1/2" x 7" x 6-1/2". The cover was made of heavy, washable plastic, in the Autumn pattern, with yellow binding on the edges. Listed as Item No. 4F190 and sold for 65¢. The tag on this toaster cover reads "Manufactured by Clarvan Corporation Milwaukee." *Byerly Collection.*

The Jewel Home Shopping Service catalog from the spring and summer of 1960 lists an Autumn-pattern seven-piece plastic cover set as Item No. 4F342. It consisted of six covers for bowls (sizes 5" to 13") and a toaster cover. The set sold for 98¢. The mixer cover was not listed.

Plastic Laundry-Basket Liner

Little is known about an exceptionally hard-to-find plastic laundry-basket liner. Many collectors believe it was available during the period of the red metal trash can, since the coloring is similar to that of the trash can. I understand the liner is solid red and the section that wraps around and over the top of the basket has the Autumn Leaf motif. Some collectors believe this section is in the red coloring of the trash can; others have told me it resembles the coloring of the plastic Autumn Leaf bib apron. If you should have this basket liner in your collection, I would appreciate hearing from you.

Jewel In Home Shopping Bag

A "Jewel In Home Shopping Service bag, displaying two Jewel trucks. *Zollinger Collection.*

Plastic Tote Bag

This plastic tote bag was introduced in the late 1970s to hold an introductory pack of Jewel's most popular grocery items. The orange tote was given to potential customers. *Author's Collection.*

CHAPTER 13
EPHRAIM

In March 1936 the following article appeared in The Jewel News:

> Did you ever stop to think that the humble mule is mighty important to you? In coffee-growing countries the mule is a beast of burden, but he is also man's servant and helper.
>
> Appreciating the importance of the mule, Jewel men have adopted one as their loyal friend. We'd like to have you know Emphraim, for he is the symbol of Jewel Coffee. Wherever his name is mentioned, you may be sure that the World's Finest Coffees are being talked about.
>
> In March 1937 a brief article appeared with what is believed to be a handcarved figurine or statuette of Ephraim. Under the picture showing this art work and the words "MORE COFFEE! MORE COFFEE!" appeared the following: "Another pose of Ephraim, the humble mule who is a symbol of coffee to all Jewel men".

No further explanation of Ephraim was included.

The exceptional 9" diameter saucer. *Hamilton Collection.*

Note the Jewel logo that appears in the bottom of this coffee cup. *Hamilton Collection.*

Emphraim was the name of the mule illustrated on the saucer along with the Jewel logo and the text "Ephraim Coffee Winner — 1939." Accompanying advertising copy read as follows:

> Jewel's mule Ephraim stands first among track immortals. No other thoroughbred has earned the winner's wreath so often. Ephraim is the undefeated champion, and now he risks his record to ring up another victory for Jewel Coffee — 9 million pounds in five periods, his goal.

On the opposite side of this large cup is an illustration of Ephraim. *Hamilton Collection.*

Ephraim Coffee Winner — 1939 cup. This cup is 6" in diameter and 3-1/2" high. Those are coffee beans around the lip of the cup! *Hamilton Collection.*

On December 19, 1938, Jewel salesmen started selling for the first deliveries of 1939. Ephraim leaves the post with the first delivery of the new year, on January 2, 1939. Ephraim's goal is to make a triumphal entry to the World's Fair on or before May 20, the end of the fifth period. He needs 9 million pounds of Jewel Coffee for admittance to the Fair. Help Ephraim strut through the gates of the World's Fair with 9 million pounds of Jewel Coffee! The following passage appeared in the Jewel Home Shopping Service on December 19, 1938:

Extra awards for outstanding coffee jobs will be made in each of the first five periods of 1939, to help Ephraim reach his goal. In each of the first two periods these awards are: 1) for 400 pounds per week average for either the first or second period, a gold coffee bean pin, engraved "400 Club"; 2) for 500 pounds per week average in either the first or second period, a $5 pair of shoes; and 3) an attractive district trophy to the branch with the best job in each district.

Route salesmen can win only one gold coffee bean, but they can win two pairs of shoes by averaging 500 pounds in both the first and second periods. The district trophy is a huge Hall China cup and saucer, six times normal size; it is decorated with coffee beans and a picture of Ephraim. The name of the winning branch in each period will be placed on the cup, and the branch with the best job for the full five periods will win permanent possession.

The "Ephraim Coffee Winner" cup and saucer set was given to salesmen and assistant managers. The enormous one-quart capacity cup and saucer was one of two versions distributed. It is estimated that less than a hundred of the above were given away.

186

400 Unique Prizes
Go To Fourth Period Winners

The other version of the award said "District Coffee Champion" and was displayed at the district office. Only four hundred were made. These were to go to 325 route salesmen and 75 assistant managers.

In February 1939, The Jewel printed the following announcement:

Selling starts this week in a campaign to boost fourth period coffee poundage and bring into 400 Jewel homes a trophy that's really different. Through special order placed with the Hall China Company, Jewel is able to offer 400 quart-capacity Hall China cups and saucers to the best coffee salesmen of the fourth period. These novel prizes are the same in design as the district trophies being awarded to branches with the best coffee jobs for the first five periods of 1939. They are different in only one respect; the insignia "District Coffee Champion" has been changed to a personal award, reading "Ephraim Coffee Winner — 1939."

This unique trophy will be a source of interest to your guests and a source of satisfaction to you. It can be ideally used in your home for growing plants. Placed on your mantel or in the china cabinet, it stands as a tribute to your standing as a coffee specialist. Here at last is a trophy that embodies the tradition and lore of the coffee business!

Every route salesman belongs to a two-man team, to handle the odd route in some branches. Each team has a coffee quota for the four weeks of the fourth period, March 27 to April 22. All winners will be decided on the basis of increased coffee poundage over these quotas. Each member of a winning team will receive a trophy. Don't let your team partner fall down on the job and don't yourself endanger your partner's chances by landing the smallest increase on your team!

The number of teams which can win, in any branch, depends upon the number of routes operated in the branch. The largest Jewel branch has been allotted eight trophies and, in that branch, all the members of the teams with the four largest increases will win trophies. In a branch with four trophies, both members of both the top two teams will win. The underlying principle is that a good individual job is not enough to win a trophy. Besides doing a good job yourself, you must belong to a hard-working team. You depend on your partner and your partner depends on you!

In addition to these team awards, which route salesmen can personally win, every Jewel salesman can help win a trophy for his assistant manager. The assistant manager of the group in each branch which has the largest coffee increase over its quota will receive a trophy. Where a branch has only one assistant manager, he will be pitted against an assistant manager from another branch.

Coffee deliveries between March 27 and April 22 determined the trophy winners!

EPHRAIM RUNS AGAIN!

CHAPTER *14*
MADRID GLASSWARE

Federal Glass Company

In 1900 the Federal Glass Company started on the south side of Columbus, Ohio with George Beatty as president. In 1902 R.J. and George Beatty sold their interest in the Atlas Glass Co. and confined their efforts to the Columbus operation. R.J. Beatty died in December 1914 and George Beatty died in 1916, at which time J.M. Beatty became president of the company.

During the Depression years of the 1930s, the Federal Glass Company produced glassware that became one of the Jewel homemakers' favorite premiums or purchases, fondly known as "Golden Glow."

Federal closed permanently on January 31, 1979.

Golden Glow

"Golden Glow" was actually a pattern called "Madrid" made by the Federal Glass Company from 1932 to 1939. The nickname "Golden Glow" came into use because of the pattern's amber color, which is also often referred to as "Topaz." Of all the Depression glass patterns, Madrid has had more publicity than any other.

The Jewel Tea Company offered this amber glassware as a premium, and also for sale. It was one of the most successful premiums of the Depression. The amber glass picked up the tone of the gold trim on Hall China pieces, so they made a striking combination.

The 1932 September issue of The Jewel News exclaimed "Just imagine! Thirty-four pieces of this Golden Glow Luncheon Set in amber glass with effective stamped design for only $2.80. Six each of: cups, saucers, salad plates, luncheon plates and fruits bowls. There are one each of the most desirable serving pieces; creamer, sugar bowl, platter and vegetable dish." This set was listed as item number 422. In the fall of 1932, many housewives would have been proud and pleased to serve a dinner or luncheon guest with her "Golden Glow" pattern glassware.

"Golden Glow Luncheon Set" advertisement from the 1933 Jewel News. *Hamilton Collection.*

Golden Glow Luncheon Set. This luncheon set will be lovely for summer parties and make the family meals seem a bit more festive, when it is used. Ideal for a gift. Thirty-four piece set. Item No. 442. $2.80

Carloads of Glassware

In 1938 Jewel purchased seven-piece cereal sets from the Federal Glass Company. This purchase was the equivalent of 33 carloads of glassware, and meant added employment for Jewel. New purchases all helped to stimulate business, though the most influential force behind Jewel's growth was the team of Jewel men who sold these products. The salesmen kept business moving — and sales meant jobs!

In 1939, Madrid glassware and Autumn Leaf china appeared in a Jewel brochure promoting Jewel Jell.

From 1939 and 1941, Jewel's auditors' lists (used for inventory purposes) show that Jewel offered the following Madrid items: Item number 442 was a 34-piece set, comprised of six each of cups, saucers, 6" plates, 9" plates, 5" plates, a serving platter, a sugar and a creamer, salad plate, and an oval vegetable dish. Though this amounts to a *35-piece* set, no explanation was given. Item number 445 was a 7-piece water set. The water pitcher and glasses differed in style from the 1932 original. The glasses changed shape in 1936, to incorporate a straightened base that made them easier to wash and dry. The ice lip was added to the 2-1/2 qt. pitcher during the middle of 1937.

In a 1935 Jewel News, another set is pictured, consisting of salt and pepper shakers, a bowl, two sets of candlesticks, and a console bowl. There is no apparent reason for there being two bowls and two sets of candlesticks.

Jewel also offered the gravy boat and platter/underplate and a serving bowl and plate. I have been unable to locate these pieces. If you should have any Madrid, I would appreciate hearing from you.

Madrid was re-issued by Federal Glass in 1976, entitled "Recollection." It bears a small '76 mark near the rim. Jewel never offered "Recollection."

In this promotional advertisement photograph, Jewel mayonnaise was the perfect dressing for asparagus salad served on a piece of Madrid glassware. Taken in late 1930s in the Jewel Test Kitchen in Barrington, Illinois. *Barrington Archives.*

The "Madrid" pattern appeared with various Autumn Leaf pieces in advertisements during the 1930s. This original 1930s photograph is an illustration of the amber Madrid with the famous Hall China Autumn Leaf pattern. The caption under the original photograph read "MATCHED SET—The Cream Pitcher and Sugar Bowl of the Hall China Service match and are appropriate with either the 8-cup Coffee Service, 9-cup Coffee Service, or the Teapot." The sugar bowl (with cover) was listed as Item No. 300B and sold for 75¢. The cream pitcher listed as Item No. 300C and sold for only 50¢. *Author's Collection.*

The above photograph was taken in the Jewel Test kitchen for promotional purposes during the late 1930s. A glass of water was served in the Madrid tumbler, a fresh cup of Jewel coffee served in the Madrid cup and saucer, and a fresh summer salad was served on a Madrid salad plate. Ivanhoe silverware completes the photograph. *Barrington Archives.*

This promotional advertisement photograph shows the Madrid creamer and sugar, along with the Madrid coffee cup and saucer. The coffee pot is a Club Aluminum Coffee Maker; the goblets are hand-cut Jewel crystal. The photograph is from the late 1930s. *Barrington Archives.*

CHAPTER 15
THE DOUGLAS PATTERN

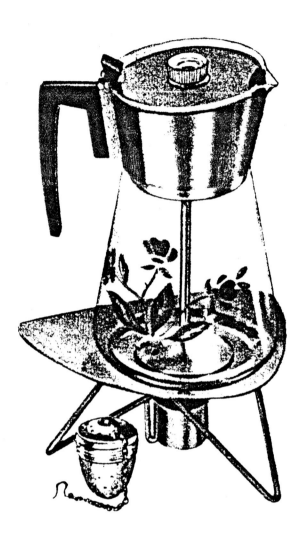

The Douglas pattern.

The Douglas ice lip pitcher. *Hamilton Collection.*

The first piece in the "Douglas" pattern, designed by David Douglas, appeared in Jewel's catalog in 1960. The pattern is a 22 karat gold-fused Autumn Leaf design. To identify a Douglas piece, look for the name "Douglas" stamped in gold near the base of the item.

By 1962 "Douglas" pieces would be discontinued. Douglas pieces seem to be among the hardest Autumn Leaf patterns to locate and can be quite costly.

There have been reports of five known Douglas ice lip pitchers. These were never offered in the Jewel catalogs, but that does not mean Jewel never sold them. Jewel usually offered promotional pieces, at the rate of three or four items per month. It is believed that the Douglas ice lip pitcher was part of this offering.

The Douglas eight-cup percolator, or twelve-cup instant coffee maker/tea maker/beverage server, first appeared in 1960. It was listed as item number 4D 30 and sold for $7.95. A housewife could add a subtle air of excitement when she served coffee or other beverages in this new carafe, which would stay piping hot. It is a 22 karat gold-fused design with a gleaming brass candle warmer, Bakelite handle, anodized aluminum lid and collar. It also included a tea ball and two candles.

The Douglas eight-cup percolator, or twelve-cup instant coffee maker/tea maker/beverage server. *Hamilton Collection.*

By fall and winter of 1961, the housewife could add other festive touches to her table with the Autumn pattern flameproof glassware by Douglas. The gleaming 22 karat gold design added elegance to any table.

In 1961, the percolator-carafe was still selling for $7.95. A graduated 1 quart serving sauce dish with goldtone collar and cover with a Bakelite handle, listed as item number 4D 43, sold for $2.98.

A pair of Douglas hurricane lamps with a seamless glass chimney, 3" in diameter x 7" high, was also offered. The chimneys were modern "Free Form" in 22 karat gold-plated bases, with four candles included. Listed as item number 4D 42, the pair sold for $5.98.

A housewife could save herself $1.96 if she bought the set: the percolator-carafe, the sauce dish, and the hurricane lamps. Though the regular price of the three items totalled $16.91, as a set they were listed as item number 4D 44 and were value-priced at $14.95.

Recently a 70-ounce Douglas Autumn Leaf iced tea maker with a tea baller was discovered at a local flea market. This exceptional piece is in the original box marked "No. 6114T, David and Douglas & Co. Inc., Manitowoc, Wisconsin." The iced tea maker was made of flame-proof glass with a wide neck and could be used as a party server.

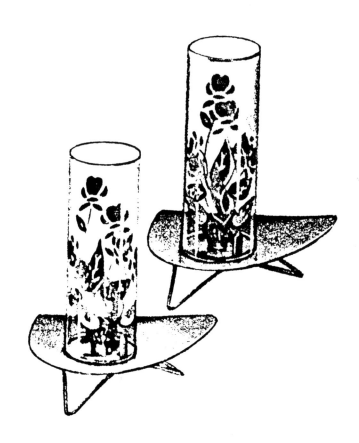

The Douglas hurricane lamps.

The modern "Free Form" Douglas hurricane lamps. *Hamilton Collection.*

Lipton® "Golden" Tea Leaf

During the time Jewel introduced the Douglas Autumn Leaf pieces, Lipton Tea introduced their Golden Tea Leaf line of kitchenware. The two lines were identical except for the different decorative motifs.

Today collectors search for the Lipton Golden Tea Leaves by David Douglas, as a "go-along" or "cross-over" for Autumn Leaf. These Lipton pieces, like their Jewel counterpart, are becoming expensive.

An original advertisement for these Golden Tea Leaf pieces reads

"Something Old...And Something New. Tea leaves like those from the legendary garden of the ancient orient adorn this streamlined modern glass tea service. It's so convenient, too. Now you can brew tea for the whole family right at your table and serve it hot or iced from this graceful glass tea maker."

Lipton offered the "Tea-Maker" server for $2.00. It had a goldtone collar and cover, and was made with a cool insulated handle. It came with a golden king-size aluminum teaball for use with loose tea.

A soup maker and server was offered for $2.25, 5" high and 5-1/4" across, with a gold-tone cover and an easy-grip finial. It came complete with a matching candle warmer stand. The warmer could be used for the tea-maker, also.

For $1.00, another offer was a 22 karat gold-decorated tea canister with a gold-tone cover and an easy-grip finial, 5-1/8" high and 4-1/4" across. The Hurricane lamp set sold for $3.50.

These pieces could be ordered from Lipton Tea for the price and a box-top from Lipton tea bags or a label from their instant tea. A brochure was included with a box of Lipton Tea; no date appears on this brochure.

One of the problems collector's face with these pieces is that the Bakelite handles were not solidly attached to the pieces, resulting in the 22 karat gold decoration being scratched or worn off. Many of these pieces are found in such conditions.

193

CHAPTER 16
SEWING, LAUNDRY, & CLEANING

Every week, American housewives, grandmothers, single women, and even bachelors are faced with some of the most difficult chores of a household. The task begins when the laundry piles high in the basket and the accumulated dust begins to appear on the mantel and furniture, and the pet hairs begin to show on the carpet. Sewing is done when the ashtray holds more odd buttons than cigarette butts and dress shirts seems to be missing more buttons than they should.

We seem to no longer take the advice of a Jewel customer from Minnesota. She suggested, "When sewing the buttons of the children's clothes use dental floss and they will stay on for the life of the garment." This customer made $1 when she sent her helpful hint to Mary Dunbar in 1946.

For many American these chores are still done just like mother instructed us. Some of us allow weeks to slip away before we undertake such tasks. But still they remain the same, as they have for generations.

When Jewel appeared on the scene, and its coffee-brown trucks began to park along the curb in front of American homes, many housewives were thrilled. They were excited not just with the products that helped feed their families, the china that graced their tables, and the furniture that decorated their homes. They were also excited about the products that assisted them in maintaining a proper and clean home, easing their task of ironing and simplifying the responsibility of laundry.

Sewing

Jewel thimbles are highly sought after by collectors. A private thimble collector has a Jewel thimble in cream-color with a blue band and the wording "Jewel Tea Co., Inc." Another thimble dates to World War II and is cream-color with red, white, and blue banding and the same wording. This one was popular in California. The two thimbles are made of a plastic material.

A third Jewel thimble is made of a soft metal with a blue band, also with the wording "Jewel Tea Co., Inc." Recently, the same thimble collector discovered a sterling silver thimble with this wording. I understand that there is additional wording on the two metal thimbles.

I have been told of a buttonhook that is marked Jewel Tea Co. Both thimbles and buttonhooks are small, and will take some time to find.

Recently, I had the opportunity to see a metal darning disc that has a paper insert on top saying: "Don't Say Darn Over Baking Failures / say JEWEL to Your Neighborhood Dealer." This darning disc is in a private collection.

A Jewel housewife in 1938 could also take advantage of the "Ruth Rutledge" patterns that were offered.

JEWEL PATTERN SERVICE By Ruth Rutledge
SCHOOL DAYS

The youngsters are sure to need a new dress or two to start out the school year. These are easy-to-make patterns and each one can be varied enough so that two or three dresses may be made from the same pattern. There's real economy in making school clothes yourself and in finding a good pattern that can be used several times.

When ordering patterns from the Fashion Magazine be sure to specify Jewel Patterns

Pattern 3055
sizes 12 to 20

2766

Pattern 2766
sizes 2 to 8

2583

Pattern 2583
sizes 6 to 12

B-3043

Pattern B-3043
sizes 11 to 19

ORDER BLANK FOR THE JEWEL PATTERNS
Patterns 10c each. Send stamps or coin (coin preferred).
JEWEL PATTERN SERVICE, 160 Fifth Ave., New York City.
Enclosed find $..............................
Please send me the Ruth Rutledge Patterns listed below:
Pattern Nos. and Sizes: ....
Name ....
Number and Street........................
City.........................State..........

SEND ME JEWEL FASHION MAGAZINE
I am enclosing 10c for the ☐ Fashion Magazine or ☐ Sewing Manual.
Name...
Number and Street........................
City.........................State..........

Ruth Rutledge patterns, with the original order blank.

Every housewife had a good variety of needles. This oval cardboard container held a selection of assorted Jewel Food Stores needles and a needle threader. *Zollinger Collection.*

During the 1940s, a woman interested in sewing would have been thrilled with the practical ideas offered in the fall and winter issue of FASHION. To get the copy of FASHION, she had to send 25¢ in coin with her name and address to The Jewel News Pattern Bureau, 530 South Wells, Chicago, Illinois.

Every seamstress owned a good pair of shears. For sewing new dresses and aprons and for repairing children's clothing, a good pair of shears was required. In April 1926, item number C-6025 was introduced: the Jewel Shears,

priced at $.50. This pair of strong, sharp, 7-inch steel shears have a good cutting edge which will stay sharp, and fine tapered points. They would cut thin or heavy materials equally well and are a very convenient size.

"The Princess" sewing basket appeared in various editions of The Jewel News, and was made with the same care as the Deluxe Hamper. It was truly the aristocrat of all sewing baskets. Quality, color and utility were artfully combined to produce a beauty of a basket.

The sewing basket would later appear in numerous Jewel Home Shopping Catalogs. It had three major advantages.

First, the sewing basket was attractive as well as useful. At that time two colors were offered: Heaven Blue or Flamingo Pink. The delicate pastel colors formed a perfect background for the bright floral decoration on the lids. The coil weave of the wicker added to its charm. Later the Princess Sewing Basket would be offered in Nile Green and Jonquil Yellow,

Second, the sewing basket was well-made. Extra heavy fiber wicker formed the sides, and both the lid and bottom were constructed of warp and crack-proof masonite. A small chrome finial was located in the center of the lid. Only the finest chip-proof enamel was used to finish the wicker.

Third, the basket was convenient to use. A spool rack for nine spools of thread was built into the basket, near the top where it was easily reached. Thread was not included. It was roomy and anyone would be amazed at how much sewing material it held. It measured 11 inches wide x 6 inches deep. It was listed as Item No. 6F60 and sold for $3.89.

Jewel Shears

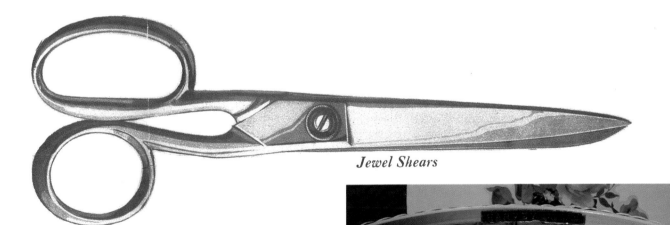

The sewing basket's spool rack, within easy reach. A paper label inside reads: "HARVEY BARRINGTON, ILL PATENT APP. FOR." Also watch for labels reading: "Princess Algonquin—Illinois REG. U.S. PAT. OFF. 2536590 - 2574371." These two numbers place the design of the basket approximately between 1951 and 1952, though this is not necessarily the date of manufacture. Patent dates and dates of manufacture may vary by several years in some cases.

195

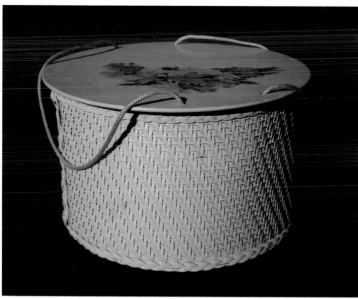

During the 1950s the selection of colors were "Heaven Blue and Flamingo Pink. *Author's Collection.*

Later the Princess Sewing Basket would be offered in Nile Green and Jonquil Yellow. The finial would be removed sometime during this period, to be replaced with matching cording.

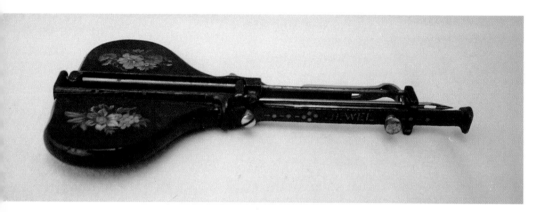

The 4-1/2" x 9-1/4" Jewel Fabric Tufting Machine. Designed to meet the wishes of ladies who desire a practical means of beautifying their homes with work from their own hands. With the tufting machine, Turkish rugs, ottomans, cushions, and lap robes could be made easily and cheaply. This machine was found in the original carton with directions for use. Manufactured by "The Oriental Pattern Co., Chicago, Illinois." At present, it is unknown if this tufting machine was ever offered by the Jewel Tea Co. *Hamilton Collection.*

Hampers and Wastebaskets

Hampers and waste baskets from the mid-40s to the mid-to-late 60s were manufactured by the Harvey Hamper Company in Barrington, Illinois. The plant later moved to Cary, Illinois. It closed in the early 1970s when Mr. Harvey died.

The Graybar Electric Sewing Machine

The Graybar sewing machine.

In the spring and summer of 1952, when the Jewel salesman arrived at the front door, he delivered a catalog offering the American housewife the Graybar Electric Sewing Machine. Listed as item number X-4G87, it sold for $73.95.

The machine required a minimum of storage space and was ideal for limited space. When the case was closed it measured about 15-1/2" long x 8-1/2" wide x 12-1/2" high and could be carried from room to room with ease. It traveled smartly in its case of durable synthetic leather: grained maroon finish accented with contrasting ivory handle and trim. The hardware was of heavy, solid brass.

Appearing with the Graybar machine was a Princess Sewing Basket.

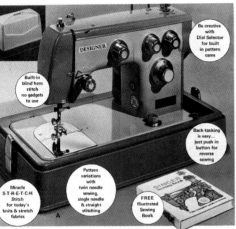
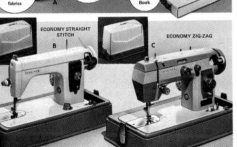

SEWING IS FUN!

(A) Super Deluxe Zig-Zag Sewing Machine. The modern machine for the modern woman who expects just a little bit more in sewing versatility. Dial a basic straight stitch or zig-zag or one of the different design stitches to create your own masterpiece. Equipped to do twin needle sewing, automatic buttonholing, automatic blind stitching...plus, miracle stretch stitch sewing for double knit materials. There's also a handy built-in light to illuminate the sewing area. Jam proof, too! High-impact plastic carrying case. FREE...Singer sewing book included. All your questions answered.
*413-0100 K5†. Built-in AC-DC motor............149.95

(B) Deluxe Economy Model Sewing Machine...straight stitch machine with built-in sewing light over work area; window dial stitch length and built-in darner. Sews over pins and needles. Automatic bobbin winder, push button forward; reverse sewing. Comes complete with extra needles, bobbins, oil, instruction book. High-impact plastic carrying case. Two-tone finish.
*413-0076 X5. 110-120 v., AC-DC.....................79.95

(C) Deluxe Economy Zig-Zag Sewing Machine. Equipped to do straight sewing, monogramming, embroidering, overcasting, appliques, button holes, blind hem and all without attachments. Built-in sew light over work area. Window dial zig-zag with control. Sews both forward and reverse. Comes complete with extra needles, bobbins, oil, instruction book and more! High-impact plastic carrying case. Sew and Save!
*413-0084 X5. 110-120 v., AC-DC.....................99.95

(D) Lightweight Zig-Zag Sewing Machine...for the woman on-the-go. Imagine only 19 pounds and still equipped to do automatic buttonholing, twin needle sewing, darning, blind stitching, sewing over pins and needles plus monogramming, all without attachments. A real treasure. Full size head with built-in sewing light over work area. High-impact plastic carrying case.
*413-0092 K5†. 110-120 v., AC-DC.................129.95

(E) Singer Sewing Book gives step-by-step instructions on how to sew dresses, suits, coats, draperies, etc.
*413-0027. Illustrated Sewing Book.....................7.95

(F) Portable Sewing Table — 18" x 40" top is of extra sturdy construction with cutout for all size portable sewing machines and when flat, this table is the proper height for a typewriter. Table top is made of Pionite woodgrain high pressure plastic laminate to resist burns and scratches. Brown baked enamel steel legs and tray.
*413-0118 X5. Use as a serving table, too!.........19.95

*No Postage Charge...item delivered by Area Manager
†Available through Jewel's Easy Payment Plan
or cash (see page 68F)

This advertisement is from the Spring and Summer 1972 Jewel In Home Shopping Service. Jewel made sewing fun!

Laundry

The Zippo Clothes Line plastic case.

In 1946, Jewel offered the Zippo Clothes Line plastic case, which held twelve feet of cotton line for light laundry and lingerie. When not in use, the clothesline wound up in the case, completely out of the way, on an easy-winding reel. The plastic case could be hung in the bathroom or kitchen on one of the two screws provided. The other end was fasten to the opposite wall for the end of the clothesline. You could use less than the full twelve feet of line by locking the line over a small plastic wedge on the Zippo case. The Zippo Clothes Line No. 47035 came in assorted colors and was available from the friendly Jewel Man.

1926 Laundry

In 1926, The Jewel Lady suggested "summer laundering with Soap Flakes. Some of your most delicate summery things, your organdie, fine white silk hose, dainty mull, georgette or silk lingerie, or your brightly colored cretonne or linen breakfast sets, are too delicately colored to submit to the regular laundry suds. You want to 'do' them yourself with utmost caution."

Jewel also suggested that a box of Jewel's Soap Flakes be kept in the bathroom; when you remove your fine silk hose at night, rinse them out at once in the wash basin, thereby removing all perspiration.

The New Improved GRANO. Marvelous for fresh clean clothes, sparkling dishes and general cleaning. Net weight 2-1/2 lbs. *Byerly Collection.*

This promotional advertisement for GRANO granulate soap taken in the Jewel test kitchen in Barrington, Illinois. GRANO was safe for fine clothing, linens, and china. *Barrington Archives.*

Jewel customers had their choice of many different laundry products. Among them were Meteor, Won, and Daintiflakes. The following is advertising copy for these brands:

METEOR SOAP FLAKES were fine soap flakes for general laundry, fine fabrics, dishes, and household cleaning. Clothes wash clean in faster time when laundered in Meteor.

WON was a washing sensation that is WONderful for laundry because WON makes suds in the hardest water, leaves no cloudy hard-water film to dull her white and colored clothes.

DAINTIFLAKES was a mild gentle soap flake used for the finest washable fabrics.

This photograph was used in a Jewel promotional advertisement for DAINTIFLAKES, taken in the Jewel Test Kitchen in Barrington, Illinois. *Barrington Archives.*

In 1929, a Jewel customer would find that all Jewel Laundry Products were strictly first quality items — as are all groceries and premiums bearing the Jewel trademark.

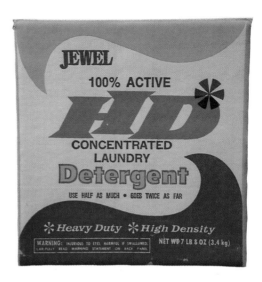

Two different packaging of Pure Gloss Starch, which irons to a satin smoothness. The net weight of each package was 3 pounds 8 ounces. On the package at right, note the Victory Package seal, which places it in the 1942-1945 era. *Hedges Collection.*

Jewel 100% Active HD Concentrated Laundry Detergent, circa 1970. The net weight was 7 lbs. 8 oz. This HD symbol appears on a wallet shown in the "For Men Only" Chapter. *Byerly Collection.*

In the early 1940s, $1.45 would buy an ironing board pad and cover that gave housewives a springy cushion to make ironing easier. The Jewel pad and cover fit any board, and was nonflammable, sterilized, deodorized, and mothproof. The Jewel ironing pad and cover were easy to put on and take off. In 1941 they were listed as item number 780.

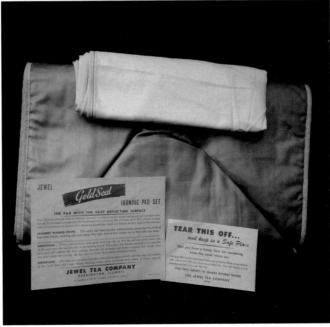

Under the wrapper we find original instructions enclosed for the pad with the heat reflecting surface. Jewel Tea Company Barrington, Illinois. *Hamilton Collection.*

A late version of a Jewel Deluxe Ironing Pad and Cover Set. *Hamilton Collection.*

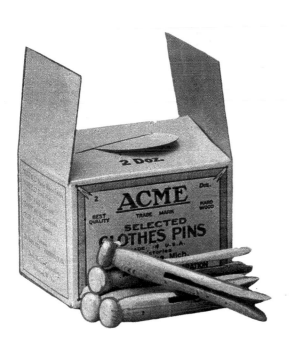

No Woman Likes to Wash Her Clothes Over

Wooden soldiers to guard your clothes-line! When clothes are "hung out," they are meant to hang, and not fall on the ground. Sturdy, well-shaped clothes pins do the trick. That is what these will do. Made of smooth hardwood, with rounded edges. Will not splinter and tear clothes, nor will they stain them. They are 4 inches long, and are packed two dozen in a box. They are a household utility which are always in demand. Price 10c. Our Item No. S-1194.

In 1927, this original advertisement and its captions appeared in The Jewel News.

Iron with "Meteor" Speed

A friend in need! Ironing day need not be dreaded when you have a good electric iron to take out the wrinkles. The "Meteor," made by the well-known Manning Bowman Co., is the last thing in efficiency. Voltage, 110, so it can be used on alternating or direct current. It is heavily nickel plated, weighs six pounds, four ounces, and has a special construction in the element, which is encased in cement. It is well balanced, with a tip-up stand. The plug fits into a special locking device, which prevents slipping. The 6-ft. cord has coiled wire at one end, to prevent wearing when iron is tipped. Price $4.45. Our Item No. 763.

This original advertisement and caption appeared in a 1927 Jewel News.

Mary Dunbar's automatic electric dry iron, item number 4G331, in its original box. The drawing of Mary Dunbar was a popular logo during the 1950s and was a mark of quality. (See Appendix 4.) *Private Collection*.

In 1960, the name of Mary Dunbar on irons stood for quality you could rely on! Each one had been made with extra care to give the customer far better service. Any customers who read the Mary Dunbar Guarantee would understand. The Mary Dunbar Dry Iron, shown here, had an automatic fabric dial which gave correct heat for all fabrics. Positively controlled temperature. *Blow Collection*.

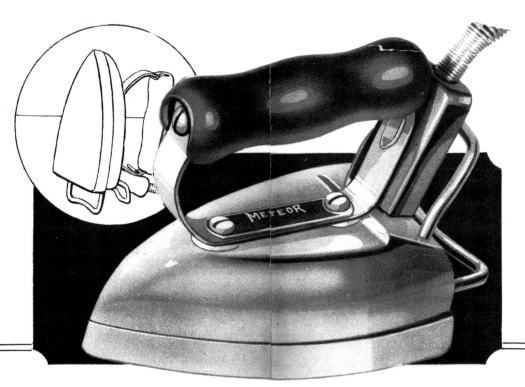

MANNING-BOWMAN ELECTRIC IRON

We are justly proud of this item! For here we offer to you an outstanding value—a 6 lb. electric iron—6⅝ inches long, beautifully nickeled, with cool comfortable handle. The makers—Manning, Bowman & Co.—need no introduction to you, as manufacturers of only the highest quality merchandise. This iron has an absolutely guaranteed heating element. The electric wires are embedded in cement, and are consequently protected from jar and breakage. It is of the tilt type, and is perfectly balanced. The cord is strong and well covered. The cool plug has a locking device which holds it firmly on the iron and prevents loosening the electric connecting posts. A coiled spring protects the cord from wear and tear just above the plug. Our Home Service Division conducted a series of tests on various irons, covering a period of months of use. With their unqualified recommendation of this iron, we know that we are offering you an outstanding value. Remember! This iron is absolutely guaranteed. 110 volts—may be used on alternating or direct current. Price $4.45 (in P. S. C. or Cash). Our Item No. 763.

This original advertisement and captions appeared in a 1927 Jewel News.

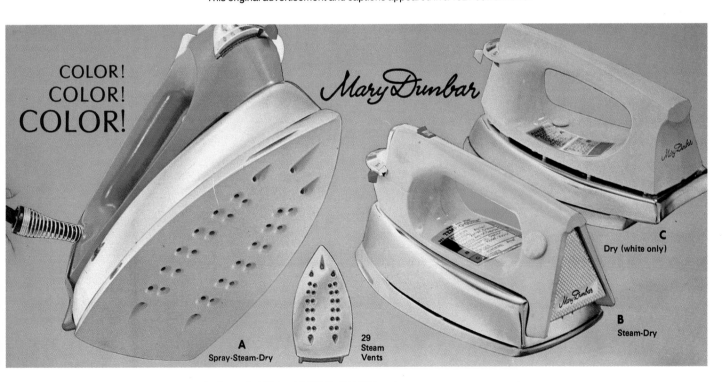

In the early 1970s, JEWEL'S BEST Mary Dunbar Irons could be chosen in either A, B or C models. The quality Mary Dunbar Iron was precision crafted for dependable performance! Fingertip temperature control with the easy-to-read ironing temperature guide. Full one year guarantee.

Cleaning

Jewel provided so many cleaning products and items for the housewife to use in cleaning her home that it is impossible to list or photograph them all. No matter how large or small the task may have been, Jewel could provide. Simply ask your Jewel route salesman.

Jewel introduced two new items that the friendly Jewel man started carrying in his basket in September 1946: Duo-Dustin Sheets and Bruce Floor Cleaner™. Some customers had an "advance" opportunity to find out what wonders these two new products performed when they purchased both of them. The Duo-Dustin Sheets—specially treated paper that picked up dust like a magnet—came in a handy roll. Dampened, Duo-Dustin Sheets even cleaned and polished. Bruce Floor Cleaner™ was a scientific cleaner for wood and linoleum floors. These products were both carried in the Jewel man's basket.

PAINT N' WALL CLEANER was a product for all painted, washable surfaces, and made everything ship shape for a clean home. Net weight is 3 pounds, 6 ounces. *Hedges Collection.*

Jewel's CEDAR FRESH MOTH CRYSTALS kill moths, eggs, larvae, and mildew, and were perfect for vacuum cleaner use. *Byerly Collection.*

For cleaning, dusting, and polishing, this dusting paper was convenient, sanitary, and labor-saving. Distributed by Jewel Tea Co., Inc. Jewel Park, Barrington, IL. The tube of dusting paper rolls from the package so that sheets could be torn off by a metal edge on packaging. The Mary Dunbar seal of approval appears on the package. It is listed in a 1942 grocery price list in the Barrington Archives. *Hedges Collection.*

A 1928 edition of The Jewel News told readers that a colorful 3-lbs. container of Jewel Cleanser was a household necessity for scouring. This exceptional cleanser can bears a Jewel logo and the wording "JEWEL CLEANSER." The illustration appearing on the can shows a kitchen sink with the Waterless Cooker sitting on it. The 1928 promotional advertisement pointed out that a can was always handy by the kitchen sink, and in the bathroom could be used to keep your enamelware spotless. Jewel Cleaner sold for 28¢.

This piece of flat metal, which will be used to make a container for the cleanser, has not yet been formed into a can. *Byerly Collection.*

From the early 1930s, Jewel New Cleanser: "No Grit - No Scratch - No Stain." Distributed by Jewel Tea Co., Jewel Park Barrington, Il. *Byerly Collection.*

A mid-1950s Jewel Rug and Carpet Shampooer with original carton and script Jewel logo. The shampooer was approved by Mary Dunbar for brightening rugs and carpets made of rayon, cotton/nylon, and wool blends. It was amazingly easy to use: just apply, let it dry, and vacuum. It offers four-way cleaning action, 30% more tank capacity, an easy-to-fill leak-proof tank, and an anodized aluminum handle. It leaves rugs mildew-proof and odor-free. In 1966-1967 the shampooer sold for $5.95, with FREE Jewel Shampoo. *Vogel Collection*

Jewel Rug Shampoo cleaned and brighten a 10' x 14' rug. *Schwartz Collection.*

Jetco (Jewel Tea Company) 15 oz. Spray Fabric Finish restores a "like-new" finish. *Schwartz Collection.*

It makes your dishes smile! 16 fl oz. of Jewel Suds for Happy Dishes. Schwartz Collection.

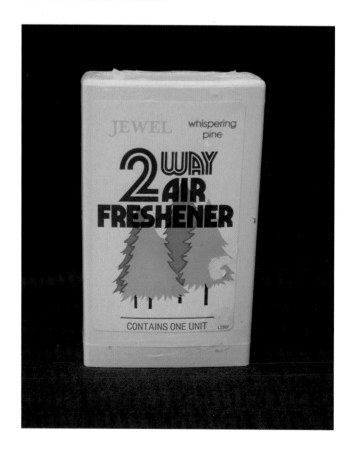

It makes glass look like new. Jewel Mr. Glass in a 12 oz. plastic bottle. *Schwartz Collection.*

Whispering Pine Jewel 2-Way Air Freshener. *Schwartz Collection.*

7 fl oz. of Jewel Furniture Cleaner and Wax Remover. *Schwartz Collection.*

16.6 oz of Jewel Odor Kil. *Schwartz Collection.*

8 fl. oz. of Jewel Moisturizing Furniture Lotion. *Schwartz Collection.*

14 oz. of Jewel Power Spray Oven Cleaner could be used for either gas or electric ovens. *Schwartz Collection.*

Sterling Carpet Sweeper

All metal construction, with disc wheels, assures that the "Sterling" Carpet Sweeper is well made and easy to keep clean. It runs silently and with little effort. The handle is held in vertical position when not in use. Will not mar furniture because of the rubber bumpers and tires. Will clean any surface easily. Price $3.95. Our Item No. 766.

This new lemon-fragrance giant sudsing Glorex Cleanser polishes and cleans porcelain sinks, bathrubs, ranges, and enamel. It dissolves dirt with sudsing action, and cuts grease faster on pots and pans. It removes spots from floors and painted surfaces. Net weight 21 ounces; distributed by Jewel Tea Co., Inc. Jewel Park Barrington, Illinois. *Eisnaugle Collection.*

In 1926 this original advertisement and caption for the Sterling Carpet Sweeper appeared in The Jewel News.

The 1903-1915 JEWEL Bissel Sweeper. *Hedges Collection.*

The underside of the Bissel Sweeper provides a listing of "Important Directions," U.S. patent dates, and "Operations Directions." *Hedges Collection.*

In the early 1970s, Jewel offered two vaccuum cleaners: Vaccuum (A), the Mary Dunbar Cordaway Vacuum Cleaner, had a powerful 'fanjet' 1-1/2 h.p. motor, for thorough cleaning in jet-speed time! Fingertip power selector turns suction up or down to match the cleaning job. Had a protective vinyl bumper and many other features. Vacuumn (B), the Mary Dunbar Lightweight 2-in-1 Vacuum, had powerful suction that really cleaned. The adjustable brush cleaned bare floors. Hand Vac gives the same powerful suction to deep clean furniture, drapes, and the family car.

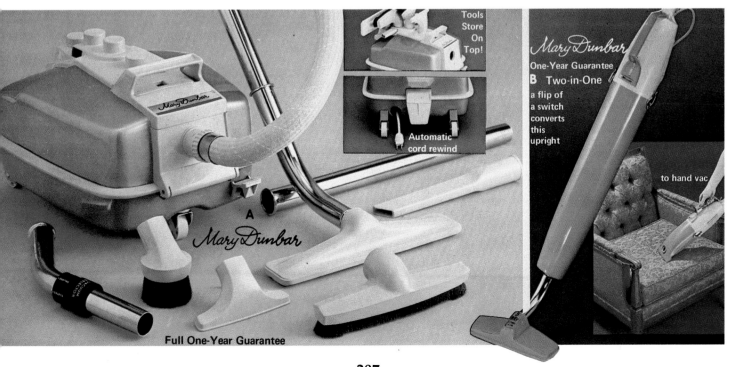

The Bissell™ Carpet Sweeper with the name Jewel on it was sold during 1959. With its all-steel construction, this sweeper adjusted to the depth of the rug. Offered only in green. *Randall Collection.*

A 27" x 54" Jewel ALL WOOL Pile Rug. *Hedges Collection.*

Did Jewel offer a broom? Yes, they did! A private collector has one, which was purchased in the early to mid-1940s by the owner's mother. The paper work and a Jewel label (reading "Distributed by Jewel") are the only indications this was purchased from Jewel—for 28¢! A section of the label is missing.

The most striking design in Autumn Leaf ever to appear (other than the Hall China) was custom-designed linoleum, installed in an Illinois home that incorporated the motif. The linoleum came in 22" squares, the center of which was identical to the round hot pad. No known photograph of the linoleum exists today. Towards the end of 1937, Jewel customers began sending the Barrington Headquarters photographs of home-made and home-decorated items incorporating the famous pattern, which they were using to decorate their homes. Jewel advised their salespeople not to use the pattern outside the organization, since Autumn Leaf was an exclusive pattern belonging to the Jewel Company.

The reverse side shows the "JEWEL" label with instructions for proper care. "Keep rug clean by using a vacuum cleaner or carpet sweep. Do not shake. Keep back of rug clean and mend any broken stitches in binding immediately." Dist. by Jewel Tea Co., Jewel Park, Barrington, Ill. *Hedges Collection.*

Jewel Homemakers' Institute Kitchen staff members had their share of sewing, laundering, and cleaning, other than the thorough testing of Jewel products and premiums. Everything had to be cleaned and returned to its proper place at the end of a working day. Mrs. Julia J. Goddard, Field Representative for Mary Dunbar, shown here, is checking how well a cleaning product works on ladies' hose. The photograph is dated from the early 1940s. *Barrington Archives.*

The daily process of laundering and ironing was undertaken by an unknown kitchen staff member in this 1950s photograph. Note that on the back kitchen wall hangs a Hall Autumn Leaf clock. *Barrington Archives.*

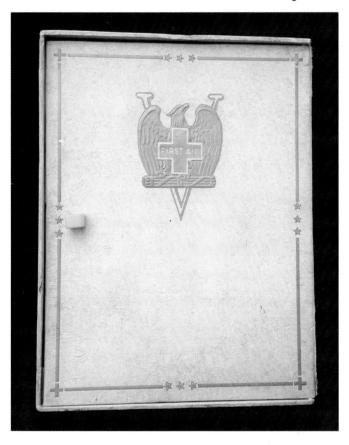

This first aid wall cabinet, No. 375, was "Packed Specially for Jewel Tea Co., Inc. Jewel Park Barrington, Ill." The cabinet contained essential first aid materials. *Hamilton Collection.*

The inside door of the first aid wall cabinet, reading "FIRST AID HELPS — and How to Use Them." The "Packed Specially" label appears below the instructions. *Hamilton Collection.*

CHAPTER 17
FOR MEN ONLY

Whether you were a grandfather, father, son, or Jewel salesman, Jewel provided numerous items useful in a man's world. It is impossible to show every item offered in the men's general gift line, men's toiletry line, men's clothing line, and the great many Jewel salesmen's awards. Various awards are covered in different sections of this publication. It is my intention in this chapter to convey the idea that Jewel did not only provided products, china, and fine linens for the lady of the house, but also provided interesting articles for the men.

The Bread-winner

In a 1938 publication titled "For Men Only," Jewel salesmen said to the head of each Jewel household, "As a bread-winner, you are the one who makes my job possible, and I want to thank you for the orders your wife gives me. These orders are not only appreciated, but respected and valued. I shall continue to give your family more for the money you spend with Jewel than you can get elsewhere."

Jewel pointed out that they seldom saw the men, and rarely had the chance to explain just why Jewel gave their wives their money's worth in good quality groceries and useful household articles.

Jewel explained that they had four ways of saving in order to give their customers valuable premiums at no extra cash outlay. First, Jewel's nation-wide business permitted them to buy in immense quantities from original sources; second, they skipped the jobber and wholesaler to sell directly to the consumer; third, Jewel did a cash business; and fourth, Jewel spent no large sums for general advertising.

I would like to point out here that the only known outside advertising was to appear in an issue of "Life" magazine on January 13, 1941. This happened four years after the appearance of the "FOR MEN ONLY" article.

The Life magazine in which Jewel placed their only outside advertisement, on January 13, 1941. *Author's Collection.*

A LETTER TO CUSTOMERS, FROM THE JEWEL MAN (1946)

As you well know, someone must pay for all advertising. Premiums were Jewel's form of advertising, and although there customers paid for this advertising, they got something useful, permanent, and attractive for this expense.

Jewel's advertising benefit came from satisfied customers who tell their friends how much they enjoyed the premiums they got by trading with Jewel. Jewel don't claim to give something for nothing. There customers pay for what they get — but in buying from Jewel, the housewife gets more than when she trades with others.

The 3,664 heads of families employed by Jewel in 42 states appreciate the orders that make possible their jobs. Thousands of workers in other industries — transportation, paper, steel, rubber, soap, agriculture, and others — likewise benefit by your wife's purchases from Jewel.

signed, THE JEWEL MAN.

The Dear Mrs. Brown advertisement from Life magazine. This advertisement also appeared on the back page of The Jewel News Premium Catalog of 1941. *Byerly Collection.*

There are numerous products for men that bear the famous Jewel name. In addition to the Jewel items offered strictly for the man of the house, there are many salesmen's awards which are highly sought after by collectors of Jewel memorabilia. I have tried to included as many items "For Men Only" in this chapter as possible, but there are so many items in the secondary market today that it is almost impossible to cover every item. I have covered only those items made available to me.

Recently, a collector wrote to me about their recent acquisition of a 1952 Jewel price guide, effective as of July 28, 1952 in branch and route stocks only. Upon close examination of this guide, they noticed a listing for No. X-4G103, which was a Jewel Radio (Table Top) in walnut finish, priced at $19.95. This same radio was also available in white. This radio was "Made by the Jewel Radio Corporation of Long Island City, New York." The ecstatic collector realized that they already had one in their home, dated 1947.

The 1952 price guide also listed numerous power tools, sewing machines, washers, sweepers, and other radios.

A 1950-1960 Jewel Radio, Model 5057U, manufactured by the Jewel Radio Corp., from Long Island City 1, NY. On the back appears "U.S. Pat. No. 2282759." This radio is in working condition. *Hamilton Collection.*

In December 1938, this was the perfect gift for Father: an attractive, efficient, modern "Royal Jewel Alarm Clock" that was easy to read and always accurate. Jewel listed the clock as Item No. 853 and sold it for $3.35. The clock is marked "Pat' USA 1568431, 1789146, 1848520 MADE IN USA." These numbers vary by several years between 1926-1933. *Hamilton Collection.*

Item number X-4G103, a Jewel tabletop radio from the 1952 price guide. *Hamilton Collection.*

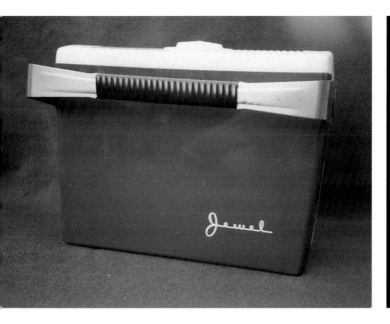 

A portable Jewel radio. The handle could be moved into a portion position for easy carrying or moved into a position that served as a stand. Note the scripted "Jewel" logo popular during l950s and 1960s. This radio never appeared in a Jewel publication and is not believed to be part of the famous Jewel Tea Co. *Private Collection.*

This Jewel radio has a walnut finish case and sold for $19.95. This appeared with an ivory-finished version in the 1952 Jewel catalog. 9-1/2" x 6" x 4-3/4" deep. The cabinet was color-molded throughout of pure Bakelite or Urea plastic. Note the "Jewel" logo. *Hamilton Collection.*

The Jewel Radio in ivory-finish case from the 1952 Jewel catalog, 9-1/2" x 6" x 4-3/4" deep. This version sold for $21.95.

It is often said that men begin their first beauty treatments with the first shave. The creamy lather of shaving soap not only helps to make a smooth shave, but penetrates to keep skin clean and clear. Neck muscles and consequently the skin stay firm with the exercise received every time the chin is raised or lowered as the razor moves briskly along. When after shave lotion is applied to the skin a fresh, tingling sensation is felt.

If a customer was at a loss for an appropriate gift in 1946, Jewel promoted the Spruce Shaving Set. The set consisted of lotion and soap with a forest-fresh fragrance that was light but bracing. Jewel believed this produced would appeal to the average man.

In 1946 Jewel offered three shaving necessities packed in a luxury Norwood gift box for men, just in time for Father's Day on June 16. The box held Norwood Liquid Shave Cream, After Shave Lotion, and After Shave Talc. The shave cream was a brushless, and gave a smooth shave. The talc was flesh-tinted and soothed irritated skin. The lotion had a definite masculine scent. This Father's Day gift set sold for $1.80.

HOUSEHOLD HAMMER

Made just right for a housewife. Good steel head, nickel plated, wedged securely into the strong handle. Just the handy tool you've wanted for hanging pictures, putting up nails in the pantry, opening boxes, or laying matting. It also has a well designed tack lifter feature. Price 85c (in P. S. C. or Cash). Our Item No. C-6024.

In this original 1926 advertisement for the Household Hammer, Jewel suggests that it is just the right tool for a housewife. Could it possibly be that a housewife had other ideas about who would be using this hammer?

HARD RUBBER COMB

A very good comb of black, hard rubber. It has both coarse and fine teeth and is both pliable and strong. Light, easy to handle and yet strong enough to carefully dress the heaviest hair. Price 25c (in P. S. C. or Cash). Our Item No. S-1174.

This advertisement for the hard rubber comb appeared in 1926.

This full Jewel Beam bottle truck is one of the commemorative items made for Jewel's 75th Anniversary celebration in 1974. The stand can also be found in red. *Author's Collection.*

In 1984, in commemoration of the Jewel Food Stores' 85th Anniversary, the Jim Beam Jewel Tea Grocer bottle was produced. *Byerly Collection.*

In 1978 an offer was published that there would be one more production run of the Jewel Tea Belt Buckle, which shows Jewel trucks. The belt was to be worn with pride, to let the world know that you, as a salesman, were a part of the Jewel Home Shopper team. *Busch Collection.*

In 1981 the "Father's Day" brown mug was filled with the original coffee milk candy. The mug could be purchased only through a Jewel route salesperson. This mug may well have been the last collectible from Jewel, as The Jewel Home Shopping Service closed their doors on May 21, 1981. *Author's Collection.*

Double-edged Blue Steel Velvet Touch razor blades were offered by Jewel in packages of 5. *Byerly Collection.*

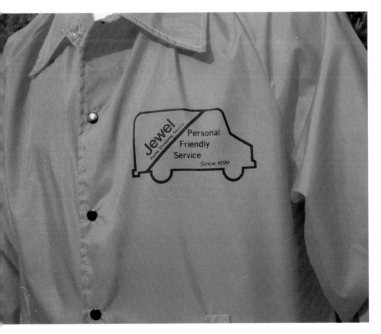

The windbreaker may have been offered to customers as well as to route salesmen. The Jewel logo appears on the front with the text "Personal Friendly Service Since 1899. Jewel Home Shopping Service." *Byerly Collection.*

Jewel offered various pocket knives for sale and as awards. In 1938 Jewel asked their salesmen "What Sales Tool Are Needed To Cut Jewel A Bigger Share Of the 1938 Consumer Dollars"—and this was the answer. This pocketknife held an assortment of blades, files, openers, corkscrews and shears. It was called a Super Multi Purpose Knife. "J.T.'s General Store" appears on the side. The knife came with special packaging. *Byerly Collection.*

The Magic Knife

—From The Jewel News (1938), based on a speech given by Jewel business counsellor and director Robert R. Updegarff at the 1938 Jewel branch managers convention.

Every business that succeeds solves some problem. Mrs. Brown's pocket-book was flatter in 1938. So Jewel's problem for 1938 was helping Mrs. Brown get along with less money. Thousands of Mrs. Browns, of course, have just as much or more money to spend this year as last year. But even many of these housewives are spending their money more carefully. *Jewel's problem for 1938 is helping Mrs. Brown get along with less money.*

In 1938 Jewel salesmen had all sorts of tools to get Mrs. Brown's dollars. Their selling tools were like the gadgets on a fine pocketknife. Their selling tools included a hook to dig out prejudices, saws for cutting off sales resistance, punches for putting holes in arguments, and cork screws for uncorking new ideas.

Those tools they had at their command were almost unlimited. Each one was designed to be used when it was needed to enter Mrs. Brown's pocketbook.

All those selling gadgets were fine — at times they might have become necessary and important. But Jewel's main job was helping Mrs. Brown get along with less money, and they relied on the two main cutting blades of the knife.

Jewel had to use the big blade — ECONOMY—and the small blades — PREMIUMS. Those two ideas was believed to solve Jewel's 1938 problem. Convincing Mrs. Brown that the money she spends with Jewel was the most wisely spent money in the world.

Mrs. Brown was in the market for economy, and they must give it to her. There were two ways to use the big blade of Jewel's knife, two ways to sell Jewel economy: (1) sell the economy of the products themselves — how much farther they go, how their tested quality avoids cooking failures and spoilage; (2) sell economical uses of Jewel products — money-saving meals built around macaroni and rice, money-saving pie crusts and money-saving home shampoos. Selling the qualities of Jewel quality made for economy.

Jewel felt the small knife blade, premium selling, cut well in good or bad times. For its 'advertising expenditures' in 1937, Jewel gave away to its customers the sum of $2,649,793 in profit sharing credits. That figure was proof of Jewel economy, and was quoted to customers as a sales tool. Premiums made it easy for Mrs. Brown to get along with less money.

In 1938 Jewel felt that their greatest selling weakness was their attitude toward the first delivery sellback (or repeat business). They wanted to Jewelize America in 1938, and they had to substitute guts for gratitude at the first call. Instead of running off thankful because an order "sticks," they felt real salesmen started selling for the future. Jewelizing the customer's habits right from the start.

In making the first sellback, Jewel regarded any order of less than a three items, including coffee, as a "short-change sellback." "Substitute guts for gratitude," they told salesmen, and cut your way into Mrs. Brown's pocketbook with the two blades of Jewel's magic selling knife — ECONOMY and PREMIUMS.

J.T.'s General Store Cooler. Easy to carry by the fiber handle; a clasp at one side keeps the cooler closed but allows for easy access. The cooler holds six cans of your favorite beverage. *Byerly Collection.*

The Barbeque Grill in its original package was offered by J.T.'s General Store. Manufactured by EHCO Mfg. Company. *Byerly Collection.*

The Jewel salesmen sold so many watches (particularly Jewel's own) that a watch repair department was established in Barrington. Consequently, whenever a customer needed a watch repaired the salesman suggested that the customer return it directly. They were reminded to be sure to insure the watch before it was returned to Barrington. Repairs were to be mailed to JEWEL HOME SHOPPING SERVICE Watch Repair Service, Jewel Park, Barrington, IL. 60010, beginning on June 1, 1969.

What man wouldn't enjoy his own J.T.'s General Store Truck and Trailer quartz clock? This metal truck/trailer reads (across the top) "J.T.'s TRUCK LOAD DETERGENT SALE," and the clock was located in the front windshield. *Byerly Collection.*

Jewel provided various salesman awards, such as the "DunDee" watch shown below. The face of this watch displays a Jewel truck. The watch is in the original packaging and with instructions. *Schwartz Collection.*

A smaller van version. The quartz clock is located in the windshield. *Byerly Collection.*

217

Jewel rings are enthusiastically sought after by collectors of Jewel memorabilia. It would be impossible to acquire every ring Jewel offered as an award. Rings with blue stones (sapphires) were award to Jewel salesmen. Here, in their original boxes, are three sapphire rings. *Schwartz Collection.*

Any salesman or man of the house would look sharp in a Jewel tie. Silhouettes of a Jewel horse and wagon appear on the tie. *Schwartz Collection.*

A gold silhouette of a Jewel horse and wagon appears on top of this ring's stone. Encircled around the stone is "Sponsor of Excellence." The box is original. Very few of these gold rings exist. *Schwartz Collection.*

A gold silhouette of a horse and wagon appears on the navy blue Jewel tie. *Schwartz Collection.*

In October of 1946, Jewel believed it would be easy to please the men on their customer's shopping lists, since they offered an assortment of Cutter Cravats from which to choose. In 1946 Cutter was one of America's foremost names in tie styling. There were many patterns to choose from. All ties were expertly tailored from fine-textured fabrics that would tie smoothly and knot gracefully. The ties were listed as item number 5407 and sold for $1.50 each.

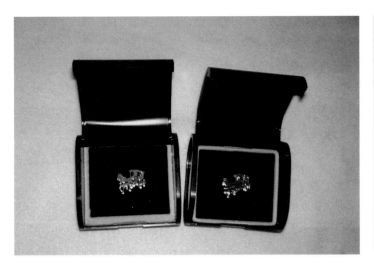

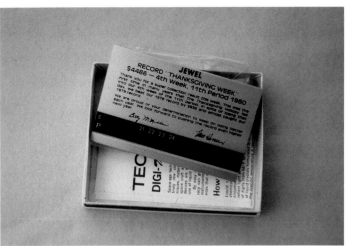

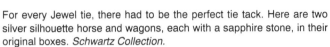

For every Jewel tie, there had to be the perfect tie tack. Here are two silver silhouette horse and wagons, each with a sapphire stone, in their original boxes. *Schwartz Collection.*

What Jewel salesman or man of the house couldn't have used this digital calculator in his home or place of business? The award reads "Jewel Record - Thanksgiving Week - $4486 - 4th Week, 11th Period 1980." The calculator is in the original box, with instructions. *Schwartz Collection.*

This miniature Jewel enamel truck could have held any tie in place. The tie tack is in the original box. *Schwartz Collection.*

The perfect Jewel key ring appears in its plastic case. An assortment of key rings is available to the collector of Jewel memorabilia. *Schwartz Collection.*

A wallet for every man. This leather wallet displays a visible symbol of a Jewel HD Detergent motto. *Schwartz Collection.*

This aluminum ice bucket would have been a perfect gift or award for any man. The ice bucket measures 8-1/2" high without bail handle and 8-1/2" in diameter. With the lid the height is 10-1/2". Marked across the front it reads: "JEWEL IN HOME SHOPPING SERVICE," the ice bucket is stamped on the bottom Made in Italy. *Author's Collection.*

The Dunbar Name

In the 1960s, Jewel frequently used the Dunbar name, mostly in clothing ranging from mens' dress shirts to seamless stretch nylons. Catalogs of that period display numerous examples of the Dunbar appeal. The "Dianne Dunbar" character was popular with women, Dan Dunbar with men, Debbie Dunbar with young girls, and Don Dunbar with boys. Baby Dunbar advertised infant's clothing. During the 1960s Dan Dunbar "Work 'n Leisure Mates" included a shirt for $3.98 and pants for $4.98.

Fleur-de-Lis Pattern Dress Shirt, shown above, was a permanent press blend of polyester and cotton. Styled with a pointed collar and long sleeves, two-button cuffs, a tapered body, and tails. This machine-wash shirt was available in small, medium, large, and extra large, and in the colors blue, burgundy, and brown. Distributed by Jewel Shopping Service., Barrington, Ill. 60010. *Zollinger Collection.*

The original DIANNE DUNBAR advertisement appeared in the Jewel Summer Specials catalog in 1966. The dress sold for $8.98 and the scarf sold for $1.98.

Dan Dunbar

WORK 'N LEISURE MATES!

- Genuine Cramerton Army cloth...rugged twill.
- 2-ply combed cotton...Sanforized, colorfast.
- Bartack reinforced at all strain points.

Top Value, Wear! Cut fuller for comfort...bend, stoop without strain! Machine wash countless times, they take it! Shirt has 2 button-thru pockets, long tail. Pants have sturdier tunnel belt loops, pressed open seams, heavy duty zipper. Pocketing and inner construction are Sanforized sailcloth.

Shirt. Neck Sizes: 14½, 15, 15½, 16, 16½, 17.
C-95B 8. State size, Tan or Gray..........................3.98

Pants. Waist Sizes: 29" (30, 32 inseam), 30" (29, 30, 32, 33), 31" (30, 32), 32 & 34" (29, 30, 31, 32, 34), 36" (29, 30, 31, 32, 33), 38" (29, 30, 31, 32), 40 & 42" (30, 32). State color: Tan or Gray.
C-95B 9. State waist, inseam; which is inseam.4.98

60 • Jewel

The original DAN DUNBAR advertisement appeared in the Jewel Home Shopping Service Spring and Summer catalog in 1966.

Baby Dunbar diapers were advertised as the nicest a customer could buy, either in a package of twelve Birdseye Diapers or a package of twelve Gauze Diapers. Other Dunbar product lines included Debbie Dunbar's finest slips or, in 1966, Dianne Dunbar's new permanent press fashions with Forrel by Celanese, in sizes proportioned to fit beautifully. For other items, see the "Children's" chapter.

It is still quite possible to find Dunbar garments or those with a Barrington label. I have been told the best location is a local used clothing store.

Shown above and below, two Jewel crew neck tee shirts. The shirt shown above displays an unusual Teapot with the Jewel van and 1980. The tee shirt below bares an illustration of a Jewel logo. *Schwartz Collection.*

Safe Driving Award

Numerous Safe Driving awards can be found. This may take some searching for. The award, shown above, was awarded for 3 years of safe driving. *Byerly Collection.*

A pewter horse and wagon appear on this clear glass. There were glasses with this design in various sizes, as well as a large brandy snifter. These pewter pieces were salesmen's awards. *Randall Collection.*

In 1933, The Jewel Tea Company commissioned Hall China to make the Newport Teapot. This was Jewel's first premium with the famous Autumn Leaf pattern. The Newport Teapot was used from 1933 to 1935, and was then retired. This collectors' item was re-introduced as an award (shown here) for Outstanding Jewel Salespeople in the 13th period of 1979. The plaque is signed "L.W. Devereaux, President." There is also an Aladdin Teapot award similiar to this Newport one. *Byerly Collection.*

Plates

This series of plates with various trucks were used for different sales campaigns during the 1980s. There are not a large supply of these nostalgic plates available.

This 14-1/2" x 10-2/4" platter is dedicated to "Charles Simpson — Presented for Sales Excellence 1984 Blanket Promotion." "J.T.'s General StoreTM*" appears above Mr. Simpson's name. In the center is the Barrington Headquarters, top left appears a 1923 Model "T" Ford, top right a 1925 Ford, bottom left a 1918 Ford Model "T" and bottom right a 1928 Ford DeLuxe Delivery. *Byerly Collection.*

A salesman award plate with an illustration of a 1925 Ford in the center. *Byerly Collection.*

J.T.'s General was waxing nostalgic during the 1980s, many sales incentive awards were a series of framed historical photographs. This photograph of Jewel salesman W.G. Donnelly was used periodically for sales campaign awards. The original background has been skillfully removed. *Byerly Collection.*

A series of four 5" diameter plates, each with a historical illustration of a Jewel truck. The original carton is 10-3/4" x 10-3/4". *Byerly Collection.*

This salesman award is engraved with a Jewel logo and "Sales Manager's Cup won by A. Dundon 1927." An illustration of this logo is also shown. The subject of Safety Awards For No Accidents has been covered in the "Jewel Salesman" chapter. *Hamilton Collection.*

In 1983, a series of nostalgic historical Jewel photographs were awarded in the Pioneer Blanket Campaign Winner. One of the series is shown here. *Byerly Collection.*

CHAPTER 18
CHILDREN

"Better Children for Our Nation; a Better Nation for Our Children."

In 1929, Leone Rutledge Carroll (Mary Dunbar) introduced her daughter Sally, shown in the small photograph here. The caption read: "Sally, Mary Dunbar's good looking daughter. It may interest you to know that the rest of the picture includes the mother, our 'Mary Dunbar', the director of Jewel Home Service, who does so much work on your problems — a practical mother, indeed. She is the head of a household much like your own."

Customer satisfaction wasn't the only concern of the numerous Mary Dunbars associated with Jewel over the years. Mary Dunbar was concerned and interested in the production and distribution of the products that were being purchased by the American housewife, for those products helped feed American children.

From the very beginning Jewel took an interest in childrearing, beginning with "The Jewel Lady" and Mary Reed Hartson.

Mary Dunbar's interest in children is evident in the short article below. The date of this article is unknown.

Eight year old Barbara Lois Leckie, from Joplin, Mo., sent Mary Dunbar her original household hint and received $1.00 for her idea, which was published in the Jewel News "IDEA EXCHANGE". Ms. Leckie wrote, "I am 8 years old and make nice doll cradles of Jewel Quick Oats boxes. I paste the open end back on and cut out a little less than half of the side of the box. This makes a nice bed for my little dolls and I can rock them in it."

Sally would appear often in photographs published in various editions of the Jewel News, sometimes with her famous mother and other time alone or with friends.

In 1938, friends Dickie and Louise loved to come to Sally's house. Pig-tailed Sally is shown offering her friends graham crackers.

Children of American families were clearly important to Jewel, evident when one looks at Jewel News covers and articles by Mary Dunbar and her associates. Her concern and care was to keep American children strong, hardy, sturdy and healthy.

Mary Dunbar calmly tolerated delay, understood confusion and inefficiency, and was patient with her staff. She observed and tested products, recipes and listened wisely when suggestions were made by her staff and management, all because Mary Dunbar cared for the customers and their children.

When the volume of mail became too large for her "Idea Exchange" column, she accepted no more correspondence until further notice. The amount of mail she received was overwhelming.

Her "Jewel News" articles were of interest to the mothers of young infants and small children. She offered advice, guidance, suggestions, directions, and warnings but was careful, cautious, solid, and observant with her advice.

During the summertime everything was at its happiest, with the children home from school, playing, or just helping mother, so Mary Dunbar offered summer advice. When the time came around for them to return to school, she helped mothers prepare lunchbox menus. Her suggestions were well-balanced lunches, not too bulky for little hands to carry, and attractively prepared. Many of her lunchbox menus were prepared from leftovers.

Holidays were important to Mary Dunbar, her staff, and Jewel management, since holidays were for children. She became interested in what Jewel could offer.

During Thanksgiving and Christmas Mary Dunbar shared her own dinner menu with readers. She felt that modern children had been cheated out of many of the old-fashioned Thanksgiving treats. While she knew that many children still had traditional treats, she recalled the days

When Jewel customers wrote to Mary Dunbar, she listened and gave advice. Mary Dunbar is shown at her desk here; the era is late 1930s. *Barrington Archives.*

when the whole family had been bundled up in leggings, warm stockings, and caps, snuggled down into a sleigh, and off they would go to spend the day with Grandmother.

Christmas was the most wonderful time of the year at Jewel. The office and kitchen of Mary Dunbar had the aroma of freshly baked sweets filling the air. She and her staff worked hard with management to give Jewel customers just a little more luxury. Children would once again become the center of attention, both with new menus and toys. Christmas at Jewel was a time when everyone became a child again, for it was magical and the Christmas catalogs were filled with everything from Christmas toys to warm winter clothing.

In December 1946, Jewel offered five Christmas tree ornaments that had been designed by an artist in Jewel's advertising division. Anyone interested in obtaining instructions for them, could write to the Advertising Division, Jewel Tea Co., Inc., Jewel Park, Barrington, Illinois.

Toys! Toys! Toys!

Jewel offered Christmas games, toys, and other items for many years. It is very difficult to identify particular items, as records are incomplete. Price lists usually consisted of listings no more specific than "000-0000 Car Game....$1.25." It would be impossible to present every toy or game Jewel ever offered. I am pleased to present those childrens items made available to me.

For children it was an even more magical time, when every "Mother Goose" character and doll came alive — when every little boy became a cowboy or a real Indian. At the same time many housewives and grandmothers purchased the year's Christmas toys from their Jewel salesmen.

Many children's dreams were built from Christmas gifts "Santa" had delivered via these salesmen. Boys became grown-ups when they received the Jewel pedal car; little girls became adult mothers with their doll, or served tea from their Jewel tea sets, or baked cakes from a fourteen-piece Jewel cake mix set which included a small cake, cookie mixes, a pan, and instructions. They became teachers when they received a series of books. Jewel allowed the children to become whatever that magical time allowed.

Whether it was Christmas, Thanksgiving, Halloween, Easter, or the 4th of July, Jewel was able to provide and Mary Dunbar was there to assist.

Shopping from a Jewel Home Shopping Service Christmas Gift Book in 1962 was a guarantee of customer satisfaction. *Byerly Collection.*

Jewel made shopping at home easy, interesting, and fun — with up-to-date and exciting merchandise they offered through their colorful catalogs, and interesting sample displays.

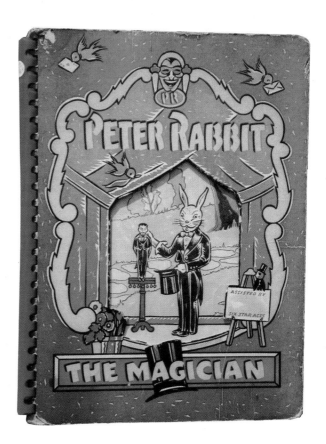

Any child would have enjoyed the above "Peter Rabbit The Magician" 16-page picture book. Manufactured for Jewel Tea Co., Inc. Jewel Park, Barrington, Ill. ©1942. *Byerly Collection.*

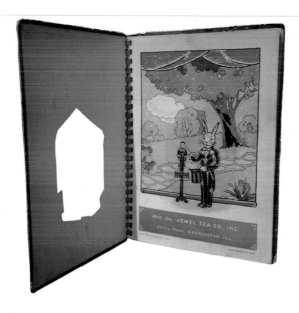

"Peter Rabbit The Magician," opened to the first magical page. *Byerly Collection.*

Jewel had its own fashion doll, appropriately named Debbie Dunbar. This glamorous fashion model was fully jointed—a total of fourteen joints at the head, shoulders, elbows, wrists, waist, legs, thighs, and knees. This allowed the doll to be posed many different ways, and made her ever so much more fun to play with. Debbie was all vinyl, 11-1/2" tall, with a curvy grownup figure, bouffant blonde-rooted Saran hairdo. Later Debbie's last name (Dunbar) was dropped and she was referred to only as Debbie.

Debbie Dunbar's friend, Don, was also introduced. Don was 12-1/2" tall, with molded hair and brown eyes. His body was vinyl, with movable head, arms and legs. A stand was also included.

Debbie Dunbar and Don were an "SPV"—a "SPECIAL PLAY VALUE." They appeared in Jewels' Christmas 1964 catalog, along with the famous Mattel Barbie® and Ken®.

IDEAL BABY DOLL—She walks! She talks!! She shuts her blue eyes tight and goes to By-Low land!!! What more could the heart of a little girl want on Christmas morning. This 14 inch doll is exceptionally well made. The head and hands are an unbreakable composition and will last a life time. The body is of cambric. Daintily dressed in lace trimmed, pale blue, crepe dress and bonnet, while socks and black patent leather shoes complete the costume. The clothes are removable so that the dollie may be easily dressed and undressed. An attractive feature is the holly and poinsettia trimmed box in which this Ideal Doll is delivered, and she only costs $1.75 (Cash only) Our Item No. C-6011.

She walks! She talks! Taken from an orginal 1925 Jewel News — any child would have enjoyed this 14" doll.

In the Jewel catalogs during the early 1960s, two of the most famous dolls in the world appeared, Barbie and Ken. *Dupler Collection.*

228

In 1964 Debbie Dunbar and Don sold for more than the Barbie and Ken dolls. A Debbie Dunbar wardrobe case was offered, similar to Barbie's. It was big and roomy and held any 11-1/2" or 12" fashion doll along with her clothes. The hardboard case had a durable patent-looking vinyl plastic covering, snap lock, and carrying handle on top. The case was 10-1/4" x 7" x 13" high and sold for $3.77.

Debbie also had her own townhouse, much like Barbie's, which folded to 26" x 8" x 13-1/2" high. Unfolded it was a sturdy corrugated townhouse with three walls and a floor, colorfully printed with realistic details inside and out.

Debbie and Don are shown in one catalog photograph sitting in Barbie's living room. The caption reads "For 11-1/2" fashion dollars, such as Debbie, Barbie, Tressy and all their friends."

In 1976, Barbie and Ken did not appear in the Fall - Winter - Christmas Jewel Home Shopping Service.

In 1962 the above "Dream House" was just right for either Debbie or Barbie, scaled to either size. The corrugated house was colorfully printed on both inside and outside with realistic detail and had a built-in wardrobe closet, a vanity table with a mirror, and a bookcase. *Dupler Collection.*

In 1962 Jewel offered "Barbie's" very own sports car shown above. Specially sized to fit any 11-1/2" fashion model and 12-1/2" boy doll. 19" long x 7-1/2" wide x 6-1/2" high overall. *Dupler Collection.*

In 1975 Debbie's Volkswagens® Camper was offered with many accessories. It easily accommodated any 11-1/2" doll or figure. The 18" x 7-1/2" x 9-1/2" camper was complete with twenty-six proportionate pieces. The above camper is complete and had never been opened. *Old Tyme Toy Mall*

The Debbie Dunbar doll is enthusuastically sought after by Jewel collectors, but there are also doll collectors looking for her (though Barbie and Ken are still the most popular among them). If you should have a Debbie Dunbar doll, I would appreciate hearing from you. At present it is not known if she came in a carton or a loose wrapper, which could give an indication of her identity.

This child's Jewel Cake Mix Set was a delight for any little homemaker. The 14-piece set included four various cake mixes, two frosting mixes, a gingerbread mix, baking pans, cookie sheet, cutters, rolling pin, and measuring spoons. The box measured 17" x 10-1/2". Distributed by Jewel Tea Co., Inc., Barrington, Illinois. *Weales Collection.*

In a 1956 Jewel Home Shopping Service catalog there appeared "Peggy Petite" with her wardrobe and furniture. Here is the complete Peggy Petite five-piece bedroom set along with the original box. The furniture was scaled for 8-inch miniature dolls like Peggy. *Kuhse Collection.*

These jigsaw puzzles appeared between 1931 and 1938. The 10" x 12" puzzle was found in an original tan envelope that says "Jewel Tea Co., Inc. Jewel Park, Barrington, IL." Since Jewel Park and Barrington came into the picture in April 1930, the puzzles cannot have been made before that date.

The finished puzzle on the right side of the package is turned; it may be wise to turn your book to see "The Great Forest Fire." The envelope printing says "This Picture is One of a Series of Jig-Saw Puzzles — Reproductions of Famous Painting." This indicates that there are other Jewel puzzles to be found. These puzzles were colorful, interesting, and fascinating. Premium price lists of the era 1939 through 1941 lists many kinds of toys and games, but no jigsaw puzzles. *Busch Collection.*

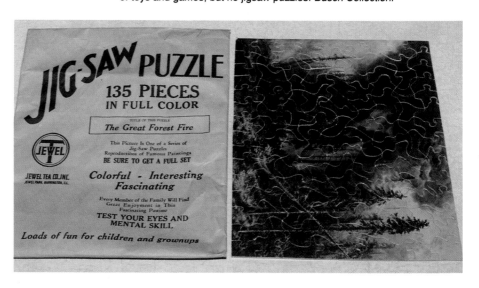

Circa 1954, Jewel Home Shopping offered the "Jewel Tea" rider truck. It was made of sturdy 20-gauge steel construction with heavy duty rubber tires, measuring 10" high x 9" wide x 22" long. It was designed just like the big Jewel delivery truck, with the true brown and tan colors, a steel steering handle, and a bell. Made by Structo. *Fausset Collection.*

The "Buddy L" brown toy truck in the original box measured 6" high x 5-1/2" wide x 11-1/2" long. *Fausset Collection.*

Come to the circus — the greatest show on earth—and see a trainload of circus animals. The only information written on the carton is "Unique Art Manufacturing Co., Inc. Newark, New Jersey." *Beguhl Collection.*

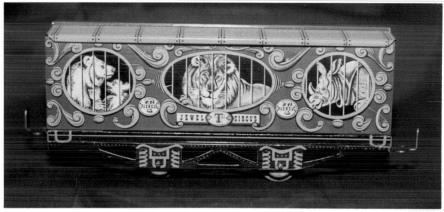

More caged animals in the train car. No date appears on the instructions which were included in the carton. Only two cars in the set have any indication of Jewel Tea on them. *Beguhl Collection.*

This Jewel Van was just like those that Jewel salespeople drove in the mid-1970s. It has the same Jewel colors with interior details, silding side door, and a back door that opens for making easy deliveries. Made of durable die-cast metal and plastic, with smooth edges and a non-toxic finish, the van measured 9" x 3-3/4" x 4-1/4". In a 1975 Fall/Winter and Christmas Catalog it sold for $4.99. *Byerly Collection.*

"J.T.'s General Store Presents Replica of Your Dealer's Truck 1899-1982." The two trucks came packaged in a handy cardboard carrying case. The "Yesterday 'n' Today" trucks were die-cast miniature metal trucks. Distributed by IHSS, Inc., Jewel Park Barrington, Ill. *Byerly Collection.*

"JEWEL - Pleasant Shopping with Friendly People." The Jewel trailer and the Jewel truck have a U.S. patent number 3307291. The large truck was made by Structo USA. *Byerly Collection.*

Available in the 1954 Jewel catalog, the 9" x 23-3/4" long Jewel Cross-Country Transport is shown below. It was just like the big Jewel trucks that traveled from coast to coast carrying groceries and other products. It was of heavy steel construction with fourteen heavy-duty truck tires. The trailer could be detached, and could stand on retractable dolly wheels. The back doors open and close. "A Better Place To Trade" appears on the side, along with "COFFEE - FINE FOODS - HOUSEWARES." On the side door to the cab appears the Jewel HOME SHOPPING SERVICE logo. *Busch Collection.*

The Buddy L Jewel Home Shopping Service Van with back doors that swing open for easy delivering. Buddy L appears across the open door in the rear. *Byerly Collection.*

The J.T. General Store's 90th Anniversary 1905 Ford delivery car bank, 1899-1989. In its original carton, this delivery bank was made by ERTL in U.S.A. *Byerly Collection.*

The Jewel In Home Shopping Service Van in the original box was distributed by Jewel Companies, Inc. Melrose Park, Illinois 60160, U.S.A. The van was made to Jewel specifications in Japan. *Byerly Collection.*

The present day Jewel truck and trailer featured flouting tandem rear axles, dual rear doors that open wide for maximum loading, fifth wheel type steering on the van, rugged steel construction, and a child-safe baked enamel finish. Made by ERTL in USA. *Byerly Collection.*

This JEWEL TEA CO., INC. van is shown in a frontal view with the side door open. Jewel Metro: 5" x 4" x 9-1/4" long, sold for $2.50. *Busch Collection.*

1954, "Here Comes the Jewel Man." This familiar brown and tan truck was reproduced for the up-and-coming salesman in any family. The front door slides open; the back gates open for easy delivery, close, and lock. This truck was true-to-life with a painted dashboard, heavy duty solid rubber tires, and sturdy steel construction. *Nemluvil Collection.*

During the 1960s, every child desired a Frisbee. Shown here is the 9" diameter Jewel horse-drawn delivery truck Frisbee in blue. *Cross Collection.*

The 1913 Model T Jewel Van with red wheels is a highly sought-after collector's item. Made by Ertl, this van is harder to find than the 90th Anniversary commemorative truck. *Byerly Collection.*

The yellow Frisbee. *Byerly Collection.*

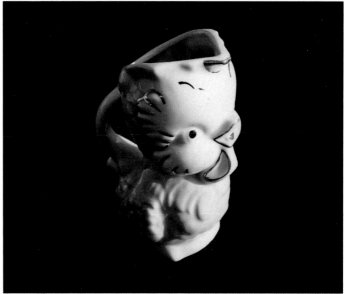

In 1946 Jewel offered the perfect milk pitcher for children. Shown above is the "Gold-Decorated Chick." Jewel believed that spring-blooming flowers make a most interesting arrangement in this unusual piece. Jewel referred to it as a hand-painted vase of white earthenware. The hat-ribbon handle and pointed lip at the front made it possible to use it as a pitcher. The colors stayed on because they were fired on under the glaze. The vase/pitcher stands 6 inches high and came in assorted colors. The gold decoration is 22 karat gold. *Author's Collection.*

A red Frisbee. An orange Frisbee is also available. *Hedges Collection.*

The exceptional all-wooden Bissell "Little Jewel" sweeper for children. The top of the sweeper reads "THIS TOY WILL REMIND YOU OF BISSELL'S FULL SIZE — "CYCO" BALL-BEARING SWEEPERS FOR THE HOME." No other information appears on this sweeper. *Hamilton Collection.*

A "Bissell's Little Jewel" sweeper for children could have been the perfect Christmas or birthday gift. No dates or patent number appears. It seems to be modeled after the large Bissell which Jewel offered. *Hamilton Collection.*

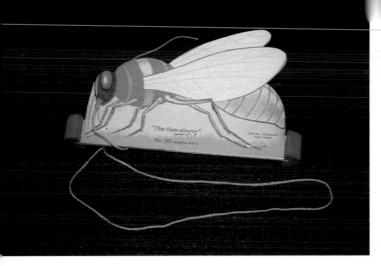

BUZZ — BUZZ — BUZZ. The exceptional child's toy "Bee Buzz" was a promotional advertisement for Honey Bee Cookies, distributed by Jewel Tea Co., Inc. *Hamilton Collection.*

The Mickey Mouse Drum Set was offered during Christmas 1977. Mickey, Minnie and the gang are strummin' and drummin' on the front. The set was listed as Item No. 359-0379X1 and sold for $19.99 complete. *Hamilton Collection.*

The reverse side of the Bee Buzz. "Make The Bee Buzz For Honey Bee Cookies—Distributed by JEWEL TEA Co., Inc. Jewel Park, Barrington, Ill" The toy would hum when the bee was swing around by the attached string. Circa late 1930s-late 1940s. *Hamilton Collection.*

In the Jewel News of November 1926, "Dizzie Lizzie" was offered. "Lizzie" was so cleverly constructed that it appeared to be falling to pieces as it shimmied across the floor. This wind-up toy car with "Wise Cracking" signs and driver was a delight for any child. Jewel listed it as Item No. C-6040, priced at 50¢. On the passenger side it is marked "STRAUSS MECHANICAL TOYS — Known the World Over." *Hamilton Collection.*

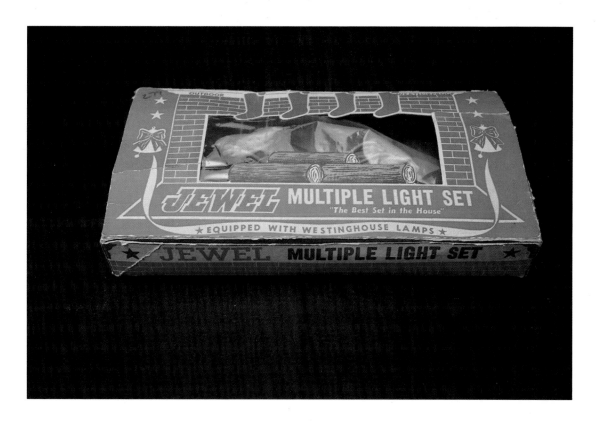

This carton contained one Jewel multiple light set, "The Best Set in the House." It could be used outdoors and was weather-proof. This set was equipped with Westinghouse lamps. Date uncertain. *Hamilton Collection.*

Children and fruitcake — no way! The bottom of this holiday fruitcake tin is marked "JEWEL." On the rim of the lid it is marked "Manufactured by Jewel Tea Company Inc. Barrington, ILL." *Barringer Collection.*

A wooden crate that held two reuseable bottles of Jewel pure honey. In the 1979 Fall — Winter — Christmas edition of the Jewel Home Shopping Service catalog, Jewel offered a crate of honey straight from the bees to the customer, in four delicious flavors: Wild Flower, Clover, Buckwheat, and Basswood. The glass jars were reusable. For Christmas of 1980, Jewel's own crate of honey was offered in three reusable 4-oz. jars. This crate was offered alongside the popular fruitcake and Autumn Leaf Tin (see *The Jewel Tea Company, Its History and Products*, pages 132-133). *Lemon Collection.*

CHAPTER 19
GRANNY HARTNEY

A famous historical photograph of Iowa resident Granny Hartney and her Jewel salesman, Harry J. Hicks.

One of the few Jewel customers to become immortalized in Jewel history was a resident of Cascade, Iowa, in 1923.

The historical picture shown here, with Granny Hartney and Harry Hicks, first appeared in a publication for Jewel employees called The Jewel, Volume 2, No. 3, on December 13, 1923.

The caption that appeared under the photograph read,

This interesting picture shows Granny Hartney and salesman Harry J. Hicks, a sub-branch salesman of Monticello, Iowa, operating out of Clinton. Granny Hartney is a regular Jewel customer who lives alone and uses two pounds of coffee every two weeks.

101 years old, Granny Hartney drinks Jewel Best Coffee five times every day and lives in Cascade, Iowa, the home of Red Faber, star pitcher on the White Sox baseball team.

Granny Hartney may have been Margaret (Mary) Hartney, a widow in Cascade, in Dubuque County, Iowa. Margaret passed away on the 16th day of June 1924—seven months after the famous photograph for The Jewel was taken.

The following obituary appeared in the Cascade, Iowa "Pioneer" paper; it appears below with spelling errors as it appeared in print.

DEATH CLAIMS AGED WOMAN

Mrs. Mary Hartry, who lived in Cascade for many years, died at her home in East Cascade Monday night, June 16th, at the age of 85 years.

She was born in Philadelphia and came to Iowa in early womanhood. She married Edward Hartry, who preceded her in death fifteen years ago. She is survived by her daughter Mrs. Robert Meader, of Dubuue, and several grandchildren.

The funeral service took place at St. Mary's Church Wednesday morning; Rev. G.A. Hauck, of Monticello, officiating. The remains were taken to Farley for burial where Rev. Hauck also had charge of the last rites at the graveside.

The pallbearers at Cascade were J.C. Davlin, John Brown, Jacob Loes, Jule Gavin, John Boland and T.J. Conlin. At Farley the casket was borne by Joseph Veach, M. O'Meara, John Kerby, Joe Breen, John Ronan and M. Connolly."

Granny Hartney's age as asserted by the obituary does not correspond with the age listed in the Jewel News. It is a known fact that many woman are cautious about giving their age; perhaps this explains the discrepancy. Or could Jewel salesman Harry J. Hicks have misunderstood her age, or intentionally misrepresented it as 101 years old? This we shall never know!

In Cascade, Iowa today, a 91 year old resident remembers the Hartney name well. "I remember she lived in the east part of town. Of course, I didn't get to town much back then, as we lived on a farm north of town and went to a country church." Today there are a number of houses in the east section of town that resemble the one appearing in the Hartney and Hicks photograph.

The Photo Plate

In the 90th Anniversary 1989 Fall and Winter J.T.'s General Store Catalog, this 10" photo plate appeared. Approximately a thousand samples were made with this most famous photograph, which had appeared 66 years earlier in a Jewel publication.

The caption that appeared under the above photograph in the catalog read "Your Favorite Photo is Reproduced on a Keepsake Plate!" Preserve a cherished moment forever on this chip-and-stain resistant, dishwasher safe, unbreakable Melamine plate! Simply give your Dealer ANY SIZE black-and-white or color photo; the picture is reproduced permanently in black-and-white on the plate. The original photo will be returned with the plate. A great gift! Allow 10 weeks for delivery." The Photo Plate sold for $24.99. *Byerly Collection.*

The 90th Anniversary 1989 Fall and Winter J.T.'s General Store Catalog. This edition is highly sought-after by collectors. *Byerly Collection.*

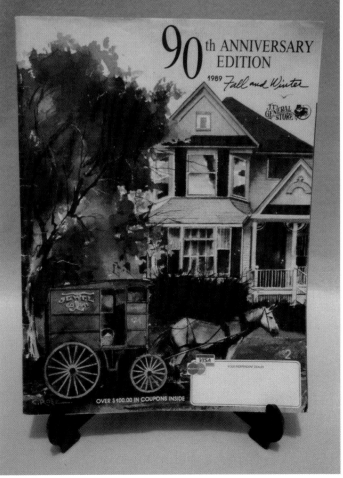

CHAPTER 20

A TWENTIETH CENTURY PIONEER

Richard E. Byrd U.S.N.

Rear Admiral Richard E. Byrd USN, a 20th century pioneer aviator and polar explorer, was born in Winchester, Virginia, on October 25, 1888. Eventually, he would be the first man to step foot on the South Pole with Jewel products!

Rear Admiral Byrd first won fame by his long-distance flights in the Arctic and over the Atlantic, and was best known for his organized expeditions to the Antarctic.

At the U.S. Naval Air Station in Pensacola, Florida he learned to fly and served in the Navy until the end of World War I. Then he turned his attention to developing navigational aids for aircrafts, developing plans for the first NC flying boat transatlantic flights.

In 1924, while in command of a naval aviation detachment with D.B. MacMilan's Arctic expedition to western Greenland, Byrd began his polar career.

Unknown Regions

A decision was announced in 1928 that Byrd was to explore the unknown regions of the Antarctic from the air. Wealthy Americans Edsel Ford and John D. Rockefeller, Jr. provided large financial backing.

Byrd's expedition, the largest and best equipped ever, set out for the Antarctic in October 1928.

In August of 1930, his picture appeared on the cover of The Jewel News. The caption under the photograph read: "The newspapers, the theatres, and the public — join in giving overwhelming praise to Rear-Admiral Richard E. Byrd, the American hero who conquered the South Pole. Guarding the health of the Rear-Admiral and his gallant party on this adventure was Jewel teas, Jewel spices, and Jewel extracts. The best for the best!"

Byrd's mother had always been a faithful Jewel shopper. She may have been the inspirational influence behind Richard's selection of Jewel productions for the expedition. At one time a brief letter from Mrs. Byrd appeared in an issue of "The Jewel News."

Facing the Dangers of an Icy World, Rear Admiral Richard E. Byrd U.S.N. made headlines when he appeared on the cover of The Jewel News in August 1930. *Author's Collection.*

Jewel Products Delivered

Jewel products accompanied Byrd on his Antarctic expedition. This photograph shows many cases of Jewel products that he took with him. Note that the cartons of products read "To-BYRD ANTARCTIC EXPEDITION — S.S. SAMSON — HOBOKEN, N.J. — From Jewel Tea Co. Inc. New York — Chicago."

At the Todd Shipyard in Brooklyn the boat "Samson" had taken on the delivered products. Incidentally, the name had been changed from "Samson" to "City of New York."

The Chief Steward of the expedition, Sydney Greason, appears on the right, talking with his assistant George Tennant as Jewel products are loaded aboard the "Samson" in this photograph.

The international hero died in Boston on March 11, 1957 at the age of 69 with full military honors. He was buried in Arlington National Cemetery, Virginia.

CHAPTER 21

THE CHICAGOLAND BOOKLET

"The History of Chicagoland"

The Jewel Tea Company entered the food store business in 1932, purchasing nearly eighty Chicagoland stores from the Loblaw Groceterians, Inc. While the Depression made these stores a terrible money-loser for Jewel, they later came out with a poster stamp booklet entitled "The History of Chicagoland." The back of the booklet reads

The origin of Jewel Tea Co., Inc. from humble beginnings and its expansion parallel those of amazing Chicagoland. In 1899, in Chicago, a "man and an idea" had $700 and a horse and buggy. Today, some forty years later, Jewel service and Jewel groceries are well known in 42 of the 48 states.

Just as the early pioneers overcame every obstacle to make Chicago a great city, so Jewel people over the years have created a great coast-to-coast service organization.

Their constant effort to serve you and serve you well has earned your confidence and friendship. They hope to be worthy of them always.

An illustration of a horse and wagon appears at the top of the booklet with the year 1899. At the bottom appears an illustration of a Jewel storefront and the year 1939.

The 1939 booklet also explained that "The Jewel Food Stores are proud to present to Chicagoland citizens of all ages a poster stamp review of their city from 1673 to 1933. The hundred subjects taken for these stamps have been selected from among thousands of interesting ones that might have been used. All have been approved by the National Poster Stamp Society."

Only available through the Jewel Food Stores, "The History of Chicagoland" was not a premium item. The booklet contained a hundred brief historical comments about Chicago with an introduction of the "Earliest Chicago" history.

On January 9, 1939, stamps were available at all Jewel Food Stores. On Monday, Tuesday or Wednesday, one stamp was issued to each person for a twenty-five cent purchase or more. One stamp was given for a twenty-five cent purchase or more on Thursday, Friday, or Saturday. One stamp was given to each customer who purchased the designated "Weekly Stamp Special." The weekly special changed each week through Thursday of the following week.

There were twenty star stamps in the series which were the most valuable. Spaces provided in the booklet were designated by a star.

One or more star stamps were packaged inside the following Jewel Products: Jewel coffees (Blue Brook, Blue Jewel, and Royal Jewel), Blue Jewel teas, and all varieties of Blue Jewel cocoa in one-pound cans.

With "The History of Chicagoland" poster stamp booklet, five free stamps were given. Over a period of twenty-five weeks, seventy-five additional stamps were given out in the Jewel Food Stores.

The stamps came in a variety of bright colors and measured 2" wide by 1-1/2" high, and could be glued onto the indicated space.

THE HISTORY OF CHICAGOLAND

PORTRAYED BY JEWEL POSTER STAMPS

A highly sought-after cover poster stamp booklet with more than 44 pages, entitled "The History of Chicagoland." This 4" x 9" stamp booklet has a 1939 copyright. *Hamilton Collection.*

FOR MORE INFORMATION

When writing to any of the individuals listed below, enclose a stamped, self-addressed, return envelope; otherwise no reply will be mailed to you in return.

Barrington Area Historical Society
Michael Harkins, Executive Director
212 West Main Street
Barrington, Illinois 60010
Write or phone (708) 381-1730 for membership
    information.

Patti Byerly, Vice President N.A.L.C.C.
4514 Errington Rd.
Columbus, Ohio 43227
Membership is $20.00 (money order or check) payable to N.A.L.C.C.

China Specialties, Inc.
P.O. Box 361280
Strongsville, Ohio 44136

Jewel Tea Company Catalog Reprints
Shirley Easley
120 West Dowell Road
McHenry, Illinois 60050
To order send $14.95 plus $2.00 UPS.

Glass From The Past (Depression Glass)
Sue and Dave McDiarmid, Owner
313 W. State Street
Fremont, Ohio 43420

The Hall China Company
The Hall Closet
East Liverpool, Ohio 43920
Tours: (self guided) Monday through Friday, 9:30 to 2:15.

Hall China Collector Club Newsletter
P.O. Box 360488
Cleveland, Ohio 44136
Subscription is $9.00 a year (money order or check) payable to Hall
    Collector Newsletter.

Olde Tyme Toy Mall (Antique Toys)
105 S. Main
Fairmount, Indiana 46928

J&B Antique Mall (Autumn Leaf China) Jerry and Beverly Nichols,
    Owners
109 West Adrian Street
Blissfield, Michigan 49228

HOW JEWEL OPERATED

Jewel Tea Co., sold groceries directly to a million American homes, with the inducement of sharing profits with customers under the Jewel plan of advancing premiums. Jewel reached the housewife in her own home through well trained salesmen who traveled over established routes by motor cars. Salesmen called on each customer every two weeks, taking orders for groceries to be delivered at the next regular call and delivering the groceries ordered two weeks before. MAKE YOUR CHOICE NOW!

COLONIAL PERCOLATOR ELECTRIC IRON

ALUMINUM SAUCEPAN 3-PC COMBINATION COOKER

MAKE YOUR CHOICE NOW!

OF

JEWEL UTENSILS OR OTHER PREMIUMS

Listed below are the fundamental principles of Jewel merchandising.

1. Distribution direct to the consumer's home.
2. Groceries sold only for cash.
3. Advertising with premiums.
4. Delivery of the premium in advance.
5. Best of quality—always.
6. Everything—groceries, premiums and service—guaranteed.

APPENDIX 3
THE LAUREL-WREATH LOGO

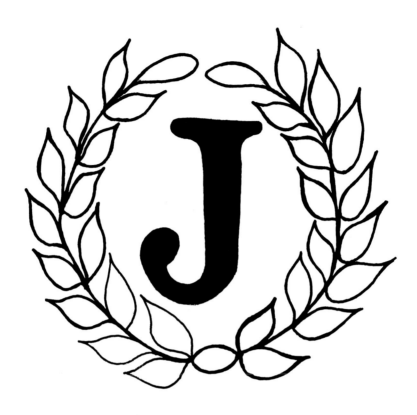

The above Laurel-wreath logo was used during the mid-1920s when Jewel had 700,000 customers and appeared on numerous pieces of Bavarian China.

THE MARY DUNBAR LOGO

The above illustration of Mary Dunbar and her famous signature would appear in numerous Jewel Home Shopping Service Catalog and was the mark of quality.

CHINA SPECIALTIES

The Hall China Company of East Liverpool, Ohio agreed to produce an exclusive line of Limited Edition Autumn Leaf Collector's items for China Specialties, Inc., in 1990. Hall utilized only shapes never before offered in the famous Jewel Autumn Leaf pattern.

The World's Largest Hall China Autumn Leaf Ice Tea Dispenser, shown here, this two-piece teapot has a 54 cup capactiy and is 18" high. The decal appears on both the front and the back of the teapot and on all four sides of the base. Trimmed in 24K gold, this teapot was first introduced by Hall China as part of their restaurant line. Limited to a production of only 299 pieces, each teapot is accompanied with a numbered certificate, also shown here. Available only through China Specialties, Inc., of Strongsville, Ohio. See Appendix 1.

China Specialties, Inc., will offer to collectors the following Autumn Leaf pieces: Square Wall Bowl, Restyled Batter Bowl, Football Teapot, Quarter Pound Butter dish, 6-1/4" Tall Bud Vase, Set of Candleholders. Boston Style Sugar and Creamer on figure eight tray and an Autumn Leaf dealer sign that is approximately 4" long by 2-1/2" high, numerous other collectible pieces worthy of any collection are planned for future release. Photographs not available.

Certificate of Authenticity

This certifies that ___SAMPLE___

has directed China Specialties Inc. to commission and secure for them from the famous Hall China Company of East Liverpool, Ohio an example of the

World's Largest Autumn Leaf Teapot

This Autumn Leaf teapot represents Number ___000___ in the limited edition series of only 299 pieces. The serial number hereon is permanently registered to the commissioner and original owner of the teapot and a record of such registration is held at the offices of China Specialties Incorporated, as well as in a leather bound, archival copy of said registrations which will be donated to the Barrington Area Historical Society's Jewel Tea Archives once this series is completed.

_____

Virginia Lee, President China Specialties, Inc.

A COFFEE ADVERTISEMENT

More American's drank Jewel coffee than any other coffee. As the illustration shown above says "AMERICA'S Favorite Drink", this illustration periodically appeared in the Jewel News.

THE N. A. L. C. C.

The 1994 N.A.L.C.C. (National Autumn Leaf Collector's Club) Autumn
Leaf syrup pitcher. This piece is marked "MADE ESPECIALLY FOR THE
AUTUMN LEAF CLUB BY THE HALL CHINA CO., 1994."

Announcements of club pieces appear in the N.A.L.C.C. newsletter, mailed to members bimonthly beginning in January. Only those pieces purchased by members are then produced by the Hall China Company. The National Autumn Leaf Collectors Club does not stock additional pieces or have additional pieces offered from past years.

Prior pieces as well as those recently offered are often available through the "Sell—Swap-Trade" section of the club newletter. As club pieces are produced in limited numbers, members pay reasonable prices. Non-members and new club members joining this organization can frequently purchase club pieces in the secondary market. Be prepared: they can be costly!

The first club piece was the New York Teapot, produced in 1983 by The Hall China Company. Today this teapot sells for between $500 and $600. The 1995 N.A.L.C.C. club piece was the Autumn Leaf Birdcage Teapot.

Membership information is available by addressing correspondence to Mrs. Patti Byerly (see Appendix 1). Enclose a self-addressed stamped envelope.

BIBLIOGRAPHY

Burness, Tad. *Auto Album* 1969 Scholastic Book Services - New York - Toronto - London - Aucklance - Sydney

China Specialties Inc., Re-issues Newsletter. Virginia Lee, President

Cunningham, Jo. *The Autumn Leaf S tory,* 1976 HAF-D Productions

_____ *The Collector's Encyclopedia of American Dinnerware,* 1982 Collectors Books

Cunningham, Jo. *The Autumn Leaf Story,* 1976 HAF-D Productions

Derwich Jenny B. and Dr. Mary Latos. *Dictionary Guide to United States Pottery & Porcelain (19th & 20th Century).*

Disasters. Arno Press New York 1976, Edited by Arleen Keylin and Gene Brown

Duke, Harvey. *Hall 2,* 1985 ELO Books

Easley, Shirley. *Jewel Tea Company Catalog Reprints - 1949 to 1982*

Florence, Gene. *Collectible Glassware from the 40's, 50's, 60's;* Collector's Books

Jewel News, 1925 - 1948

Jewel Home Shopping Cataloges, 1949 - 1950 - 1960 - 1970.

J.T.'s General Store IHSS, Inc. Jewel Home Shopping Service, Annual Report 1982.

Kovels, *Depression Glass & American Dinnerware,* Fourth Editions 1991, Crown Publishers, Inc. New York.

LIFE, January 13, 1941

Illinois Manufacturers Directory, 1993

Mary Dunbar's Cook Book, ©1927 Jewel Tea Co., Inc., New York, Chicago

Mary Dunbar's Favorite Recipes, Jewel Tea Co., Inc., Jewel Park, Barrington, Ill.

Mary Dunbar's New Cook Book, ©1933 Jewel Tea Co., Inc.

Million Dollar Directory, 1992

476 Tested Recipes by Mary Dunbar, Published for and dedicated to the American homemaker by Jewel Tea Co., Inc., Barrington, Illinois.

N.A.L.C.C., Newsletters

Needlecraft, "The Magazine of Home Arts." December 1931

Ohio Manufacturers Directory, 1989 Manufacturers News, Inc.

Oak Leaf, Newspaper January 1947 - March 1947, Oak Park Public Library

Opportunties For Determined Women At Jewel, 1974

Peterson's Guide to Four-Year Colleges, 1990

Schneider, Mike. *The Complete Cookie Jar Book.* 1991 Schiffer Publishing Ltd.

Sharing, Jewel Companies Inc.

The Jewel Cook Book, Jewel Tea Co., Jewel Park, Barrington, Illinois

The Jewel Crusader, 1948 Vol. 7 No. 8 and 1949 Vol. 7 No. 13

The World Book Encyclopedia Edition, 1992

Whitmyer, Margaret & Kenn. *The Collector's Encyclopedia of Hall China,* 1989 Collectors Books

PRICE GUIDE

Values vary immensely according to the condition of the piece, the location of the market, and the overall quality of the design and manufacture. Condition is always of paramount importance in assigning a value. Prices in the Midwest differ from those in the West or East, and those at specialty antique shows will vary from those at general shows. And, of course, being at the right place at the right time can make all the difference.

All these factors make it impossible to create an absolutely accurate price list, but we can offer a guide. The prices reflect what one could realistically expect to pay at retail or auction.

The left hand number is the page number. The letters following it indicate the position of the photograph on the page: T=top, L=left, R=right, TL=top left, TR=top right, CL=center left, CR=center right, B=bottom, BL=bottom left, BR=bottom right. Sequential numbers following immediately after these letters indicate the position of the piece in a series of pieces reading from left to right or top to bottom. The right hand column of numbers are the estimated price ranges in United States dollars.

Page	Position	Value in Dollars
2	C/TR	L: 10-15 ea.
2	C/BR	L: 20-25; C: 25-30; R: 9-11 set.
4	BC/T	10-15
	BC/B	10-11 set.
6	TC	20-25
8	TR	18-20
8	BC	50-60 set.
10	BC	10-15
26	TL	45-75
32	BL	100-120
32	BR	10-12
33	TL	5-10
33	TR	20-25
33	BR	100-120
34	TL	100-120
34	C	150-175
34	BC	150-175
35	BL	20-24
35	TR	20-24
35	CR	20-24
39	CR	15-20
39	BR	15-20
40	TL	15-20
40	BL	15-20
40	TR	20-25
41	TR	10-15
41		Coffee As a Flavoring (No Photograph) 20-25
42	TL	10-15
42	BL	10-15
42	TR	10-15
43	BL	15-20
43	CR	15-20
44	TL	15-20
44	BL	10-15
44	TR	15-20
45	CL	10-15
45	TR	3-5
45	BR	5-7
46	TC	5-7
46	BL	10-15
47		Mary Dunbar's Trunk; UND
47	BR	Pan 20-25; Colander 15-20
48	TL	Pan 20-25
48	TR	Measuring Cup 15-20
48	CL	Utensils vary from 10-20 ea.
48	CR	Measuring Cup 15-20
48	BL	Utensils vary from 10-20 ea.
48	BR	Green Handled Beater; 15-20
49	TL	Utensils vary from 10-20 ea.
53	BL	20-25 with original paper.
53	BR	300-350
54	TL	300-350
54	BL	50-75 with original paper.
54	TR	100-125
54	BR	50-75 with original paper.
55	TL	40-50 with original box.
55	BL	100-125
55	BR	100-125 complete
56	TL	65-85
56	TR	20-25
56	BL	40-50 ea.
56	CR	50-75 complete
56	BR	Item (E) 40-50
57	BL	40-50 with original paper.
57	TR	40-50 with original paper.
57	BR	150-175
58	TL	150-175
58	BL	125-150
58	CR	40-50 with original paper.
59	TL	15-20 with original paper/box.
59	BL	15-20 with original paper/box.
59	TR	45-55 with original paper.
59	BR	150-175
60	TL	20-25 with original paper.
60	CL	35-45
60	BR	35-45
61	TL	35-45 ea.
61	TR	45-65
61	CL	35-45
61		20-25 Pizza Cutter
61	BL	30-35 with original paper/box.
62	TL	10-15 ea. Oval Head 15-20.
62	CL	40-50 complete
62	TR	40-50 complete
62	BR	5-10
63	C	UND
63	BL	UND
63	BR	5-10
64	TL	5-10
64	BL	1-2
64	CR	3-5
65	C	25-30
65	BR	75-100 with original paper/box.
66	TC	75-100 with original paper/box.
66	BL	Water Bottle 50-60; Cookie Jar 75-100 with original sticker.
66	BR	25-30
67	TL	50-75 with original paper.
67	BL	5-10 Cookbook.
67	TR	40-50 with original paper.
67	CR	50-75
68	TL	45-50 (3 pieces)
68	CR	4-6 (holder only)
68	CL	8-12
68	BR	10-12 ea.
69	TL	30-35
69	CL	50-75 Glass Dripper.
69	BL	30-35
69	TR	200-250
69	CR	200-250
70	TL	100-150
70	CL	100-150
70	TR	100-150
70	CR	100-150
70	BR	30-45 (Creamer); 10-12 Jewel News
71	TL	75-85 complete.
71	CL	75-85 complete.
71	BL	60-75 without inserts.
71	TR	75-85 complete.
71	BR	80-100
72	TL	25-35 ea.
72	CR	15-20
72	BL	15-20
73	TR	L: 10-12; R: 8-10
74	TL	12-15
74	CL	10-12
74	TR	50-60 complete.
74	CR	L: 15-20 R: 10-15
74	BR	80-90 set.
76	CL	150-175
76	TR	20-25
76	CR	45-55
77	TL	350-400
77	CL	125-150
77	TR	75-100
77	BR	150-165 complete.
78	TL	40-50
78	BL	40-50
78	BR	30-40 ea.
79	TL	Fatigue Mat. UND
80	CL	30-35 ea.
80	CR	20-25 ea.
82	TL	10-12 ea.
82	CR	10-12 ea.
82	BR	25-30 ea. (Glasses); 45-55 (Cloth)
83	TL	15-18
83	CL	25-30
83	TR	30-35 ea.
83	CR	30-35

Page	Pos	Price
83	BR	L: 40-45 R: 30-35
84	TL	50-55 ea.
85	TL	15-20
85	BL	50-60 set; casserole 30-40 (not shown)
85	TR	75-100 set.
85	CR	75-100 set.
86	TL	12-15
86	TR	9-11
86	CL	8-10
86	CR	10-12 ea.
86	BR	L: 20-25; R: 18-22
87	TL	15-20
87	CL	80-100 set with labels.
87	BL	55-75
87	TR	35-45
88	BR	10-12 in original box.
89	BL	20-25 ea.
89	CR	15-20
90	TL	Top row. L: 20-25;C: 15-20; R: 20-25
90	TL	Bottom row. 20-25
90	CL	8-10 with original paper/box.
90	BR	15-20 with original paper/box.
91	TR	15-20 with original paper.
92	CL	100-150 complete.
92	TR	5-8 with original paper.
92	BR	450-550
93	TL	450-550
93	BL	20-25 with original paper.
93	TR	8-10
93	CR	150-200
94	TL	350-400
94	TR	125-150
96	TL	150-175
96	CL	75-100
96	TR	90-100
96	BR	90-100
97	TL	15-20
97	CL	15-20
97	TR	20-25 with original paper/ box.
97	BR	15-20 with original paper.
98	TR	6-8 ea.
98	CL	25-35
98	CR	50-60 with sticker.
98	BR	25-35
99	BL	2000-2500
99	TR	2000-2500
99	CR	2000-2500
99	BR	2000-2500
100	TL	2000-2200
100	CL	2000-2200
100	TR	L: 1800-2200; R: 2000- 2200
100	BR	400-600 ea.
101	TC	200 ea.
101	C	Miniature 1800-2200 pair; Regular 20-25 pair.
101	BR	200-400
101	TR	1500-1700
102	TL	UND
102	CL	UND
102	TR	Small decal 175-200; Large decal 150-175
102	BR	1800-2000 ea.
103	TL	1600-1800
103	CL	1600-1800
103	BL	L: UND R: UND
103	TR	1800-2000 ea.
103	BR	UND
104	TL	UND
104	TR	UND
104	C	L: UND C:UND R: 6-8 set.
104	BC	L: UND C: UND R: 10-12
105	TL	2500-2800
105	CL	2500-2800
105	BL	2500-2800
105	TR	2500-2800
105	BR	1200-1500
106	TL	1800-2000
106	CL	1800-2000
106	TR	800-1000
106	CR	800-1000
106	BR	18-20
107	TL	55-70 ea.
107	CR	250-300
107	BL	T-B; 5-8; 35-45; 500-600; 120-125; 14-18; UND.
107	BR	500-600
108	TL	75-100
108	CL	75-100
108	TR	250-300
108	BR	250-300
109	TR	10-12
109	BR	8-10
110	TL	5-8
110	TR	12-15
110	CL	5-8 set.
110	CR	15-20
110	BL	5-8
111	TL	15-20
111	TR	10-15
111	CL	20-25
111	CR	8-10
111	BR	L: 4-6; R: 5-8
112	TL	15-20
112	BL	10-15
112	CR	20-25
112		Open-Handled Pitcher (not shown) 50-75
113	BL	10-15
113	TR	5-8
113	BR	8-12
114	TL	25-35
114	CR	Top row. L: 25-35; C: 8-12; R: 10-15. Bottom row. L: 5-8; C: 8-10; R: 8-10.
114	BL	5-8 ea.
115	CR	25-35 complete.
116	TC	30-35 ea.
116	CL	30-35 ea.
116	BR	30-35
117	CL	30-40 complete.
117	TR	45-50
117	BR	50-55
118	TL	50-60
118	BR	50-60
119	CL	70-80
119	TR	70-80
119	BR	70-80
120	TL	70-80
120	CR	70-80
121	TL	45-50
121	CR	50-60
122	CL	45-50
123	CL	45-50
123	TR	70-80
124	BL	40-45
124	TR	50-60
125	TL	25-30
125	BL	25-30
125	CR	25-30
126	BL	25-30
126	CR	15-20
127	C	15-20
128	TL	5-10
128	TR	5-10
128	BR	5-10 ea.
129	TR	10-15
129	BR	10-15
130	TL	10-15
130	TR	10-15
131	CL	10-15
131	TR	10-15
131	BR	10-15
132	CL	10-15
132	TR	10-15
132	BR	10-15
133	TL	10-15
133	BL	20-25
133	CR	10-15
134	TL	20-25
134	BR	10-15
135	TL	10-15
135	CR	10-15
135	BL	10-15
136	TL	20-25
136	BL	10-15
136	BR	10-15
137	TL	20-25
137	BR	20-25
138	CL	10-15
138	TR	10-15
138	BR	10-15
139	TL	10-15
139	BL	10-15
139	CR	10-15
140	CL	10-15
140	TR	10-15
140	BR	10-15
141	TL	10-15
141	BR	10-15
142	CL	10-15
142	TR	10-15
142	BR	10-15
143	TL	10-15
143	CR	10-15
143	BL	10-15
144	CL	10-15
144	TR	10-15
144	BR	10-15
145	TL	10-15
145	BL	20-25
145	TR	10-15
145	BR	10-15
146	CL	10-15
146	TR	10-15
146	BR	20-25
147	TL	10-15
147	CR	20-25
148	TL	10-15
148	BR	10-15
149	TL	10-15
149	BL	20-25
149	CR	10-15
150	CL	20-25
150	TR	10-15
150	BR	10-15
151	TL	10-15
151	BL	10-15
151	CR	10-15
152	TL	10-15
152	CR	10-15
153	TL	10-15
153	CR	10-15
153	BL	10-15
154	CL	10-15
154	TR	10-15
154	BR	10-15
155	TL	10-15
155	TR	10-15
156	CL	10-15
156	TR	10-15
156	BR	10-15
157	TL	10-15
157	BL	10-15
157	CR	10-15
158	TL	10-15
158	TR	10-15

Page	Pos	Value
158	BL	10-15
158	BR	10-15
159	TL	10-15
159	TR	10-15
159	BL	10-15
159	BR	10-15
160	CL	10-15
160	TR	10-15
160	BR	10-15
161	TL	10-15
161	CR	10-15
161	BL	10-15
162	TL	10-15
162	TR	10-15
162	BL	10-15
162	BR	10-15
163	TL	10-15
163	TR	10-15
163	BL	10-15
163	BR	10-15
164	TL	10-15
164	TR	10-15
164	BL	10-15
164	BR	10-15
165	TL	10-15
165	BL	10-15
165	CR	10-15
166	TL	10-15
166	BL	10-15
166	CR	10-15
167	TL	10-15
167	CR	10-15
168	CL	10-15
168	TR	10-15
168	BR	10-15
169	TL	10-15
169	BL	10-15
169	CR	10-15
170	TL	10-15
170	BL	10-15
170	CR	10-15
171	TL	10-15
171	BC	20-25
172	TL	15-20
172	TR	15-20
172	BL	15-20
172	BR	15-20
173	TL	10-15
173	TR	15-20
173	BL	15-20
173	BR	10-15
174	CL	10-15
174	TR	10-15
174	BR	5-10
175	TL	10-15
175	TR	10-15
175	BL	5-10
175	BR	10-15
176	TL	Top row. L: 150-175; C : 20-25; R: 150-175 Bottom row. C: 10-15
176	TR	150-175
176	BL	20-25
176	BR	20-25
177	TL	50-60
177	BL	16-17
177	CR	25-35
178	TL	25-35
178	BL	25-35
178	CR	25-35
179	TL	25-35
179	TR	25-35
179	BC	25-35
180	TC	25-35
180	BC	25-35
181	TL	20-25
181	BL	25-30
181	TR	25-30
181	BR	25-35
182	CL	55-65 complete set.
182	BR	55-65 complete set.
183	TL	5-10
183	BL	25-35
183	CR	25-35
184	BL	5-10
184	CR	3-6
185	TR	450-500 set.
185	BR	450-500 set.
186	CL	450-500 set.
186	TR	450-500 set.
188	BC	60-75 complete set.
189	BL	150-200 complete set.
189		68 Madrid cup/saucer.
191	CR	400-425
192	CL	145-155
192		70 oz. not shown in original box. 150-200.
193	C	550-650 pair.
193		Golden Tea Leaf Tea Maker - 100-125; Soup Server - 75-100; Tea Canister - 50-75; Hurricane Lamps - 75-100.
195	TL	10-12
195	BR	18-20
196	TL	18-20
196	TR	18-20
196	CL	25-35
196	BR	50-75 with original paper.
198	TR	30-40
199	TL	L: 50-60; R: 60-70
199	TR	15-20
199	BL	50-60
199	BR	50-60
200	TL	10-15 with original paper.
200	TR	20-25 with original paper.
200	BL	100-125 with box.
200	BR	35-45
201	TC	20-25 with original paper.
201	BC	35-45 ea.
202	CL	25-30
202	TR	20-25
202	BC	80-90
203	TL	30-35
203	TR	45-55
203	BL	95-100 with original box.
203	CR	8-10
204	TL	8-10
204	TR	8-10
204	BL	8-10
204	BR	8-10
205	TL	6-8
205	TR	8-10
205	BL	6-8
205	BR	8-10
206	TL	25-30
206	BC	475-500
207	TC	475-500
207	BC	L: 40-50; R: 35-40
208	TL	75-100
208	TR	75-85
208	CR	75-85
209	BL	50-60
209	BR	50-60
210	TR	10-15
211	C	10-15; Framed 25-35
212	TR	20-25
212	CR	35-45
212	BL	35-40
213	TL	20-25
213	TR	20-25
213	CR	35-45
213	BL	35-45
214	BL	120-135
214	BR	135-150
215	TC	25-30 ea.
215	CL	15-20 with candy.
215	CR	5-7
215	BL	20-25
215	BR	20-25
216	TR	50-75
216	BR	75-100 with box.
217	TL	5-10
217	BL	5-10
217	CR	160-175
218	TL	175-185 ea.
218	TR	20-25
218	CL	150-175
218	BR	20-25
219	TL	20-25 ea.
219	TR	10-15
219	CL	15-20
219	CR	10-15
219	BC	10-12
220	TL	25-35
220	BL	15-20
221	TR	5-10
221	BR	5-10
222	TL	10-15
222	TR	175-225 with stand.
222	CL	5-10 ea. Brandy Snifter - 20-25
222	BR	40-50
223	TL	20-25
223	TR	25-30
223	BR	50-60 set.
224	TL	L: 45-75; R: 75-100
224	BC	25-30
227	TR	10-15
227	BR	25-35
228	TL	25-35
228	BL	80-100 with original paper/box.
228	BR	L: 60-90; R: 35-50
229	TR	40-80
229	CL	25-50
229	BR	40-70
230	TR	250-375
230	CL	125-175
230	BR	60-75
231	TL	1200-1500
231	CR	100-160
231	BL	300-400
232	TL	300-400
232	CL	75-100
232	CR	15-20 set.
232	BC	150-225
233	TC	800-1000
233	CL	100-150
233	CR	20-25 with original box.
233	BL	100-150 with original box.
234	TC	25-35 with original box.
234	CL	100-150
234	CR	100-150
234	BL	25-30
234	BR	10-20
235	TL	10-20
235	TR	8-12
235	CL	10-20
235	CR	75-100
235	BL	55-75
236	TL	20-30
236	TR	135-145 complete.
236	CL	20-30
236	BR	200-250
237	TC	20-25
237	BL	10-15
237	BR	25-35 complete.
238		Historical photographs vary 1-100
239	CL	25-35
239	BR	10-15
240	CR	10-12

INDEX

158	BL	10-15	181	BR	25-35	215	CL	15-20 with candy.
158	BR	10-15	182	CL	55-65 complete set.	215	CR	5-7
159	TL	10-15	182	BR	55-65 complete set.	215	BL	20-25
159	TR	10-15	183	TL	5-10	215	BR	20-25
159	BL	10-15	183	BL	25-35	216	TR	50-75
159	BR	10-15	183	CR	25-35	216	BR	75-100 with box.
160	CL	10-15	184	BL	5-10	217	TL	5-10
160	TR	10-15	184	CR	3-6	217	BL	5-10
160	BR	10-15	185	TR	450-500 set.	217	CR	160-175
161	TL	10-15	185	BR	450-500 set.	218	TL	175-185 ea.
161	CR	10-15	186	CL	450-500 set.	218	TR	20-25
161	BL	10-15	186	TR	450-500 set.	218	CL	150-175
162	TL	10-15	188	BC	60-75 complete set.	218	BR	20-25
162	TR	10-15	189	BL	150-200 complete set.	219	TL	20-25 ea.
162	BL	10-15	189		68 Madrid cup/saucer.	219	TR	10-15
162	BR	10-15	191	CR	400-425	219	CL	15-20
163	TL	10-15	192	CL	145-155	219	CR	10-15
163	TR	10-15	192		70 oz. not shown in original	219	BC	10-12
163	BL	10-15			box. 150-200.	220	TL	25-35
163	BR	10-15	193	C	550-650 pair.	220	BL	15-20
164	TL	10-15	193		Golden Tea Leaf Tea Maker	221	TR	5-10
164	TR	10-15			- 100-125; Soup Server -	221	BR	5-10
164	BL	10-15			75-100; Tea Canister - 50-	222	TL	10-15
164	BR	10-15			75; Hurricane Lamps -	222	TR	175-225 with stand.
165	TL	10-15			75-100.	222	CL	5-10 ea.
165	BL	10-15	195	TL	10-12			Brandy Snifter - 20-25
165	CR	10-15	195	BR	18-20	222	BR	40-50
166	TL	10-15	196	TL	18-20	223	TL	20-25
166	BL	10-15	196	TR	18-20	223	TR	25-30
166	CR	10-15	196	CL	25-35	223	BR	50-60 set.
167	TL	10-15	196	BR	50-75 with original paper.	224	TL	L: 45-75; R: 75-100
167	CR	10-15	198	TR	30-40	224	BC	25-30
168	CL	10-15	199	TL	L: 50-60; R: 60-70	227	TR	10-15
168	TR	10-15	199	TR	15-20	227	BR	25-35
168	BR	10-15	199	BL	50-60	228	TL	25-35
169	TL	10-15	199	BR	50-60	228	BL	80-100 with original
169	BL	10-15	200	TL	10-15 with original paper.			paper/box.
169	CR	10-15	200	TR	20-25 with original paper.	228	BR	L: 60-90; R: 35-50
170	TL	10-15	200	BL	100-125 with box.	229	TR	40-80
170	BL	10-15	200	BR	35-45	229	CL	25-50
170	CR	10-15	201	TC	20-25 with original paper.	229	BR	40-70
171	TL	10-15	201	BC	35-45 ea.	230	TR	250-375
171	BC	20-25	202	CL	25-30	230	CL	125-175
172	TL	15-20	202	TR	20-25	230	BR	60-75
172	TR	15-20	202	BC	80-90	231	TL	1200-1500
172	BL	15-20	203	TL	30-35	231	CR	100-160
172	BR	15-20	203	TR	45-55	231	BL	300-400
173	TL	10-15	203	BL	95-100 with original box.	232	TL	300-400
173	TR	15-20	203	CR	8-10	232	CL	75-100
173	BL	15-20	204	TL	8-10	232	CR	15-20 set.
173	BR	10-15	204	TR	8-10	232	BC	150-225
174	CL	10-15	204	BL	8-10	233	TC	800-1000
174	TR	10-15	204	BR	8-10	233	CL	100-150
174	BR	5-10	205	TL	6-8	233	CR	20-25 with original box.
175	TL	10-15	205	TR	8-10	233	BL	100-150 with original box.
175	TR	10-15	205	BL	6-8	234	TC	25-35 with original box.
175	BL	5-10	205	BR	8-10	234	CL	100-150
175	BR	10-15	206	TL	25-30	234	CR	100-150
176	TL	Top row. L: 150-175;	206	BC	475-500	234	BL	25-30
		C : 20-25; R: 150-175	207	TC	475-500	234	BR	10-20
		Bottom row. C: 10-15	207	BC	L: 40-50; R: 35-40	235	TL	10-20
176	TR	150-175	208	TL	75-100	235	TR	8-12
176	BL	20-25	208	TR	75-85	235	CL	10-20
176	BR	20-25	208	CR	75-85	235	CR	75-100
177	TL	50-60	209	BL	50-60	235	BL	55-75
177	BL	16-17	209	BR	50-60	236	TL	20-30
177	CR	25-35	210	TR	10-15	236	TR	135-145 complete.
178	TL	25-35	211	C	10-15; Framed 25-35	236	CL	20-30
178	BL	25-35	212	TR	20-25	236	BR	200-250
178	CR	25-35	212	CR	35-45	237	TC	20-25
179	TL	25-35	212	BL	35-40	237	BL	10-15
179	TR	25-35	213	TL	20-25	237	BR	25-35 complete.
179	BC	25-35	213	TR	20-25	238		Historical photographs vary
180	TC	25-35	213	CR	35-45			1-100
180	BC	25-35	213	BL	35-45	239	CL	25-35
181	TL	20-25	214	BL	120-135	239	BR	10-15
181	BL	25-30	214	BR	135-150	240	CR	10-12
181	TR	25-30	215	TC	25-30 ea.			

INDEX